CREATIVE TENSION:

THE SPIRITUAL LEGACY
OF
FRIEDRICH VON HÜGEL

CREATIVE TENSION:

THE SPIRITUAL LEGACY
OF
FRIEDRICH VON HÜGEL

BY

ELLEN M. LEONARD

Scranton: University of Scranton Press

© 1997 By the University of Scranton Press

Library of Congress Cataloging-in-Publication Data

Leonard, Ellen M., 1933–   .
    Creative Tension : the spiritual legacy of Friedrich von Hügel /
by Ellen M. Leonard.
        p.   cm.
    Includes bibliographical references and index.
    ISBN 0–940866–66–8. — ISBN 0–940866–67–6 (pbk.)
    1. Hügel, Friedrich, Freiherr von, 1852–1925. I. Title.
BX4705.H78L46   1997
230'.2'092--dc21   97–17784
                                                                                          CIP

Marketing and Distribution
Fordham University Press
University Box L
Bronx, NY 10458

PRINTED IN THE UNITED STATES OF AMERICA

TABLE OF CONTENTS

"God, the Divine Spirit, is indeed before, within, and after all our truest dignity and deepest disquiet."

Friedrich von Hügel, Note to the Second Impression of *The Mystical Element of Religion,* March 1909.

In memory of Norah Veronica Kemp, CSJ

sister and friend

who lived joyfully and creatively.

ACKNOWLEDGMENTS

I wish to thank the many people who have helped me with this book: my family and friends who have supported me, especially my sister Anne and the members of the Congregation of the Sisters of St. Joseph of Toronto; the University of St. Michael's College, Toronto, which granted me a six month research leave in 1995 and a travel grant from the Social Sciences and Humanities Research Council of Canada which enabled me to work on original documents in England and Scotland; my colleagues at the Faculty of Theology and particularly Professor Michael A. Fahey for their interest and encouragement; Professor Lawrence S. Cunningham and the members of the Theology Department of the University of Notre Dame, especially Professor Mary Rose D'Angelo, for welcoming me as a visiting scholar in the spring term of 1995; Professors Richard Schiefen, Mary Rose D'Angelo, and Kevin Kelly who read sections of the manuscript and offered timely advice; Sister Mary of St. Philip, Prioress of the Carmelite Monastery in London, and Sister Jane of Mary who shared their recollections of Sr. Thekla von Hügel; Evelyn Collins, reference librarian at the University of St. Michael's College, and the librarians at the University of Notre Dame; Anne Leonard for proofreading, Heather Chappell for preparation of the index and Dorothy McDonald CSJ for assistance with the computer.

I acknowledge and thank those who allowed me to work with unpublished materials and to quote from these: Rev. Ian Dickie, Archivist of the Archdiocese of Westminster, with the permission of the Cardinal; Rev. Michael Clifton, Archivist of the Diocese of Southwark; the Abbot and Community of Downside Abbey; Dr Norman H. Reid, Keeper of Manuscripts, University of St. Andrews Library; Keeper of Manuscripts of the British Library; Keeper of Manuscripts, Bodleian Library, University of Oxford.

Permission from J. M. Dent Publishers to reproduce photos from Michael de la Bedoyère's *Life of Baron von Hügel* is gratefully acknowledged as well as permission to quote from that work and the following books all published by Dent: Friedrich von Hügel, *The*

Mystical Element of Religion as Studied in Saint Catherine of Genoa and Her Friends; Essays and Addresses on the Philosophy of Religion; Essays and Addresses on the Philosophy of Religion. Second Series; Letters from Baron Friedrich von Hügel to a Niece, ed. Gwendolen Greene; *Selected Letters 1896–1924*, ed. Bernard Holland; *The Reality of God and Religion and Agnosticism*, ed. Edmund Gardner; Maude Petre, *My Way of Faith* and *Von Hügel and Tyrrell: The Story of a Friendship*. Passages from von Hügel's *Eternal Life* are reprinted with permission of T&T Clark Ltd. Passages from *Baron von Hügel and the Modernist Crisis in England* by Lawrence Barmann are reprinted by permission of Cambridge University Press. Passages from *Letters of Baron Friedrich von Hügel and Professor Norman Kemp Smith* edited by Lawrence Barmann are reprinted with permission of Fordham University Press.

ABBREVIATIONS

AAW	Archives of the Archdiocese of Westminster
BL	British Library
Bo	Bourne Papers
*EA*1,2	*Essays and Addresses on the Philosophy of Religion* Series one and Two
EL	*Eternal Life*
EU	Evelyn Underhill
GS	*The German Soul and the Great War*
GT	George Tyrrell
KS	Kemp Smith
Letters KS	*Letters of von Hügel and Norman Kemp Smith*
LTN	*Letters to a Niece*
Life 1	Autobiography of George Tyrrell, 1861–1884
Life 2	Life of George Tyrrell from 1884 to 1909
LP	Lilley Papers
*ME*1,2	*The Mystical Element of Religion as Studied in Saint Catherine and Her Friends*, 2 vols.
MP	Maude Petre
PP	Petre Papers
RG	*The Reality of God and Religion and Agnosticism*
SAUL	Saint Andrews University Library
SL	*Selected Letters*
VC	Vigilance Committee
vH	von Hügel
vHP	von Hügel Papers
vHT	*von Hügel and Tyrrell: The Story of a Friendship*
WW	Wilfrid Ward
WWP	Wilfrid Ward Papers

INTRODUCTION

I n this age of the laity the life and writings of Friedrich von Hügel (1852–1925) offer a source of wisdom. At a time when theology was done almost exclusively by clerics, von Hügel, a lay Catholic, devoted his life to the academic study of religion. He belonged to no school or university but wrote as an independent scholar.[1] He did this consciously as a Catholic during the period known as "Roman Catholic Modernism" and the anti-modernist period that followed. For many years he was involved in dialogue with Christians from other churches and with persons of other religions during a period prior to the entrance of the Catholic Church into ecumenical and interfaith relationships.

Von Hügel devoted his life to bringing together the world of religion and the world of scholarship. He is best remembered as a student of mysticism and as a leader in Roman Catholic Modernism. Often these two aspects of von Hügel's life have been seen as distinct, or even contradictory. His philosophy of religion has been emphasized and his involvement with the modernist movement interpreted as "an unfortunate phase" in his life; or his role in the modernist movement has been highlighted in a way that has eclipsed other aspects of his life.

This study is particularly interested in Friedrich von Hügel's spiritual legacy, a legacy that includes his writings and the example of his life. I consider that "spirituality" encompasses all one's relationships: to God, to self, to others, to all of creation. Von Hügel's spiritual legacy must be seen in a wider context than the modernist and anti-modernist movements but cannot be separated from them. We have no choice about *when* we live but only about *how* we live.

In a letter written in 1918 von Hügel distinguished between two "distinct subject-matters which could be described under the term 'Modernism'," the first was the "permanent, never quite finished, always, sooner or later, more or less, beginning set of attempts to express the old Faith and its permanent truths and helps—to interpret it according to what appears the best and the most abiding elements in the philosophy and the scholarship and science of the later and latest

1

times." The second "modernism" was "a strictly circumscribed affair, one which is really over and done. . . ."[2] Von Hügel, who has been described as "the Erasmus of the modernist movement," was a leader in both these "modernisms."[3] His spirituality was developed and lived out, at least in part, in response to these movements. Modernism and the ecclesiastical response to it provided the context in which von Hügel developed his philosophy of religion and his spirituality.

Various attitudes were taken toward modernism during the period in which it developed (1896–1907), as well as during the anti-modernist period (1907–1960).[4] Different attitudes persist. For many it is the errors presented in *Pascendi*, the encyclical which condemned it as "the synthesis of heresies." For others it is a movement for theological renewal within Catholicism which was considered misdirected by the ecclesial authorities. Over the last thirty years scholars have studied modernism both from a historical and a theological perspective and offered their diverse interpretations.[5] It is a complex movement which may be viewed in many different ways. The persons involved in the movement themselves had different concerns. Those in France focused on the biblical question and on philosophy while in Italy the issues were primarily political. In England the interest in all of these areas was their relevance for the spiritual life. English "modernism" was primarily a movement of spirituality.

Sandra Schneiders, in a study on spirituality, maintains that "only a theology that is rooted in the spiritual commitment of the theologian and oriented toward praxis will be meaningful in the Church of the future."[6] In his own context of Catholicism in England at the beginning of this century Friedrich von Hügel struggled to articulate his philosophy of religion out of a deep spiritual commitment. During a period when theology and spirituality were separated, and theology limited to an often sterile neo-scholastic mode, von Hügel's philosophy of religion integrated theology with what we now call praxis although it may be argued that praxis involves social analysis, a component that was not present in his work. What was present was a grounding of his philosophy of religion in experience. His experience as a lay Catholic, a husband and parent, shaped his philosophy of religion and his spirituality. In addition von Hügel used psychology and the comparative study of religion in an approach which was truly interdisciplinary.[7]

Since experience is a primary locus for the philosophy of religion and spirituality of von Hügel, I draw on material from his life and from those with whom his life was interwoven. The scholar who wishes to study Friedrich von Hügel has no lack of primary sources. Von Hügel left forty-three volumes of diaries covering the years 1877–79, 1884–1900, and 1902–24 in which he gave detailed accounts of his daily activities. In addition much of his correspondence is preserved in various archives. His practical advice on how to live an integrated religious life is recorded in his extensive correspondence with countless persons during his long life.[8]

Simply citing the events of von Hügel's life does not reveal the personality of this figure who was in many ways larger than life. At times his family and friends seem to have had some difficulty in understanding him. Those who have written about him since his death have struggled to make sense of apparently contradictory character-istics. How does one reconcile his piety and his criticism, his respect for authority and his independence? Maisie Ward, writing in 1937, referred to two von Hügels whom she was tempted to describe as "the von Hügel of faith and the von Hügel of history!"[9] Nicholas Sagovsky expresses the conflicting interpretations of von Hügel which have been given:

> To some the great master of the spiritual life and teacher of prayer who remained faithful to his church throughout the modernist storm and beyond; to others a man of immense but ill-articulated knowledge, so deficient in judgement that he failed to spot the radical implications of Alfred Loisy's biblical criticism and blithely waved his friend George Tyrrell on as he pitched ever nearer to destruction.[10]

These interpretations fail to recognize how von Hügel was able to integrate the various aspects of his life within a creative tension.

Von Hügel himself provides a clue to understanding his complex personality in his presentation of the three elements of religion which he developed in his great two-volume work, *The Mystical Element of Religion as Studied in St. Catherine of Genoa and Her Friends.*[11] These three elements, 1) the authoritative, historical, institutional; 2) the critical, speculative, philosophical; 3) the intuitive, volitional, mystical, must be present in the mature religious person. The struggle to keep the three elements in a creative tension lies at the heart of von Hügel's spirituality. The "friction" and "costliness," to use von Hügel's terms, which this struggle entailed, undergird his spirituality.

Part I of this study focuses on von Hügel's own spiritual journey. It is divided into five periods: his early years (1852–1870), his years of study (1871–1896), the crucial years in which he was deeply involved in the modernist movement (1897–1907), the years marked by the publication of his greatest work (1908–1912), and his later years during which he shared the fruit of his years of study and personal struggle (1913–1925). Of course these periods overlap. Von Hügel was always a student and so this aspect cannot be confined to the period 1871–1896, although it may be argued that these were the years in which the young von Hügel laid a foundation for further scholarship. Nor should his critical study of the bible be separated from his study of mysticism. He wrote his book on mysticism during the years in which he was involved in the modernist struggle using the same critical tools as he used in his biblical studies. His work as a spiritual guide and teacher began with his own children and continued throughout his life. In each period I consider the events of von Hügel's life within the ecclesial context of that period emphasizing the ways that the intellectual and mystical elements interact with the institutional in his religious response.

The second half of the book focuses on von Hügel as spiritual guide for others. Chapter Six observes von Hügel as spiritual companion by studying his relationship with Wilfrid Ward, Juliet Mansel, Evelyn Underhill, and Gwendolen Greene. Chapter Seven considers von Hügel's lay spirituality based on his experience as spouse, parent, and friend, a spirituality which was both ecclesial and ecumenical. Chapter Eight offers a systematic view of his spirituality as it reflects the historical, intellectual, and mystical elements of religion. The final chapter assesses von Hügel's spiritual legacy and how it might be expanded in ways that would address our age.

A number of previous works have presented aspects of von Hügel's spiritual legacy. The earliest one, which continues to be widely read, is Gwendolen Greene's *Letters from Baron Friedrich von Hügel to a Niece,* published in 1928 just three years after von Hügel's death.[12] Douglas Steere's *Spiritual Counsels and Letters of Baron Friedrich von Hügel* (1964) emphasized von Hügel's role as spiritual counselor.[13] A more systematic presentation of *The Spirituality of Friedrich von Hügel* was made by Joseph Whelan in 1971.[14]

Our world is very different from the world of Baron von Hügel and even from that of his earlier commentators. As Louis Dupré points out: "Not merely our thinking about the real changes: reality itself changes as we think about it differently."[15] For this reason much of von Hügel's philosophy of religion seems outmoded in a postmodern world. At times he appears to have been both overpowering and chauvinistic. Much of this may have been his personality and his cultural context. He was a Victorian gentleman whose style belonged to that age. In spite of the cultural differences between von Hügel and late twentieth century Christians, there is wisdom to be gleaned from his writings.

It is particularly as a lay theologian and spiritual guide that von Hügel's life, with its ups and downs, his writings based on a lifetime of study and reflection on religion, and his spiritual advice may be useful to late twentieth- and twenty-first-century Christians. He lived a lay spirituality in which family relationships and friendship formed the basis for his approach to religion. He integrated scholarship, including the critical study of religion with spirituality, thus offering not only a lay approach to spirituality but a spirituality for students of all academic disciplines. In a world which is becoming increasingly aware of the interconnectedness of our universe, von Hügel's convictions about the material world can contribute to an ecological spirituality. In an ecumenical age, von Hügel, who was a pioneer in interreligious dialogue, offers some insights into an ecumenical spirituality.[16] Finally, his insistence that the mystical element is part of every person's religious response, while emphasizing that the mystical should be rooted in a faith community, continues to be helpful. These strands, which can be corrected and expanded in the light of contemporary concerns, provide a rich resource for a contemporary spirituality.

NOTES

1. Nicholas Lash in *Easter in Ordinary: Reflections on Human Experience and the Knowledge of God* (Charlottesville: University Press of Virginia, 1988), p.175, n.63, refers to von Hügel as an "immensely learned amateur."

2. Von Hügel's letters to Maude Petre are in the Petre Papers (PP) in the British Library (BL), Add. MSS 45361–45362. This letter, written 13 March 1914 (MS 45362), is published in *Selected Letters 1896–1924*, ed. Bernard Holland (London: Dent & Sons, 1927), p 248; hereafter *SL.*

3. Martin Green, *Yeat's Blessings on von Hügel: Essays on Literature and Religion* (London: Longmans, 1967), p.8.

4. For example, compare *Catéchisme sur le modernisme d'après l'encyclique Pascendi Domininici Gregis de S.S.Pie X* (Paris: Libairie Saint-Paul, 1907) by J. B. Lemius, the systematic

theologian who wrote much of the actual encyclical and the anonymous defense of the modernist positions, *The Programme of Modernism: A Reply to the Encyclical of Pius X, Pascendi Dominici Gregis*, tr. from the Italian with an Introduction by A. Leslie Lilley (London: J. Fisher Unwin, 1908), or Jean Rivière's standard interpretation, *Le Modernisme dans l'église: Etude d'historire religieuse contemporaine* (Paris: Letouzey et Ané, 1929), and the more sympathetic presentation by Maude Petre, *Modernism: Its Failure and Its Fruits* (London: T. C.& E. C. Jack, 1918).

5. One of the most helpful theological studies has been Gabriel Daly, *Transcendence and Immanence: A Study in Catholic Modernism and Integralism* (Oxford: Clarendon, 1980). For a historical study see Marvin R. O'Connell, *Critics on Trial: An Introduction to the Catholic Modernist Crisis* (Washington: Catholic University of America, 1994).

6. Sandra M. Schneiders, "Spirituality in the Academy," *Theological Studies* 50 (December 1989), pp.676–97; quote from p.677.

7. Patrick Sherry in "Von Hügel: Philosophy and Spirituality," *Religious Studies* 17 (1981), pp.1–18 emphasizes the way that von Hügel keeps philosophy, theology, and spirituality together.

8. The von Hügel archives (vHP) are at Saint Andrews University Library (SAUL). For earlier works on von Hügel, see: James J. Kelly, *Baron Friedrich von Hügel's Philosophy of Religion* (Lueven University Press, 1983); Lawrence F. Barmann, *Baron Friedrich von Hügel and the Modernist Crisis in England* (Cambridge University Press, 1972); Michael de la Bedoyère, *The Life of Baron von Hügel* (London: J. M. Dent & Sons, 1951); Maurice Nédoncelle, *Baron Friedrich von Hügel: A Study of His Life and Thought*, trans. by Marjorie Vernon (London: Longmans, Green & Co., 1936). See also *Selected Letters 1896–1924*, ed. with a Memoir by Bernard Holland (London: J. M. Dent & Sons, 1927).

9. Maisie Ward, *The Wilfrid Wards and the Transition: Insurrection versus Resurrection* (London: Sheed & Ward, 1937), p.489. This work emphasizes Loisy's influence on vH. There is a chapter on vH (pp.489–515).

10. Nicholas Sagovsky, "Von Hügel and the Will to Believe," in *The Critical Spirit and the Will to Believe: Essays in Nineteenth-Century Literature and Religion*, ed. by David Jasper and T. R. Wright (London: Macmillan, 1989), p.206.

11. (London: Dent, 1908; 2nd edn, 1923; reprint edn, 1927); hereafter *ME* 1 and *ME* 2. See Appendix for the second chapter of this work in which vH developed his understanding of the three elements of religion.

12. Edited with an Introduction by Gwendolen Greene (London: J. M. Dent & Sons, 1928); hereafter *LTN*. This work has been reissued as a Fount paperback by Harper Collins (1995) to commemorate the seventieth anniversary of vH's death. Keith Mitchell comments on its reappearance in "Avuncular Counsels: Von Hügel and his *Letters to a Niece*," *The Month* 29 (February 1996), pp.68–71.

13. Edited with an Introductory Essay by Douglas V. Steere (London: Darton, Longman & Todd, 1964).

14. Joseph P. Whelan, *The Spirituality of Friedrich von Hügel* (London: Collins, 1971).

15. Louis K. Dupré, *Passage to Modernity: An Essay on the Hermeneutics of Nature and Culture* (New Haven: Yale University Press, 1993), p.6.

16. Von Hügel's contribution to spirituality in ecumenical perspective has been noted in a book by that title: *Spirituality in Ecumenical Perspective*, ed. E. Glenn Hinson (Louisville, Kentucky: Westminster/John Knox Press, 1993). See especially the essays by Morton T. Kelsey, pp.15–31, and by E. Glenn Hinson, pp.161–76.

PART I

THE SPIRITUAL JOURNEY

PREPARING FOR THE JOURNEY (1852-1870)

1

T his chapter has a two-fold purpose: to present von Hügel's family, educational, and religious background and to consider the ecclesial context of English Catholicism. Although he was eventually recognized by the academy, the church was the matrix in which von Hügel would develop his philosophy of religion and his spirituality. English Catholicism became his spiritual home.

Family and Educational Background

Friedrich von Hügel was born in Florence in May 1852 and spent the first seven years of his life in that city. At the time of Friedrich's birth his father, Baron Carl von Hügel, an Austrian diplomat and the minister at the Grand Ducal Court of Tuscany, was fifty-seven years old having had a military career before joining the diplomatic service. In addition, Carl von Hügel was a recognized scientist. In 1836 he had been named an Honorary Foreign Member of the Royal Geographical Society of London in recognition of the research he had done during a six-year journey in Asia, Africa, and Australia.[1] Friedrich's mother, Elizabeth Farquharson, a Scottish woman and convert from Presbyterianism, was twenty-one when their first child was born on 5 May 1851. He was named Friedrich after his godfather, Prince Liechtenstein.[2] There were two other children, Anatole born in 1854 and Pauline in 1858.

Friedrich's earliest religious memories go back to Florence and

11

even at an early age he seems to have combined the mystical and the
institutional aspects of religion:

> At five and six years of age, I possessed a sense, not only of
> God in the external, especially the organic, world, but of a
> mysterious divine Presence in the churches of Florence.[3]

At the outbreak of revolution in 1859 the family fled to Vienna.
In 1860, when Friedrich was eight years old, Baron Carl von Hügel was
appointed Austrian Envoy Extraordinary in Brussels where the family
lived until their father retired from public life in 1867. They then
settled in Torquay, England. Friedrich was fifteen when his family
moved to England. It became his home but he always maintained a
special love for Florence as his birthplace.

Friedrich did not become an English citizen until 1914 and
throughout his life he remained in many ways more European than
English. He never quite belonged, a fact that he attributed both to his
Scottish and German background:

> This consciousness of difference and of isolation, with its
> sadness, all but wholly and promptly disappears in the society
> of Scotch men, so that it probably springs as much from my
> Scottish blood as my German.

Nevertheless, he was in "social and political outlook and sym-
athies . . . thoroughly, consciously, gratefully English."[4]

Unlike his younger brother Anatole, who was educated at
Kalksburg, Vienna, and Stonyhurst, Friedrich was educated solely at
home, never having "the advantages—nor the disadvantages—of an
institutional education at any period of his life."[5]   His teachers
included a Protestant woman, a Lutheran pastor, a German Catholic
historian, and a Quaker geologist. These educators must have
communicated to Friedrich a love for religion, history, and geology
which he carried throughout his life. The elder von Hügel son was
shaped by a childhood spent in private tuition, with an emphasis on the
classics and on science, and by the fact that he lived in three different
cultures during his formative years with the result that he was fluent in
Italian, French, German, and English.

This unusual formation developed an unusual scholar. If one
contrasts von Hügel's education with that of Roman Catholic priests
in nineteenth-century England one can appreciate just how unusual

von Hügel's formation was. The future clerics were taught clearly defined textbook theology along with a suspicion of secular knowledge.[6] Few had any desire to continue their studies after ordination. Von Hügel, whose mind had been opened to the riches of the Western classics as well as to the mysteries of the world around him, believed in lifelong learning and continued to study in a formal disciplined way throughout his life. It has been suggested that the lack of a seminary or Catholic university background resulted in "a certain innocence in von Hügel's approach to the Vatican, particularly concerning its dispositions and common methods of procedure."[7] This was true not only as regards political matters but also approaches to the study of religion. Because he had not been trained either in a seminary or in one particular discipline with its own methodology, he freely explored new avenues of study and new methods. He seems to have had an almost childlike delight in learning. This freedom, openness, and enthusiasm characterized his scholarly work throughout his life, and may be found even in his last book, published posthumously.

Religious Conversion

Von Hügel looked back to events that took place when he was eighteen as particularly significant in his life. His father died in Brussels on his way to Vienna in 1870 and shortly afterward Friedrich caught typhus, an illness which permanently damaged his hearing. This was a crucial time for young Friedrich. The death of his father thrust von Hügel into adulthood. As the oldest son he assumed responsibility in the family and received an income which provided him with a livelihood.[8] At this time of uncertainty he turned to a Dutch Dominican, Father Raymond Hocking, who helped him to come through what he called his first conversion. Years later, in a letter to Edmund Bishop, he corrected the latter's impression that he was a convert to Catholicism but he claimed a different kind of conversion.

> I am a convert only in the sense of having, owing to a variety of circumstances, had to regain and to conquer for myself, morally, spiritually, and intellectually, a positive faith in the Catholic religion: from 13 to 18, I would have hesitated as to affirming a positive adherence to the Church; and I had considerable interior work to go through even after those early years.[9]

An incident in Mainz Cathedral convinced him of the efficacy of prayer. A woman whose baby had just died threw herself before the altar and wept bitterly. Gradually her sobs subsided and as she left the church Friedrich saw the radiance of her face. Many years later he recalled this scene and its effect on his own spirit.[10]

This was a period of searching in which von Hügel, who had been uprooted a number of times as he was growing up, found his true self by struggling to become free from what he described as "my poor, shabby, bad, all-spoiling *self*." Looking back as a seventy-year-old man he shared his struggles and subsequent freedom with a young Anglican friend on the occasion of her confirmation:

> Yet it remains most true that our religion begins to be our romance—our most solid, sustaining romance—only on the day on which it becomes adult and quite real—that is, only on the day on which we wake up to self and determine to fight it.[11]

In this task he was grateful to God for the "noble-hearted, gladly self-immolating Dominican Friar, whom God sent me, to seek and save me when I was eighteen."[12] With Father Hocking's direction, Friedrich resolutely rejected what he came to recognize as false freedom and embarked wholeheartedly on the religious quest that characterized his life.

In contrast with his father who had pursued a military, a scientific, and a diplomatic career, and his brother Anatole who chose an academic profession, becoming curator of the University Museum of Archaeology and Ethnology at Cambridge in 1883, a post he retained until 1921, Friedrich chose to spend his entire adult life in the study of religion.[13] He did this as a devout lay Roman Catholic during a period in which there was little encouragement and support for such a vocation.

Ecclesial Context: English Catholicism

Friedrich von Hügel was in many ways an international person, a European at home in different languages and countries. He had a very Catholic understanding of the Church as universal, but he lived his adult life as a Catholic in England. To understand von Hügel it is helpful to situate him in the context of nineteenth-century Catholicism as it found expression in England.

A Second Spring

From the Reformation until 1850, just two years before Friedrich's birth, the Catholic Church in England had been a mission from Rome under the leadership of vicars apostolic.[14] The Catholic faith had been preserved by a number of families whose ancestors had remained faithful to Rome during and after the Reformation, surviving persecution and suffering numerous disabilities which excluded them from the political life of the nation. Although these "Old Catholics" were looked upon with suspicion by their Protestant neighbors, they had been able to remain both Catholic and English, maintaining a double loyalty to pope and monarch.

As a result of the potato famine in Ireland large numbers of destitute Irish Catholics arrived in England in the 1840s, creating the need for ecclesiastical reorganization. There was also the hope that many more converts would follow Newman into the Catholic Church. As a response to changing pastoral needs, and at the request of the vicars apostolic who wished to bring proper order into the Catholic community, Pius IX restored the diocesan hierarchy in 1850 by appointing Catholic bishops to twelve dioceses. Nicholas Wiseman, vicar apostolic of London since 1849, became the first cardinal archbishop of the newly established metropolitan see of Westminster.[15]

The restoration of the Catholic hierarchy, under the leadership of Cardinal Wiseman, was greeted with joy by most Catholics. Wiseman joyfully, if rather imprudently, proclaimed:

> Catholic England has been restored to its orbit in the ecclesiastical firmament, from which its light has long vanished, and begins now anew its course of regular adjusted action round the center of unity, the source of jurisdiction, of light, and of vigor.[16]

But for many members of the Church of England this change was seen as an act of "papal aggression." Angry mobs burned effigies of the pope and cardinal. In a more ecumenical age it is difficult to imagine how upsetting the restoration of the Catholic hierarchy was not only to many of the general population but also to the bishops of the Church of England who protested to the Queen against "this attempt to subject our people to a spiritual tyranny from which they were freed at the Reformation."[17] Wiseman's *Appeal to the Reason and Good Feeling of the English People* helped to reassure those who feared a Roman take-over. The cardinal explained that his charge would not be the Abbey of Westminster but the poor people who lived in the area, most of whom were at least nominally Catholic. "This is the part of Westminster which alone I covet."[18] The anti-papist demonstrations died down, although anti-Catholic sentiments remained and left their mark on English Catholicism.

The restoration of the hierarchy introduced England belatedly to Tridentine Catholicism with its rigid practices and uniformity. Norman describes the effect this had on English Catholics:

> To the exultant converts, anxious to luxuriate in everything which differentiated themselves from the English religion they had abandoned, this was splendid; to the Old Catholics, however, it was a lamentable and insensitive renunciation of a religious tone which echoed centuries of sacrifice and common-sense adjustment to Protestant sensibilities.[19]

The influence of the clergy over the laity was extended, and the Old Catholics who had remained loyal to Rome after the Reformation no longer enjoyed the hegemony that had been theirs for over three centuries.

John Henry Newman, who had been received into the Roman Catholic Church in 1845, preached his famous sermon on "The Second Spring" at the first Provincial Synod of Westminster on 13 July 1852, just two months after Friedrich von Hügel was born. In colorful language Newman described his vision of the Catholic Church in England at the beginning of the second half of the nineteenth century as a "second spring"—but a particular kind of spring:

> Have we any right to take it strange, if, in this English land, the spring-time of the Church should turn out to be an English spring, an uncertain, anxious time of hope and fear, joy and suffering—of bright promise and budding hopes, yet withal, of keen blasts, and cold showers, and sudden storms?[20]

This accurate description of the English spring conveys the sense of excitement experienced by Catholics who for centuries had been largely "invisible" in English society. Their numbers were increasing, both by the conversions of influential people, like Newman himself, and by the influx of Irish immigrants swelling the Catholic population of the cities, particularly London, Birmingham, and Liverpool. The number of

Catholics was still small (about 3½% of the population in England and Wales in 1850) but there was a sense of expansion.[21]

The growing Catholic population was by no means homogeneous. As a result of the French Revolution many priests, religious, and lay people had fled to England, some of them staying and helping to transform the Catholic Church in that country. A number of religious orders set up monasteries and schools in England. The Old Catholic families continued as a small but influential group with their own quiet English spirituality. Increasing numbers of converts to Catholicism, some, like Newman, connected with the Oxford Movement, formed a third group.[22] Finally, there was the influx of Irish immigrants who greatly increased the Catholic population. Catholics in each of these groups had their own needs and priorities. The second half of the nineteenth century was marked by massive building of churches and schools to provide for this rapidly growing and diverse population. The mix of persons from different social classes who worshiped side by side became a characteristic mark of English Catholicism.

Von Hügel and his friends, George Tyrrell and Maude Petre, reflect three of the different backgrounds which shaped English Catholicism. The von Hügels, both Friedrich and his brother Anatole, represented the European Catholics who brought their own international flavor and breadth to English Catholicism. Maude Petre was an articulate representative of that strong, independent group of lay Catholics who had kept Catholicism alive in England during and after the Reformation and whose courage she praised in her work on *The Ninth Lord Petre*.[23] George Tyrrell, himself a convert, joined the Society of Jesus with the expressed desire to work with others who, like himself, had to struggle to come to faith. Much of his ministry of writing and spiritual direction was directed to those who were interested in becoming Catholics or who had recently joined the Church.

The bond which united the disparate groups who made up English Catholicism was a strong allegiance to Rome, and to the person of the pope. This made them different from their neighbors and caused them to be looked at with some suspicion by their Protestant neighbors who saw them as a "church of outsiders."

A Church of Outsiders

In general the English Catholic community in the nineteenth

century remained socially and politically isolated. Although Catholic Emancipation had been achieved during the early nineteenth century, after great struggles and amidst fear of "popery," suspicion of Catholics continued. Holmes describes the view held by many: "Catholics were unenlightened, intolerant bigots whose religion was opposed to sound economic progress and liberal political development."[24]   Owen Chadwick describes the Catholic community as putting out "prickles against its environment."

> For it mostly consisted of working men who felt half-foreigners and knew that they were disliked; and where it did not consist of Irish, it consisted either of old-fashioned recusant aristocrats with a long tradition of quiet separateness, or of a small number of converts from other churches who knew themselves disapproved as converts by the main body of society.[25]

An attitude of social and political isolation was encouraged by the clergy and particularly the hierarchy. Even when Catholics were no longer excluded from admission to the old universities, the bishops discouraged their attendance, fearing that such an environment would be dangerous to faith and morals. Manning, who succeeded Wiseman as Archbishop of Westminster in 1865, attempted unsuccessfully to provide a Catholic University for English Catholics in Kensington. Under his leadership English Catholics were encouraged to be "more Roman than Rome, and more ultramontane than the Pope himself."[26] The clergy were to be romanized, even in their dress. Rather than seeing itself as a component of English Christianity, the Roman Catholic Church in England saw itself as "a (beleagued) outwork of 'The Church', a divine institution founded by Christ in person and entrusted to Peter and his successors in Rome."[27]

Von Hügel was an "outsider" in his own way. He chose England for his home, but his German name and accent set him apart within his adopted country. Gradually he found a place within the larger religious milieu of his day and through his writings and lectures he challenged the perception of Catholics as removed from the mainstream of religious life and thought. He also developed a more inclusive understanding of Catholicism than the narrowly Roman version of Manning and his successor Vaughan.

An Ultramontane Church

George Tyrrell called the Catholicism that took shape during the pontificate of Pius IX "Vaticanism." When Pius IX was elected in 1846 he was considered a liberal pope but the revolution of 1848 and the establishment of the Republic of Rome profoundly changed him. He refused to renounce the temporal power of the papacy and took refuge in Gaeta in the kingdom of Naples. In 1850, supported by European diplomacy and a French expeditionary force, Pius reentered Rome and the papal regime was restored in an atmosphere of resentment. From that time until the end of his long pontificate in 1878 he viewed Catholicism as diametrically opposed to the contemporary world. His *Syllabus of Errors* in 1864 set the Church against the modern world while the definition of papal infallibility in 1870 strengthened the spiritual authority of the pope. With the outbreak of the Franco-Prussian War in 1870, Italian troops occupied Rome and ended the papal temporal power. Pius IX considered himself a prisoner in the Vatican. He did not see himself as a sovereign defending his kingdom but as a leader responsible before God for the defense of Christian values. Pius was venerated by the faithful as a true martyr, inspiring a personal devotion which was new in the history of the Church.

Improved communications, combined with a strong ultramontane spirit and a distrust of liberal ideas, enabled the Vatican to exert rigid control over the Catholic Church in different countries. Those chosen as bishops were men who were strongly committed to carrying out Vatican policy. This seems to have been particularly true of English Catholicism, which was Roman and militantly ultramontane. Wiseman, and his successors Manning and Vaughan, had been educated in Rome and were deeply committed to ultramontane attitudes and policies.

While von Hügel was going through his personal struggles in 1870, the bishops of the world were involved in decisions which would determine the future shape of the Catholic Church. Manning was one of the most enthusiastic supporters of papal infallibility both before and after its proclamation at the first Vatican Council in 1870. Newman, who believed in papal infallibility, was opposed to its definition. There were other Catholics in England also opposed to the definition, but the majority of English Catholics, following the leadership of Manning, overwhelmingly favored it.

When the carefully nuanced definition of papal infallibility was accepted by the Vatican Council, some in England questioned whether a person could be both a good and a loyal English citizen. Newman provided an eloquent answer to this question in his famous *Letter to the Duke of Norfolk*, a work which influenced the young von Hügel.[28]

Holmes comments on the increasing emphasis on the Roman aspect of the Catholic Church not only in England but throughout the world.

> The triumph of Ultramontanism was reflected not so much in the definition of papal infallibility as in the transformation of Catholicism within a generation. By establishing a Roman approach to devotion, discipline and theology throughout the Catholic Church, the Roman authorities were able to take over the leadership of the Church, while the first Vatican Council simply defined the structure of the Church in accordance with their understanding of it.[29]

It was in this ecclesiastical climate that von Hügel, with great dedication and enthusiasm, embarked on his career as a scholar of religion. He saw himself as an ultramontane, but not in the narrow political sense of the late nineteenth century. In 1892 he wrote to Wilfrid Ward: "Personally, I have never been anything but an Ultramontane, in the old and definite sense of the word, ever since I have been a convinced Catholic at all."[30]

Whereas Tyrrell would look to the "church of the future" during a difficult period in the history of the Church, von Hügel looked to the church of the past for his inspiration. Through his study of history he discovered in the pre-Reformation Catholic tradition wisdom which helped him to relativize the difficulties which he experienced in late nineteenth-century Catholicism. The Catholic Church in England during this period has been described as "aggressive and exclusive" with an "appetite for contentious dogma, authoritarian rubric, clerical omnicompetence and an often tasteless obsequiousness towards the papacy."[31] These were characteristics which contrasted with von Hügel's spirit. And yet he knew that it is only in the present that the church in each generation must respond to its own challenges. For him nineteenth-century English Catholicism provided the background against which he developed his philosophy of religion and his spirituality.

NOTES

1. *Charles von Hügel (1795–1870)*, a biographical sketch edited by Anatole von Hügel and translated from the German by Friedrich von Hügel (Cambridge, printed privately, 1903). The work is a compilation of sketches about this remarkable man who was a horologist, botanist, ethnographer, anthropologist, geographer, statesman, and military leader.

2. Ibid.

3. *The Reality of God and Religion and Agnosticism*, ed. by Edmund G. Gardner (London: J. M. Dent & Sons, 1931); hereafter *RG*, p.80.

4. *The German Soul in its Attitude towards Ethics and Christianity* (London, Paris, Toronto: J. M. Dent, 1916), p.123; hereafter *GS*.

5. Barmann, p.1.

6. For a description of seminary education in the nineteenth century, see Peter Doyle, "The Education and Training of Roman Catholic Priests in Nineteenth Century England," *Journal of Ecclesiastical History* 35 (April 1984), pp.208–19.

7. John A. McGrath, *Baron Friedrich von Hügel and the Debate on Historical Christianity (1902–1905)* (San Francisco: Mellen Research University Press, 1993), p.235.

8. Barony had been conferred by the Holy Roman Empire and the title was used by all members of the family.

9. Quoted by Barmann, p.2.

10. De la Bedoyère, p.18.

11. *SL*, pp.351–52.

12. vH to GT, 26 December 1900; PP, BL, Add. MS. 44927. O'Connell describes von Hügel's "first" conversion in *Critics on Trial*, pp.44–45.

13. Peter Gathercole provides an interesting sketch of Anatole von Hügel's career in "Baron Anatole von Hügel (1854–1928): Collector, Curator and Benefactor," *St Edmund's Record* 7 (1992–93), pp.49–53. Anatole had no formal academic qualifications (he was made an honorary MA on appointment), but he was an expert on the cultures of the Southwest Pacific, especially Fiji, where he had spent two years. Anatole played an important role in the foundation of St Edmund's College, Cambridge.

14. For the history of English Catholicism prior to 1850, see John Bossy, *The English Catholic Community 1570–1859* (New York: Oxford University Press, 1976).

15. For a biography of this gifted churchman, see Richard Schiefen, *Nicholas Wiseman* (Shepherdstown: Patmos Press, 1984).

16. From Wiseman's pastoral, *Out of the Flaminian Gate*, quoted by J. Derek Holmes, *More Roman Than Rome: English Catholicism in the Nineteenth Century* (London: Burns & Oates, 1978), p. 75.

17. Quoted by Holmes, p. 76. In a different ecumenical climate, the Catholic Cardinal Archbishop of Westminster, Basil Hume, read the scriptures at the enthronement of the Anglican Primate, Archbishop George Carey, in Canterbury Cathedral in 1991.

18. Schiefen, p.190.

19. Edward Norman, *Roman Catholicism in England from the Elizabethan Settlement to the Second Vatican Council* (Oxford: Oxford University Press, 1985), p.84.

20. J. H. Newman, "The Second Spring," a sermon preached in St. Mary's, Oscott, at the first Provincial Synod of Westminster, 13 July 1852. *Sermons Preached on Various Occasions* (London: Longmans, Green, & Co., 1892), pp. 163–82; quote from pp.179–80.

21. Edward Norman, *The English Catholic Church in the Nineteenth Century* (Oxford: Clarendon Press, 1984), p.3.

22. This growth continued throughout the nineteenth century. In the 1890s the number of converts was estimated at ten thousand a year. Walter L. Anstein, *Protestant Versus Catholic in Mid-Victorian England: Mr. Newdegate and the Nuns* (Columbia & London: University of Missouri Press, 1982), p.216.

23. Maude Petre, *The Ninth Lord Petre: Pioneers of Roman Catholic Emancipation* (London: SPCK, 1928).

24. J. Derek Holmes, *More Roman Than Rome*, p.44.

25. Owen Chadwick, *The Victorian Church* Part II (London: Adam & Charles Black, 1970), pp.402–3.

26. H. E. Manning, "The Work and the Wants of the Catholic Church in England," *Dublin Review* n.s.1 (1863), p.162.

27. Gerard Connelly, "The Transubstantiation of Myth: Towards a New Popular Nineteenth Century Catholicism in England," *Journal of Ecclesiastical History* 35 (January 1984), pp.78–104; quote from p.96.

28. John Henry Newman, *A Letter Addressed to His Grace the Duke of Norfolk on the Occasion of Mr. Gladstone's Recent Exposition* (London: B. M. Pickering, 1875).

29. J. Derek Holmes, *The Triumph of the Holy See: A Short History of the Papacy in the Nineteenth Century* (London: Burns & Oates, 1978), p.135.

30. Wilfrid Ward, *William George Ward and the Catholic Revival* (London: MacMillan & Co., 1893), p.371.

31. Connelly, p.94.

THE YOUNG SCHOLAR (1871-1896)

2

I n this chapter we follow von Hügel in his vocational choice of family life and scholarship. These were important years in which he grew intellectually and spiritually, influenced by a number of scholars but in a particular way by the lay scholar William George Ward, by John Henry Newman, and by his spiritual director, Abbé Huvelin. During these years von Hügel began his own scholarly activity and supported that of others. His aristocratic background and financial independence gave him access to the ecclesiastical and scholarly world of western Europe.

A New Life

Following his father's death and his own illness the young Baron von Hügel returned to England. In the autumn of 1873 the twenty-one-year-old Friedrich became engaged to Lady Mary Herbert, from a famous Anglican family.[1] Her father, Sidney Herbert, England's Minister of War during the Crimean campaign, died in 1861. His widow, Lady Herbert of Lea, Mary's mother, became a Catholic in 1865, and was a close friend of Henry Edward Manning and Herbert Vaughan, both of whom became Archbishop of Westminster.[2] Although the children were brought up in the Church of England, Mary became a Catholic in 1873 a short time before meeting Friedrich.

The happiness, as well as the deep religious commitment of the young Friedrich, is expressed in a letter to "My Molly."

23

Darling, darling, pray that our own sweet Lord may be the ultimate object and end of all our desires. . . . Don't forget that our Lord is Lord of sweet things as well as bitter. . . . I never *dreamt* of such happiness; for my life hitherto has been based on the supposition that not even a foretaste of that was to be got here, and even in Heaven somehow, it would be the sort of satisfaction that a laborer has in receiving scanty wages for a bit of extra-tough work.[3]

Friedrich appreciated the gift of celibacy within the church but recognized that his gift was marriage and parenthood, experiences which would shape his spirituality.[4] Friedrich and Mary were married on 27 November 1873. John Henry Newman wrote to Lady Mary thanking her for the news of this event and promising to say Mass for the couple on their wedding day.[5] The spouses were devoted to each other, but had different interests. Friedrich would have liked his wife to read and study with him but Lady Mary did not share her husband's enthusiasm for philosophical and religious studies. Her faith seems to have been simple and uncomplicated while his was always critical and aware of the complexities of life. Both Friedrich and Mary suffered from poor health throughout their lives, one reason why they spent many winters in Italy, sometimes together, at other times separately. They seem to have been able to support one another in their various activities and to have provided the necessary space that each required.

The couple had three daughters, Gertrud born in 1877, Hildegard born in 1879, and Thekla born seven years later in 1886.[6] Von Hügel firmly believed that parents were responsible with God for both the physical existence and the spiritual growth of their children.[7] His diaries reveal an attentive father who carefully recorded the first time he heard baby laugh, the first time she sucked her toe, and the appearance of her first tooth.[8] There are references to walks with the children, often including a visit to the library and to the church, outings to the zoo and to the toy shop as well as to art galleries and book shops. Hildegard's earliest recollection was of her father carrying her on his shoulders while singing Gilbert and Sullivan.[9]

Catechism classes were an important activity for the three daughters as well as for their father who took seriously his responsibility for the religious education of his children.[10] He carefully prepared each child for the reception of the sacraments, taking each one to her first confession, instructing her for confirmation and first reception of communion. Catechism classes were replaced by bible study and more advanced religious education as the children matured. The preparation and teaching of these lessons was carefully noted in his daily diary.

In addition to personally undertaking the religious education of his daughters, von Hügel carefully supervised all their education and conducted regular examinations on their progress in various subject areas. His diary notation for 21 December 1889 reveals the scope of these examinations which sometimes lasted several days: "Began children's examinations; G's German, grammar, recitation; reading; and history. H's sums, German, reading." There were also lessons in French, English, and Latin, and reading aloud of Shakespeare and Plato. In a letter to Bernard Holland many years later he commented on the bonding aspect of doing Latin with Gertrud. "In looking back I note that perhaps no one thing knit me so closely to my eldest as just the Latin we did and loved together."[11]

The income from his father's estate enabled von Hügel to spend his life as an independent scholar, reading widely, writing, and carrying on an extensive correspondence.[12] Lady Mary also had an independent income. Because he did not have an academic base for his scholarship, it was particularly important for von Hügel to be in dialogue with other scholars. Throughout the years the von Hügels welcomed persons from many different backgrounds to their home. The diaries list the names of visitors for lunch, tea, and dinner as well as overnight guests. Friedrich and Lady Mary were personal friends of such leading Catholic figures as Cardinal Manning, Bishop Hedley, Bishop Vaughan, Father John Henry Newman, William George Ward and his son Wilfrid Ward. Through Lady Mary and her family the young couple also had connections with the English establishment. Nor was their circle of friends limited to England but included many in France, Germany, and Italy, among them cardinals, bishops, and scholars. De la Bedoyère only partially exaggerated when he claimed that von Hügel had an "intimate acquaintance with all the leading religious figures in Britain, France, Italy, and Germany, to all of whom he could speak and write in their own tongue."[13] These included leading Protestant scholars such as Heinrich Julius Holtzmann, Ernst Troeltsch, and Rudolf Eucken, and Jewish scholars such as Julius Spira and Claude Montefiore.

New Influences

Among the early intellectual influences on the young man who had determined to become a scholar and a saint were two Englishmen, William George Ward and John Henry Newman. W. G. Ward had been a follower of Newman at Oxford where he was deprived of his degree because of his religious views. He gave up his Anglican orders and became a Catholic. Wiseman appointed him as lecturer in moral philosophy and later as professor of theology at St. Edmund's College. The involvement of a married layman and recent convert in the education of future priests shocked some Catholics.[14] Throughout the 1860s Ward edited the *Dublin Review*.

Von Hügel met Ward in 1873 and for the next nine years as neighbors they carried on lively discussions while enjoying rambling afternoon walks across Hampstead Heath. The example of an independent Catholic lay scholar must have inspired the twenty-one-year-old von Hügel. Although he disagreed with the extreme ultramontane positions of W. G. Ward, he learned a great deal from him. The bond between the two men is symbolized by Wilfrid Ward's dedication of his father's *Essays on Theism* to von Hügel: "My dear Baron von Hügel, in offering these volumes of my father's philosophical essays for your acceptance, I am doing what I believe he would himself have done had he lived to republish them. They treat for the most part of subjects which you frequently discussed with him, and on which I know he valued your opinion."[15] Wilfrid Ward included a letter from von Hügel in his biography of his father, *William George Ward and the Catholic Revival*, in which von Hügel described his relationship with W. G. Ward, ending with the words, "a friend of friends, a father and a playfellow to one so all but utterly unlike himself."[16] In an address given in 1920 von Hügel referred to W. G. Ward as the one who first taught him that the supernatural should not be measured by its conscious, explicit references to Christ or even to God, an insight which would have far-reaching implications which he would develop in his philosophy of religion.[17]

Even more formative for the young scholar was his relationship with John Henry Newman.[18] In December 1874 the twenty-two-year-old von Hügel expressed his gratitude to the seventy-four-year-old Newman:

The reading of *Loss and Gain*, *The Apologia*, *Anglican Difficulties* and *The Grammar of Assent* has, at different times and in different ways formed distinct epochs in my young intellectual and religious life. Such intellectual discipline as I have had, I owe it to your books. They have I hope, made up to me, at least somewhat, for the absence in my youthful years of any systematic training, any sympathetic and reliable teacher.[19]

Newman replied by sending von Hügel a copy of his *Letter Addressed to His Grace the Duke of Norfolk*, his response to the question whether one could be both a faithful Catholic and a loyal citizen, a work which von Hügel found very helpful. Newman also invited the young man to visit him at the Oratory in Birmingham. He added: "It is a great consolation to an old man to be told that his writings have been of service to any of the younger generation, especially to those who have a foremost place in it."[20] Von Hügel did visit Newman for a few days in June 1876 and they discussed a number of topics which would be of enduring interest to von Hügel: religious certainty, the vicariousness of Christ's suffering, scholastic theology, papal infallibility, and the temporal power of the papacy.[21]

A letter from Newman written in January 1880 commented on von Hügel going to Cambridge. The Cardinal supported the idea but questioned whether Friedrich had the health for such study:

I may have been wrongly informed, but it was commonly said that your long illness was owing to the hard work and excitement unavoidable when you were reading for your examination abroad. If this is the case, can I view your setting about a second course of that *exciting* study, which an examination demands without anxiety?[22]

The Cardinal was indeed misinformed about the cause of von Hügel's illness, but Newman's letter may have influenced him not to undertake a university degree.

Although von Hügel did not pursue studies at a university, he did undertake an exacting program of reading and study during his twenties and thirties, a discipline which he continued throughout his life. His diaries indicate the breadth of his reading which included all the major works of English literature as well as philosophical works beginning with Plato. His disciplined approach to study is evident in the various lists at the beginning of each year's diary indicating works to be read as well as summaries at the end of each diary noting work accomplished during that year. For example, the list for 1888 included works by authors as diverse as Kant, Butler, Pascal, Eucken, Tennyson, Arnold, Thomas Aquinas, Möhler and Döllinger to mention only a few.

Language study was an important preparation for von Hügel's scholarly work. There are references to the reading of German, Latin, and Greek. In 1879 he undertook the study of the Greek New Testament and its scholarly commentaries and in 1890 began his study of Hebrew. His first ten lessons were given by Dr. Gustav Bickell, an orientalist and biblical scholar from Innsbruck who was visiting London. Hebrew lessons continued under the tutorship of the Jewish scholar Julius Spira. In 1892 he laid out his plan for six hours of Greek and twelve hours of Hebrew plus five hours of Religion teaching each week. In 1895 while in Rome he studied Aramaic under Professor Ignazio Guidi of the Collegio Urbano.

These were primarily years of study. Von Hügel did not begin to write until the 1880s with his first article published when he was thirty-one. It was a brief introduction and translation of a work by his father, "The Story of the Escape of Prince Metternich," published in *The National Review* (June 1883).

During these years of study, von Hügel was growing, not only intellectually, but spiritually. His diaries reveal a man for whom the liturgical life of the church provided a framework for his daily activities. Feast days of saints are noted. The entry for each week begins with Sunday Mass and often compline. Many weekdays, particularly Wednesday and Friday, also begin with Mass which he attended sometimes alone, at other times with Molly, and later with the children. Confession and communion, stations of the cross, and benediction are also recorded as well as special times of retreat, often lasting four or five days.[23] In addition to works of criticism, philosophy, and literature, he read the writings of various saints including among his favorites Augustine, John of the Cross, and Francis de Sales.

Von Hügel's spiritual growth was facilitated by his relationship with the Abbé Henri Huvelin, a Parisian diocesan priest whom the thirty-two-year-old von Hügel met in 1884. Huvelin was forty-six, and an experienced director. Huvelin's wisdom and holiness supported von Hügel for many years, encouraging him in his search for truth.[24] The priest recognized God's action in the young man: "God has given you the grace of seizing you at the very core of your being." At the same time he encouraged von Hügel in his intellectual work: "Never regard your studies—their ideal—as insignificant."[25] It was Huvelin's understanding of the role of spiritual guide which von Hügel would adopt as his own.

> God who might have created us directly, employs, for this work, our parents, to whom He joins us by the tenderest ties. He could also save us directly, but He saves us, in fact, by means of certain souls, which have received the spiritual life before ourselves, and which communicate it to us, because they love us.[26]

Huvelin communicated to von Hügel a spiritual wisdom which not only supported him through many difficult periods in his life, but which he in turn was able to share with others.

Von Hügel was always deeply grateful for the support that he had received from Huvelin. When he died in 1910 von Hügel wrote to Maude Petre that he stood out "as the deepest and most salutary religious influence exercised upon me by any man known to me in the flesh."[27] Von Hügel continued to quote Huvelin as a source for his own wisdom although he avoided too close a connection with him in print because he hoped that the holy man would be beatified and did not wish to be an obstacle in this process.[28]

It was Huvelin who directed von Hügel toward the Catholic tradition of the late seventeenth century where he discovered a rich spirituality and the beginnings of historical-critical scholarship. From the French spiritual tradition he appropriated the ideal of the scholar-saint. A passage in an article on "The Spiritual Writings of Père Grou, S.J.," written by von Hügel in 1889, describes Jean Nicholas Grou and suggests the ideal toward which von Hügel himself strove:

> Sober, silent, solid, simple; a solitary, laborious, claimless scholar, gentleman and saint; passing, with overgrowing serenity, through ever-thickening storms and sufferings, exterior and interior; driven back and pressed down upon the very foundations and mainsprings of faith and love, he speaks with his whole being in accents large and calm.[29]

The opening of this essay gives us an insight into how the young von Hügel saw his world and longed for "something more."

> In a transition period such as our own, and an age of hurry, of noise, of restlessness and self-consciousness, and in which

even the most direct and earnest find it specially difficult to
rise to something more positive and more persuasive than
some more or less contentious anti-Protestantism. . .[30]

At such a time one needed to look to the past for wisdom. And this is
what von Hügel did—but always with an eye on the present reality.

At the same time as von Hügel was looking to the past for
inspiration, he was studying contemporary scholarship, especially the
historical critical work of German authors. Not only did he read their
works but he corresponded and visited with many of them. In addition
to Catholics such as Franz Xaver Kraus, von Hügel became friends
with Rudolf Eucken, Heinrich Holtzmann, and Ernst Troeltsch.[31] The
work of German critics had a significant influence on von Hügel's
intellectual formation. He in turn was able to make the work of
German scholarship accessible to English readers.

Michael De la Bedoyère sums up his description of von Hügel at
this time as "an unusually devout, unusually deep, unusually broad
Catholic," one with "unusual tastes, unusual health, and unusual likes
and dislikes in regard to both his Church and his fellow Catholics."[32]

A New Pontificate

The beginning of the pontificate of Leo XIII in 1878 awakened
hope for a more liberal climate within the Church following the long
reign of Pius IX. One of the new pope's first actions was to open the
Vatican archives to scholars. At the request of the Duke of Norfolk on
behalf of English Catholics, and in spite of opposition from suspicious
Roman officials, he made Newman a cardinal. His first encyclical,
Aeterni Patris (1879), insisted on the works of Thomas Aquinas as the
basis for Catholic philosophy and theology. Although this action
inspired some excellent studies of Thomism, the usual form that
theological studies assumed was narrowly apologetic and ahistorical, as
may be seen in the neo-scholastic textbooks of the period.
Theologians were limited by this insistence on Thomism from
responding creatively to the changing situations facing the Church in
the late nineteenth century. Leo's encyclical, *Rerum Novarum* (1891),
called on Catholics to respond to the social problems of the day, but
in a way that did not challenge the structures of society. While taking
account of the modern world, the pope continued to look to medieval
Europe for his vision. His encyclical on biblical studies, *Providentissimus*

Deus (1893), encouraged contemporary methods but was based on a narrow definition of inspiration.

Leo XIII had hoped for a corporate reunion of the Church of England with the Catholic Church. Such a possibility was supported by the historian Abbé Louis Duchesne who argued for the validity of Anglican Orders. However, any recognition of Anglican Orders was strongly opposed by Cardinal Vaughan along with the other English bishops as well as the Irish and Scottish bishops, and the influential English member of the Vatican, Rafael Merry del Val, secretary of the Commission on Anglican Orders, later to become Secretary of State for Pius X.[33] The hope for reunion on the part of some Catholics and Anglo-Catholics was squelched when Leo issued his papal bull, *Ad Anglos* (1895), calling for the conversion of England followed by another papal bull the following year, *Apostolicae Curae*, declaring Anglican Orders to be null and void, defective in form and intent.

Biblical Studies and Advocacy

In the climate of cautious hope that marked the pontificate of Leo XIII, von Hügel's passionate interest in religion and in scholarship found expression in his critical study of the bible.[34] In May 1884 von Hügel met Abbé Louis Duchesne, professor at the Institut Catholique, and founder and editor of the *Bulletin critique*. Duchesne encouraged the young scholar in his critical study of the historical origins of Christianity. At Duchesne's invitation von Hügel wrote a number of short chronicles about scriptural research in England which were published in the *Bulletin critique*.[35] Von Hügel soon realized how far Catholic scholarship lagged behind the work done by Protestant scholars in the critical study of the bible. This awareness inspired him to work for tolerance within the Catholic Church so that Catholic biblical scholars might freely undertake an open investigation of the sources.

Von Hügel found encouragement for his own study from Newman's work, "An Essay on the Inspiration of Scripture." The Cardinal had written:

> I am desirous of investigating for its own sake the limit of free thought consistent with the claims upon us of Holy Scripture; still, my especial interest in the inquiry is from my desire to assist those religious sons of the Church who are engaged in

biblical criticism and its attendant studies, and have a conscientious fear of transgressing the rule of faith.[36]

Von Hügel wrote to the Cardinal to express his appreciation and the Cardinal replied: "My dear Baron, it pleased me to think that my Article in the xixth century was acceptable to you. Of course it is an anxious subject. It is easy to begin a controversy—and difficult to end it."[37]

In addition to his own critical study of the bible, von Hügel supported others who were involved in this task, most notably the French priest and scholar, Alfred Loisy, whose work he began to read in 1890 and whom he met for the first time in October 1893. Loisy, five years younger than von Hügel, was already under ecclesiastical suspicion for his writings. When *Providentissimus Deus*, Leo XIII's encyclical on the study of sacred scripture, appeared, Loisy sent the pope a letter of submission to the encyclical and a memorandum on the biblical question as he saw it. Cardinal Richard, Archbishop of Paris, ordered Loisy to suspend his periodical, *Enseignement biblique*. At the same time Loisy's article, "La question biblique et l'inspiration des Ecritures" in the last issue of *Enseignement biblique*, was the occasion for his dismissal from his teaching position at the Institut Catholique. Loisy spent the next six years as chaplain at a convent in Neuilly where he had the time to apply the method which he had used in his study of the bible to the development of the church, an exercise which resulted in his famous little book, *L'Evangile et L'Eglise*.[38]

Von Hügel firmly believed in Loisy's ability to further Catholic biblical scholarship and he did everything in his power to support Loisy in this task. The two scholars corresponded and von Hügel visited Loisy at Neuilly each year on his way to and from Italy. Von Hügel used his influence to try to prevent Loisy's condemnation, pointing out to the various Roman authorities the harm that would be done in England by a denunciation of Loisy's work, an action which would discredit the Catholic Church in the eyes of the educated. Barmann has described von Hügel's persistent campaign on Loisy's behalf undertaken on different fronts from 1890 to 1908.[39] It included letters and direct interviews with ecclesiastical authorities, reviews of Loisy's work, efforts to rally others in support of Loisy, and a number of published statements on Loisy.[40] This campaign not only supported Loisy but was the way that von Hügel worked for acceptance, or at least tolerance, by ecclesiastical authority for historical-critical methodology in Catholic biblical studies.

During the 1890s von Hügel was also involved in the question of the validity of Anglican Orders. Many English Catholics, including Cardinal Vaughan, worked against the recognition of Anglican Orders fearing that such an action would discourage individual conversions. Von Hügel himself was uncertain about the question but was opposed to an absolute negative ruling. In a brief letter to the editor of the *Tablet* he pointed out that the more significant issue was the question of jurisdiction and of unity.[41] He added that the consensus over the past twenty years was that Anglican orders were "not certainly invalid, yet not certainly valid." His views on biblical issues were expressed more strongly. In discussions of biblical criticism and the issue of Anglican Orders, von Hügel used all his diplomatic skills and his many contacts to plea for greater openness within the Catholic Church, arguing that such freedom would be for the good of the Church.

Among those with whom Von Hügel discussed the need for a climate of freedom if Catholic scholars were to carry on their work was Cardinal Herbert Vaughan.[42] The Cardinal allowed von Hügel to write his articles on scripture, but he did not really understand the biblical issues and he did not want to become involved in Loisy's defense. A more helpful bishop with whom von Hügel discussed his concerns was Eudoxe Irénée Mignot, Bishop of Fréjus and later Archbishop of Albi. Mignot shared von Hügel's conviction that liberty was necessary for Catholic scholars to pursue their critical studies.[43]

Von Hügel also tried to obtain support for his causes in Rome where he met with Cardinal Rampolla, Leo XIII's Secretary of State, who asked him to prepare a memorandum for the pope on the topics which they had discussed, i.e., Anglican Orders, the admission of Catholics to Oxford and Cambridge, and biblical scholarship in England. Many years later von Hügel heard indirectly that his memorandum was referred to by Cardinal Ledochowski as "un impertinenza" on the part of a layman.[44] In February 1896, accompanied by Duchesne, von Hügel had an audience with Leo XIII himself. He had carefully prepared a paper for the pope which he presented during his twenty-two-minute audience.[45] During this period von Hügel also met a future pope, Eugenio Pacelli, who would become Pius XII.

These attempts to influence Vatican policy on Anglican Orders and on biblical criticism do not seem to have been effective. Certainly they were not appreciated by Merry del Val, secretary of the Commission on Anglican Orders, who played a key role in preparing the papal bull, *Apostolicae Curae* (1896), which declared Anglican Orders to be null and void. In a letter to Vaughan, Merry del Val revealed his assessment of von Hügel's contribution:

> I hear Bn von Hügel is leaving next week and I am not sorry, for he seems to have the art of helping to throw confusion, without possessing any theological or historical knowledge of the question at issue.[46]

These harsh words do not reflect von Hügel's contribution or the recognition which he received in Rome. He participated in the *Sodietà degli Studi Biblici* and in March 1896 he read a paper to the group on "Certain Transpositions of Facts which Are Noticeable in the Gospel of Luke."[47] His opinion was respected by many scholars and church leaders who visited him or whom he visited during his yearly trips to Italy.

The positions taken by Leo XIII concerning Anglican Orders and biblical criticism discouraged von Hügel who was deeply committed to the Catholic Church but convinced that the pope's responses, particularly to biblical scholarship, were not only inadequate but disastrous for the Church. He offered his own broad interpretation of *Providentissimus Deus* in "The Papal Encyclical and Mr. Gore," published in *The Spectator* (19 May 1894) and three articles on "The Church and the Bible" published by the *Dublin Review*.[48] In 1897 when the Holy Office issued a statement on "The Comma Johanneum," von Hügel pointed out to the readers of the *Tablet*, which had suggested that the matter was now settled because Rome had spoken, that he himself had talked about the decision "either directly or at but one remove, with twenty and more Catholic specialists, fellow-Biblicists, Church historians, theologians," all of whom treated the decision as *ad interim*.[49] Von Hügel believed that there was a science of the bible which had its own methods and that scholars needed freedom in order to carry out their research effectively.

Von Hügel's efforts attracted the attention of Dom Cuthbert Butler, later Abbot of Downside Abbey, who wrote to him after reading his second article on scripture in the *Dublin Review*, noting how impressed he was by von Hügel's "wide reading and solid learning" but particularly by the "skill and discretion" with which the author was "unostentatiously making 'elbow room'." Butler's words of gratitude "for having given the Church this admirable and scholarly essay" must have pleased von Hügel.[50]

Barmann described von Hügel's motivation in working for change within the Catholic Church:

> To him *loyalty* meant working constantly to achieve within the church an ever-increasing openness and positiveness in attitude and spirit in the effort to live an ever fuller life of faith in truth; the negativism and condemnatory attitude of official Rome to most modern developments, good as well as questionable, was increasingly something he could not simply accept and acquiesce in as final.[51]

Von Hügel shared some of his concerns about the Church with his daughter Gertrud with near disastrous results. As a result of her father's outspoken critical approach to religion, the nineteen-year-old woman suffered a crisis of faith which affected her health. Although Gertrud was not ready for her father's critical approach, there were others for whom he provided liberation from the narrow constraints of nineteenth-century theology and spirituality.

One such person was Maude Petre who as a young woman wrote to von Hügel for information concerning the German mystics. Von Hügel replied with a detailed list of works to read and instructions on where to find the books.[52] Throughout her life Petre was an avid reader, and for many years von Hügel served as a mentor in her selection of works. He also read the books and essays which she wrote, providing meticulous critique which was always both encouraging and constructive. In her memoirs Maude Petre acknowledged that von Hügel had been for her as for countless others "'a great liberator' opening the door to many imprisoned souls."[53] This ability to empower others is a characteristic mark of his spirituality.

As a scholar it was important for von Hügel to work with others for a common cause. Since he was not officially related to any school or university but worked independently, he searched for persons with whom he might share his ideas. During his winters in Rome he was introduced to leading scholars from Europe and North America, many of whom became lifetime friends. These included the Barnabite scripture scholar Padre Giovanni Semeria and the lay philosopher Maurice Blondel.[54] As Maude Petre expressed it: "Von Hügel was ever on the watch for kindred minds; for men and women who shared his religious fervor and his intellectual breadth, his love of religion and truth."[55]

Von Hügel's sojourns in Rome were not totally taken up with ecclesiastical politics. There were visits to shrines, especially to St. Catherine's in Genoa, Mass offered by Abbé Duchesne in the catacombs, dinner parties with important dignitaries, and outings with the children. Although these years were primarily devoted to intellectual activities, they were supported by the institutional practices of Catholic life and a profound love for the truth. As von Hügel continued his study and writing, the historical, intellectual, and mystical were coming together in his response to life.

By 1896 von Hügel was a mature scholar, deeply committed to Catholicism but aware of the historical problems which were not being addressed in Catholic scholarship. We turn now to the crucial years 1897–1907, years in which the scholar was plunged into controversy at the same time as he researching and writing his major work on mysticism.

NOTES

1. See Marvin O'Connell, *Critics on Trial,* pp.45–48, for a description of Lady Mary's background and conversion to Catholicism.

2. Vaughan's letters to Lady Herbert have been published; *Letters of Herbert Cardinal Vaughan to Lady Herbert Lea, 1867–1903,* ed. Shane Leslie (London: Burns & Oates, 1942). There are no letters from Christmas 1871 to January 1874, the period of Friedrich von Hügel and Mary Herbert's courtship and marriage. Vaughan and Lady Herbert are buried beside each other at Mill Hill, the College of Foreign Missions founded by Vaughan with support from Lady Herbert. She is described on her epitaph as "The Mother of the Mill."

3. Letter to Lady Mary quoted by de la Bedoyère, p.9.

4. Duncan McPherson points out that vH considered celibacy a form of prophetic witness. "Baron von Hügel on Celibacy," *Tablet* 223 (August 1969), pp.757–58. Chapter 7 below will discuss the impact of marriage and parenting on vH's spirituality.

5. *The Letters and Diaries of John Henry Newman,* eds. Charles Stephen Dessain & Thomas Gornall, v. 26 (Oxford: Clarendon Press, 1974), p.388. Newman's letters to vH (1874–1884) are in the vHP, SAUL, MSS 2884–2899.

6. Newman sent his congratulations when Gertrud was born and promised to say Mass for the Baroness and the little child. vHP, SAUL, MS. 2888; published in *Letters and Diaries,* v. 27, p.187.

7. *Essays and Addresses on the Philosophy of Religion,* first series (London: J. M. Dent & Sons, 1921), p.106; hereafter *EA* 1.

8. Diary of 1877; SAUL, MS. 36362.

9. "Rough Notes by Baroness Hildegard von Hügel," *SL*, Appendix 3, p.66.

10. vH's convictions concerning parenting are revealed in a lengthy letter to Margaret Mary Petre Clutton, youngest sister of Maude Petre, written in June 1912. The letter was published, with notes by Joseph P. Whelan, under the title "The Parent as Spiritual Director," *Month* n.s.2 (1970), pp.52–57, 84–87.

11. 7 January 1919, *SL*, p.263.

12. In a letter written toward the end of his life (29 May 1923) to a young friend, Henri Garceau, who had won an award, von Hügel reflected on money: "Of course, all money is the result of toil on the part of someone—even though it be a someone centuries ago. But we remember this better if we have seen the money being earned, as I saw mine being earned by my Grandfather, and better still, if oneself has toiled for it, as you have now done repeatedly." *SL*, p. 366.

13. De la Bedoyère, p.124.

14. E. E. Reynolds, *The Roman Catholic Church in England and Wales: A Short History* (Wheathampstead: Antony Clarke Books, 1973), p.341.

15. W. G. Ward, *Essays on the Philosophy of Theism*, 2 vols. (London: K. Paul Trench, 1884), dedicatory page.

16. Wilfrid Ward, *William George Ward and the Catholic Revival* (London: MacMillan & Co., 1893), pp.365–75; quote from p.375.

17. "Christianity and the Supernatural," *EA*1, p.280.

18. See David Tracy, "Recent Catholic Spirituality: Unity amid Diversity," *Christian Spirituality: Post-Reformation and Modern*, eds. Louis Dupré and Don E. Saliers (New York: Crossroad, 1989), pp.143–150 for an analysis of Newman's and vH's contribution to modern Catholic spirituality and Newman's influence on vH.

19. vH to Newman, 13 December 1874; *Letters and Diaries*, v.27, pp.189–90. See also R. K. Browne, "Newman and Von Hügel: A Record of an Early Meeting," *Month* (1961), pp.24–33.

20. Newman's letter of 15 January 1875; vHP, SAUL, MS. 2885.

21. Kelly, p.44. See also "Newman and Von Hügel," pp.27–33.

22. Newman to vH, 3 January 1879; vHP, SAUL, MS. 2898.

23. The diary for 26 August 1884 notes that he went to Manressa for his sixth retreat. On 26 August 1896 he notes an informal eight-day retreat at the Benedictine monastery of Downside.

24. See Appendix 1, *SL*, pp.57–63 for "Some of the Sayings of Abbé Huvelin." This was advice written down by vH from his visit to Huvelin in May 1886. Also James J. Kelly, "Counselling von Hügel: A Selection of Some Advice Given to Baron von Hügel by the Abbé Huvelin in 1886 and 1893," *Tablet* 228 (1974), pp.693–95. O'Connell describes Huvelin's influence on vH in *Critics on Trial*, pp.51–53.

25. "Counselling von Hügel," p.692.

26. Von Hügel quoted this passage from Huvelin's *Conferences on Some of the Spiritual Guides of the Seventeenth Century* in *Eternal Life* (Edinburgh: T.& T. Clark, 1912), p.376; hereafter *EL*.

27. vH to MP, 15 December 1910, PP, BL, Add. MS 45362,

28. *LTN*, p.xv. See also James J. Kelly, "The Abbé Huvelin's Counsel to Baron Friedrich von Hügel," *Bijdragan* 39 (1978), pp.59–69.

29. *Tablet* 74 (December 1889), p.900. This essay by vH was included as an Appendix in John Nicholas Grou, S.J., *Spiritual Maxims*, newly translated and edited by a Monk of Parkminster (London: Burns & Oates, 1961), pp.265–93.

30. Ibid.

31. For background on the influence of German scholarship on vH see Hans Rollmann, "Liberal Catholicism, Modernism, and the Closing of the Roman Mind: Franz Xaver Kraus and Friedrich von Hügel," *Downside Review* 109 (July 1991), pp.202–16; "Holtzmann, von Hügel and Modernism," *Downside Review* 97 (1979), pp.128–43; 221–44.

32. De la Bedoyère, p. 64.

33. Rafael Merry del Val (1865–1930) became a cardinal in 1903 and served as Secretary of State for Pius X (1903–1914) and as Secretary of the Holy Office from 1914 until his death in 1930. Because of his English background he took great interest in the Church in England and exercised a powerful influence on English ecclesiastical life. For a discussion of this influence, see J. Derek Holmes, " Cardinal Raphael Merry del Val—An Uncompromising Ultramontane: Gleanings from his Correspondence with England," *Catholic Historical Review* 60 (1974), pp.55–64; Gary Lease, "Merry del Val and Tyrrell: A Modernist Struggle," *Downside Review* 192 (1984), pp.133–56. See also O'Connell, pp.211–13.

34. For von Hügel's involvement in critical biblical studies, see Barmann, pp.18–53.

35. Chronique, *Bulletin critique* 6:2 (May 1885), pp.175–78; 7:6 (March 1886), pp.117–18; 7:7 (April 1886), p.135; 7:24 (December 1886), pp.477–78; 12:6 (March 1891), pp.119–20; 12:24 (December 1891), pp.278–79.

36. John H. Cardinal Newman, "An Essay on the Inspiration of Scripture," *Nineteenth Century* 15 (February 1884), pp.185–99.

37. vH to Newman, 1 July 1884; Newman to vH, 21 July 1884; *Letters and Diaries*, v.30, pp.382–84.

38. Alfred Loisy, *L'Evangile et L'Eglise* (Paris: Alphonse Picard et fils, 1902); *The Gospel and the Church* (London, Pitman, 1904).

39. Barmann, pp.79–137.

40. The following list of publications indicates vH's advocacy of Loisy: "A Proposito dell'Abate Loisy," *Studi Religiosi* 1 (July-August, 1901), pp.348–50; "The Case of Abbé Loisy," *The Pilot* 9 (9 January 1904), pp.30–31; "The Case of M. Loisy," *The Pilot* 9 (23

January 1904), p.94; "The Abbé Loisy and the Holy Office," *The Times* (2 March 1904), p.15 (signed Romanus); "Introduction to letters by Bailey Saunders and Loisy," *The Times* (30 April 1904), p.6; "Discussions: M. Loisy's Type of Catholicism," *The Hibbert Journal* 3 (April 1905), pp.599–600; "The Abbé Loisy," *The Tablet* 3 (7 March 1908), pp.378–79; Review, *Les Evangiles Synoptiques*, *The Hibbert Journal* 6 (July 1908), pp.926–30; "L'Abate Loisy e il problema dei Vangeli Sinottici," *Il Rinnovamento* 3 (January-June 1908), pp.209–34; 4 (July-December 1908), pp.1–44; 5 (January-June 1909), pp.396–423 (signed H).

41. "L'Abbé Duchesne and Anglican Orders," *Tablet* 83 (2 June 1894), pp.857–58.

42. Diary of 1892 notes that Vaughan came to stay with the von Hügels on 28 January and that they had two talks about biblical criticism.

43. vH first met Mignot 22 November 1893. vH described their meeting in his obituary, "Eudixe Irénée Mignot," *Contemporary Review* 113 (1918), p.519.

44. C. L. Wood (Lord Halifax) to vH, 5 September 1911, quoted by Kelly, p.69, n.59.

45. Diary, 7 March 1896.

46. Merry del Val to Vaughan, 2 April 1896, Archives of the Archdiocese of Westminster (AAW), Vaughan Papers 1/14, 36.

47. Diary 6 February, 5 March 1896. Barmann comments on vH's paper, p.63.

48. "The Church and the Bible: The Two Stages of Their Inter-Relation," *Dublin Review* 115 (October 1894), pp.313–41; 116 (April 1895), pp.306–37; 117 (October 1895), pp.275–304.

49. "The Comma Johanneum," *Tablet* 89 (5 June 1897), pp.896–97.

50. Butler's letters to vH are at SAUL, MSS 2359–2373. vH's letters to Butler are in Downside Abbey Archives (uncatalogued). See J. J. Kelly, "On the Fringe of the Modernist Crisis: The Correspondence of Baron Friedrich von Hügel and Abbot Cuthbert Butler," *Downside Review* 97 (October 1979), pp.275–301. This first letter from Butler was written 22 June 1895.

51. Barmann, p.42.

52. vH to MP, 5 December 1899. PP, BL, Add. MS. 45361. Von Hügel suggested that Petre should begin with selected works of Plotinus and Dionysius and emphasized the importance of reading only works that had been translated from the original text. For a study of this remarkable woman, see Ellen Leonard, *Unresting Transformation: The Theology and Spirituality of Maude Petre* (Lanham: University Press of America, 1991).

53. Maude Petre, *My Way of Faith* (London: Dent & Sons, 1937), p.255.

54. vH's diary notes his first meeting with Semeria, 14 November 1894, and with Blondel, 14 March 1895.

55. Maude Petre, *Von Hügel and Tyrrell: The Story of a Friendship* (London: J. M. Dent & Sons, 1937), p.10; hereafter *VHT*.

THE CRUCIAL
YEARS
(1897-1907)

3

T he next ten years were crucial ones for Friedrich von Hügel. During this period he wrote his great work on religion, the two-volume study on mysticism. At the same time he was deeply involved in the religious crisis known as "modernism." Because of his role as a networker, bringing people from different countries and backgrounds together, he has been called the "lay bishop" of the "modernist" movement.[1] Not only did he welcome people into his home both in London and in Rome, but he circulated articles written by himself and others among a large network from different countries. An illustration of the scope of this activity may be seen in his diary entry for 6 January 1904 where he lists nineteen persons to whom he sent off prints of his article on "The Case of Abbé Loisy." These included Genocchi and Minocchi in Italy, Loisy, Houtin, and Mignot in France, Troeltsch, Holtzmann, Sauer, and Eucken in Germany, Jacks in England, and the American Bishop Spalding.[2]

In September 1903 the family moved from Hampstead to 13 Vicarage Gate in Kensington, a large house which would be home for the remainder of von Hügel's life. During this period von Hügel spent considerable time in Europe, visiting Loisy and Huvelin in France, Eucken and Troeltsch in Germany, and making numerous contacts in Rome. In July 1903 Leo XIII died and was replaced on 3 August by the more conservative Pius X. As Marvin O'Connell points out, von Hügel risked nothing professionally in the scholarly wars which were raging during these years, because he had no profession to risk. He was "a well-fixed private layman, free to indulge his interests in a private manner and free also to encourage, cajole, and admonish others less advantageously positioned than himself."[3]

Von Hügel, following the advice of Huvelin, continued to look for truth in wholeness, although his efforts to hold together competing claims did not always succeed. For him the tensions involved were part of the "costliness" of discipleship.

Friendship with George Tyrrell

At the beginning of this period von Hügel met George Tyrrell, a thirty-six-year-old Jesuit, eight years younger than himself, a priest who was becoming well known as a spiritual writer and confessor.[4] The two men, together with Maude Petre, worked closely together for a time on what they saw as a common cause, the renewal of Catholic Christianity. Von Hügel was grateful for the friendship and support of people who shared his passion for religion and his concern for the Church. In a letter to Maude Petre he explained why these friendships were important for him:

> Here in England I have, just at present, got so few Catholic friends (whom I am seeing sufficiently often and closely to be able to judge about) who strike me as growing and opening out *mentally;* and yet growth as deepening and expansion of the whole being, head and heart, are about the one profound refreshment which one soul can itself experience, and in doing so, can in some measure hand on to another.[5]

All who knew von Hügel and Tyrrell were struck by the sharp contrast between the two men. De la Bedoyère describes them as "the orderly, scrupulous, intensely concentrating, deeply devout, German-Scottish scholar, and the temperamental, volatile, skeptical-mystical, Irish convert-priest."[6] Maude Petre, who knew them both so well, portrayed them as sharing a fundamental aim, the spiritual welfare of humankind, "through the instrumentality of the Catholic Church," but emphasized "the great difference between the grave, cautious German and the generous but incautious Irishman; between the mind of system and the mind of intuition; between virtue and heroism."[7]

The story of the friendship of these two very different personalities is important, not only in the study of modernism, but in understanding von Hügel and his spirituality. Von Hügel's friendship with Tyrrell has sometimes been played down or interpreted as an "unfortunate incident in the Baron's life." In response to this interpretation, Maude Petre maintained that the friendship was a misfortune for Tyrrell, because it involved him in historical studies for which he was not prepared and which led ultimately to his condemnation. In response to this interpretation De la Bedoyère pointed out:

> It is rather hard to accuse a theologically untrained layman, however learned and keen, of corrupting, through the introduction of new friends and writers of common interest and through completing his education, a trained Jesuit selected by his superiors for the highly responsible work of spiritual writing in the society's name for the good of souls.[8]

O'Connell suggests that if von Hügel led Tyrrell into waters that were too deep for him, the cause was lack of judgment, not malice.[9]

Tyrrell had already experienced some difficulties within his order. After only two years he had been removed from his teaching position at St. Mary's, Stoneyhurst. The young teacher had argued that his critical approach to St. Thomas was faithful to the intent of Leo XIII in *Aeterni Patris*, although the practice within the society was to study Aquinas through his Jesuit commentator Suarez. In 1896 his superiors reassigned Tyrrell to the scriptorium of the Jesuit periodical, *The Month*, a position in which he became widely known as a spiritual director and writer.

After reading Tyrrell's *Nova et Vetera*, von Hügel wrote to invite the author for lunch or tea at the von Hügel home in Hampstead.[10] Barmann comments on the significance of this first meeting during October 1897 of the two men whose lives were to impact on one another:

> At even this first meeting they seem to have recognized in one another the shared sources of hopes and aims toward which they would work together in the following years—the common desire to eliminate the sectarian spirit in its various manifestations within Roman Catholicism.[11]

At von Hügel's request, Tyrrell undertook the direction of his eldest daughter, Gertrud, a young woman of twenty whose faith had been disturbed by her father's imprudent sharing of his own religious problems with her, a situation which Tyrrell pointed out to von Hügel.

> You neglect St. Paul's caution against giving babes the solid food of adults. The result is indigestion. . . . We must give minds time to grow and feed them suitably to their age. . . . If you want your daughter's company you must shorten your steps and walk slowly, else she will lose her breath in her desire to keep up with you.[12]

Tyrrell carefully noted that he had not said anything "that would not be equally true were it a question of a son rather than a daughter."[13]

Von Hügel accepted Tyrrell's judgment of the situation. His grief is apparent in his letter from Rome written in January 1898:

> If only I had looked out against the selfishness of leaning on one whom I ought to have propped still for many a day! I have dropped my own child, my first-born, whom God gave me to carry and to guard.[14]

It was a lesson which von Hügel never forgot and one which helped him in his guidance of others.

Von Hügel was not only deeply concerned about his daughter, but he was aware that Gertrud's situation might create difficulties for himself and for his work, an anxiety which he confided to Tyrrell.

> I just simply live for my work, and that work requires as a *sine qua non* of, I will not say, success, but even of existence, a reputation of substantial orthodoxy, and even prudence, sufficient to stand a good deal of strain.[15]

This concern for what he called his "little reputation" would continue to be a cause of anxiety in the years ahead. Tyrrell had already pointed out to Gertrud "the danger of scandal, and also the triumph your defection will be to those who are hostile to your father's attitude as a liberal Catholic, and who will, not unnaturally, point to his own daughter as the fairest fruit of his opinions."[16] With help from Tyrrell and Abbé Huvelin, and understanding from her father who assured her that "it will make not the shadow of a difference to your old Father's love and sympathy," Gertrud was able to work through the difficulties she was experiencing.[17]

The friendship that grew between von Hügel and Tyrrell was

important for the development of each of them. They read one another's work and discussed problems together. In 1898 von Hügel was already writing a paper on St. Catherine of Genoa which would grow into his two-volume book. He counted on Tyrrell's advice at the various stages of the work. From Tyrrell's perspective, von Hügel opened up for him a world of scholarship, both Catholic and Protestant. He gratefully acknowledged von Hügel's influence:

> All the vast help you have given me—and surely I have grown from a boy to a man since I knew you—has been in opening my eyes to an ever fuller and deeper knowledge of the data of the great problem of life.[18]

The two scholars became partners in grappling with what they saw as the "great problem of life."

Just as Loisy provided a focus for von Hügel's concern over Catholic biblical studies, Tyrrell became a focus for his concern about the exercise of ecclesiastical authority. An article on hell, entitled "A Perverted Devotion," brought Tyrrell into conflict with his superiors which led to his departure from the Farm Street community in London.[19] In June 1900 he took up residence in a quiet Jesuit mission in the town of Richmond in Yorkshire where he had ample time to read and write. Von Hügel kept in touch with his friend through letters and visited him each August for two to three weeks. There they would read together, often joined by Maude Petre.

At the end of 1900 Cardinal Vaughan and the bishops of the Province of Westminster issued "A Joint Pastoral Letter on the Church and Liberal Catholicism"[20] which both men found upsetting and which stimulated their reflections on the nature of ecclesiastical authority. Tyrrell's reflections found expression in *The Church and the Future* printed and privately circulated under the name of Hilaire Bourdon.[21] Von Hügel's thoughts on the topic were first given in an address to a group of Anglican clerics in January 1904. The work was further edited by von Hügel with helpful suggestions from Tyrrell, but not published until after von Hügel's death.[22]

Tyrrell's position within the Society of Jesus became increasingly difficult as restrictions were placed on his writing and pastoral work. Von Hügel worried about what would happen to Tyrrell if he left the society. In a letter written a few months before Tyrrell left the society in February 1906, von Hügel expressed to his friend his deep affection and his concern about the future:

> I love you—can you doubt it?—as I love at most four or five souls now living our poor earthly life throughout many a country, race, position, sex, and religion. And I feel saddened and benumbed when the vivid and ever recurring impression seizes me that what looks like a coming deliverance is, at bottom, a diminution of your utility in and for the Church, and through it, for religion at large.[23]

Von Hügel tried to use his influence to find a bishop who would be willing to take Tyrrell into his diocese but he was no more successful in this endeavor than he had been in his efforts to find ecclesiastical support for Loisy.

Other Influences

Within his own family, von Hügel's sister Pauline provided an example of a saintly life. She died in 1901 at the age of forty-three and was buried in the little cemetery of the parish church near Downside Abbey where her mother and brother Friedrich would also be buried. Like her brother, she was a writer, although she had a more lucid style. Three of her works were published as books, two of them stories on religious themes and the other a biography of Prince Demetrius Gallitzin (1770–1840).[24] Pauline was known as a generous and talented woman who cared deeply for the things of God.[25] Her suffering and death must have had a profound impact on her older brother. In an unpublished letter to his second daughter, Hildegard, he described Auntie Pauline's burial day and his own prayer by the coffin before the Requiem Mass.[26]

In 1904 von Hügel became involved in a debate between his two friends, the exegete Loisy and the philosopher Blondel over history and dogma, especially as these disciplines touched upon Christology. As one who worked as an exegete and a philosopher, von Hügel tried to help the two scholars to understand each other's position. He appreciated the work of both scholars but in this debate his sympathies were more with Loisy than with Blondel. He attempted, without success, to find a mediating position between the two positions.[27] From the exchange among the three scholars von Hügel wrote his own response: "Du Christ éternel et de nos christologies successives."[28]

In addition to Tyrrell, Loisy, and Blondel, there were other influences and numerous persons with whom von Hügel carried on an intensive correspondence and friendship. In November 1897 while he was in Rome he met the American Protestant scripture scholar Dr. Charles Augustus Briggs with whom he coauthored *The Papal Commission and the Pentateuch* (London, 1906). In May 1898 and again in May 1902 he visited Rudolf Eucken in Jena, Germany. During the same trip he visited Ernst Troeltsch for the first and only time. Scholars from different countries and traditions often found hospitality in the von Hügel home. Von Hügel would show them the sights of London, take them to visit scholars in Oxford and Cambridge, and often arrange for them to deliver an address. One such guest was Archbishop Mignot who visited England in July 1904.[29] Duchesne and Briggs both visited in June 1906 and Briggs again in 1907.[30]

In addition to European and American scholars there were many English scholars with whom von Hügel maintained close contact including the Catholic layman Edmund Bishop, religious scholars like Edward Cuthbert Butler, and Anglicans like Alfred L. Lilley and Clement C. J. Webb.[31] Von Hügel was keenly aware of the need for collaboration in the task which he had undertaken. As he wrote to Tyrrell:

> It is *quite* certain that we, tiny group of English lang(uag)e R.C.'s must not *dream* of working alone. We must *either* amalgamate with broad Anglicans and such-like, in England, or with large R.C.'s abroad.

He saw the second alternative as "more effective for our direct purposes," but also recognized the difficulties, particularly the fact that they would be "more exposed to being somehow tracked down and captured by our opponents" than if they worked "together with various sorts of non-Catholics."[32]

Von Hügel tried to do both. He sent Loisy's and Tyrrell's writings to a number of Anglican and Protestant scholars, sometimes suggesting that they might promote both the scholar and the work. Percy Gardner, Professor of Classical Archeology at Oxford, was one whose influence von Hügel courted.[33] When Gardner requested "one or two broad Roman Catholics" to write papers for the *Hibbert Journal,* von Hügel checked with Cardinal Vaughan, who suggested Dr. Robert F. Clarke. Von Hügel added his own suggestions: Mr. Edmund Bishop,

Dom E. Cuthbert Butler, Rev. Dr. William Barry, and Mr. Wilfrid Ward.[34] In another letter von Hügel explained his own situation to Gardner:

> I have so few *English* friends who, laymen, care deeply for religion and yet apply critical method to its documents and phenomena. It is this that binds me, in spite of any differences, so sincerely and abidingly to Edward Caird and James Ward and also yourself.[35]

Edward Caird, Master of Balliol in Oxford, was one of a number of prominent scholars to whom von Hügel sent Loisy's *L'Evangile et L'Eglise*, noting that Loisy had quoted from Caird and referred to him as "un savant Anglican." Although Caird was a Presbyterian, von Hügel expressed his conviction that he was indeed " 'catholic' using the word in my sense, from a large minded but very convinced Roman Catholic perspective." Caird thanked von Hügel for Loisy's book and graciously acknowledged that he was enriched by those whose religious life had developed under different conditions from his own.[36]

During this period von Hügel, along with Tyrrell and Petre, was involved in an ecumenical project to publish a number of "Tracts." Von Hügel wrote to Maude Petre, "I love collaboration wherever we can get it, with self-respect and duly guarded."[37] But it seemed that the timing was wrong. Von Hügel was seeking what he described as "a *cordially equal footing* of collaboration between the Anglicans and the Roman Catholics in this combination."[38] After demanding that Roman Catholic papers should be included, von Hügel was worried that Tyrrell was too upset to "speak in his own full tones at this time" and he was concerned about his own "first and probably last great work being myself very decided not to break with the authorities."[39] The project finally had to be abandoned.

Von Hügel also helped to found the Italian periodical *Il Rinnovamento*, published by a number of laymen in Milan. Von Hügel described them to Maude Petre as "acting out of faithful love and inalienable devotion to the Church," adding that he would not write for them until his book was out.[40]

These projects took a great deal of time and energy during the period when von Hügel was trying to complete his book on St. Catherine. He himself was often unwell. His diary notes "white nights" and "empty mornings." Not only his wife, but also his daughter Gertrud, suffered poor health. Gertrud had to postpone her marriage because of illness. These difficulties, along with the growing reactionary forces within the Church, caused much suffering, but von Hügel tried to maintain hope in the midst of these trials. He cautioned Maude Petre not to dwell too much on the difficulties:

> ... the thought of God and of His patient, slowly victorious truth, and of the many souls that in humble, prayerful frankness face the painful blissful light and love that come from and that lead to Him and this, with much work, shall strengthen us.[41]

Although the issues related to historical study within the Roman Catholic Church were the focus of von Hügel's concerns at this time, he was also reaching out to the larger religious world. In 1904 he helped to form the London Society for the Study of Religion, an interfaith group who were interested in the scholarly and scientific study of religion. As Barmann points out: "For a Roman Catholic to acknowledge the truth or legitimacy of other religious systems was at this historical moment considered by Roman authorities to be, if not formal heresy, at least a manifestation of heretical leanings and of 'indifferentism.' "[42]   Von Hügel did not want to be the only Roman Catholic involved. He tried, unsuccessfully, to interest both Wilfrid Ward and Edmund Bishop in the project. As he explained to Ward: "my own feeling so far is, that tho' no doubt the scheme might turn out unworkable, or, at least, impossible for Catholics, there is nothing so far to show that this will or must be the case. The scholarly and careful Catholics might do much good, while themselves learning useful things."[43] This last sentence describes the actual experience of von Hügel who, through the society, was able to establish contact with scholars from different traditions who shared his concern about the role of religion in their world.

The London Society for the Study of Religion (LSSR) as well as the Synthetic Society founded in 1896 to consider agnostic tendencies and to contribute to a philosophy of religious belief, provided von Hügel with a forum for the exchange of ideas. Many of his papers were read to these groups and he responded to his colleagues who, in consideration of his deafness, would present their papers for him to read before each meeting. In May 1903 he delivered his address on "Experience and Transcendence" to the Synthetic Society. This was an important work, which was revised and published in *Dublin Review* (1906).[44]

Von Hügel not only helped to establish the LSSR but he served for many years on its planning committee which often met in his home. The diaries carefully describe each meeting and list the names of the members present. The LSSR gave von Hügel access to scholarly colleagues and provided a wider vision of the religious quest as well as personal support and friendship which he would need as the situation in his own church became more tense.

The Modernist Storm

Von Hügel's hope for an ecclesiastical climate that would encourage free historical and critical enquiry, or which would at least provide what he called the "elbow-room" required to carry out critical studies, became slimmer as Loisy's work was placed on the Index and Tyrrell was dismissed from the Jesuits. One last effort by von Hügel to draw up an "address of support" for Loisy composed of signatures of leading laymen from England, France, Italy, Germany, Austria, and even Russia proved impossible to achieve.[45] Von Hügel feared that it would appear that Cardinal Merry del Val was the true, sincere type of Catholic and that "none of our group are, then, Catholic at all."[46]

A number of events in 1907 reinforced this fear. In January the first issue of the Milanese Review *Il Rinnovamento* appeared, edited by the laymen Alfieri, Casti, and Gallarati Scotti. In April Cardinal Steinhuber, Prefect of the Index, instructed Cardinal Ferrari, Archbishop of Milan, to call for its suspension as "notoriously opposed to the Catholic spirit and teaching." He deplored the pride with which such writers as Fogazzaro, Tyrrell, von Hügel, Murri, and others posed as masters and doctors of the Church.[47] In July *Lamentabili sane exitu*, a syllabus of sixty-five condemned propositions, was promulgated followed in September by the encyclical *Pascendi dominici gregis* which presented a systematic analysis of "modernism" and prescribed remedies for correcting these errors. As Barmann points out,

> . . . from its opening paragraphs to its conclusion, the encyclical presumed bad-faith and evil motives on the part of these adversaries of scholasticism whom it aimed to smite with God's own right hand of papal authority.[48]

The differences between von Hügel and Tyrrell show up most

clearly in their reactions to *Pascendi*. Tyrrell responded immediately
with articles in the *Giornale d' Italia* and *The Times*, actions which
brought him ecclesiastical censure. Amigo, Bishop of Southwark,
reported the articles to the Roman authorities who ordered that Tyrrell
should be deprived of the sacraments and his case reserved to the Holy
See. Von Hügel supported Tyrrell, but in his letter of appreciation to
Tyrrell for his articles, the Baron expressed some concern over the
"personal tone" which was "very hot, vehement, and sarcastic." He
admitted that he himself "in spite of everything" had

> . . . a feeling as to the pathetic position of the Pope, holding
> that most difficult of posts not through his own choosing, a
> peasant of simple seminary training and speaking to some 200
> million souls of whom doubtless, a good nine-tenths, at least,
> are even less cultured than himself, and whom he is sincerely
> trying to defend against what he conceives to be deadly
> error.[49]

Von Hügel understood the pressures on his friend but urged him to be
patient amidst the difficulties:

> You are born to be daring, deeply independent; just because
> of that, do not let any over-swiftness, any unlimitedness, any
> impatience with that dearest and greatest of the disguises
> under which God works in man—I mean love of friction and
> our poor bovine, humble slownesses, of a goodly dose of
> stupidity—get into or find any lodgment in that amazingly
> rapid nature of yours.[50]

In August, just before the publication of *Pascendi*, von Hügel had
met in Molteno with a group of Italian modernists to discuss strategies.
In his diary he noted that he had pointed out the "necessity of sincere,
thorough, critical work; of deep self-renouncing Xtian life; & of careful
charity & magnanimity to'rds our opponents."[51] It was advice which
he tried to follow, but in the atmosphere of suspicion generated by the
condemnations, this was not easy.

Von Hügel believed that there were times when resistance to
ecclesiastical authorities was justified and even argued in a letter to
Wilfrid Ward that "the Church itself is demonstrably based upon such
a 'disobedience' on the part of Our Lord Himself." He continued:

We can only maintain (and indeed are strictly bound to hold) that the *presumption* is ever on the side of the authorities and obedience to them; that only under pressure of obedience to even higher and still more costing claims and obedience to them can any "disobedience" ever be licit; and that the "disobedient" individual so acts ever at his own risk and peril to be justified or not in time and by God's own spirit working and expressing itself in and thro' the Church.[52]

Von Hügel was aware that his family did not share his views and that he had a responsibility toward them. As he wrote to Tyrrell on an earlier occasion concerning his need to be discreet: "I have not myself only to think of, but a dear wife, only by affection with me in this attitude, and three good girls to marry."[53] Although Lady Mary did not share her husband's concerns, she did speak up for Loisy at her audience with Pius X in January 1906.[54] In April of 1907 von Hügel's youngest daughter, Thekla, entered the Carmelite monastery and on 7 December 1907 his oldest daughter Gertrud married Count Francesco Salimei in Genoa in a civil ceremony followed by a Nuptial Mass the next day on the Feast of the Immaculate Conception at the Shrine of St. Catherine of Genoa. Francesco had wanted Padre Semeria, who had taught him catechism and was a friend, to preside at the wedding but Pius X forbade it. Both Semeria and von Hügel were considered suspect.[55] These momentous family events, along with the ecclesiastical developments of 1907, must have made the year an extremely stressful one for von Hügel.

In addition to family concerns, von Hügel also had his book to think about, the work of over ten years which was soon to be published, and which he feared might be placed on the Index. Tyrrell had already suggested that his name should not be associated with the book, although he had acted as a resource at every stage of its development, including final proofreading and editing of the over 2000-page typescript. Von Hügel was grateful for Tyrrell's willingness not to be acknowledged, realizing that the book would probably have "a good deal of suspicion or hostility to encounter, and to make such a declaration might just finish off its chances with our people, even before it was well out."[56]

Von Hügel had struggled unsuccessfully for intellectual freedom within the Catholic Church. After the publication of *Pascendi* many of those whom he had encouraged felt deserted by him. They interpreted as cowardliness von Hügel's determination to avoid anything which might be seen as a conspiracy. When Tyrrell challenged his friend's cautious attitudes, noting that he himself "as an extra-social animal" was freer to "mix with strayed sheep than a layman with a Catholic family," von Hügel's response reveals a person who was always ready to learn from criticism.[57] He accepted Tyrrell's comments as "a most valuable appeal to me to grow and modify myself," but while he was ready to reflect on Tyrrell's words, he stated his own conviction:

> A good deal of what I love with all I am will have to die, for good and all—in me as truly as in anyone—and again that which will survive, will have to do so, just as an element in a larger whole, larger than I can see.[58]

What survived from those difficult years was von Hügel's great work, *The Mystical Element of Religion as Studied in Saint Catherine of Genoa and her Friends*. After some difficulty in finding a publisher willing to undertake the publication of such an unwieldy work it was finally accepted by Dent on 3 March 1908 and published in November 1908, just a year after the condemnation of Modernism.

NOTES

1. Paul Sabatier, *Modernism: The Jowett Lectures 1908*, trans. by C. A. Miles (London: T. Fisher Unwin, 1908), pp.40–44.

2. Diary for 6 January 1904.

3. O'Connell, *Critics on Trial*, p.51.

4. Biographers and scholars have found the personality of Tyrrell difficult to capture. The most recent attempt is Nicholas Sagovsky, *"On God's Side": A Life of George Tyrrell* (Oxford: Clarendon Press, 1990). Maude Petre was the first to undertake this task, publishing Tyrrell's own description of his first twenty-three years written for her when he was forty: *Autobiography of George Tyrrell 1861–1884*, vol.1 of the *Autobiography and Life of George Tyrrell* (London: Edward Arnold, 1912). Petre arranged and added supplements to the first volume and wrote the second volume, *Life of George Tyrrell from 1884–1909*. The first volume will be referred to as *Life* 1, the second as *Life* 2.

5. vH to MP, 26 September 1900, PP, BL, Add. MS. 45361; published in *SL*, pp.88–95; quote from p.88.

6. De la Bedoyère, p.100.

7. Maude Petre, *Von Hügel and Tyrrell: The Story of a Friendship* (London: J. M. Dent & Sons, 1937), pp.2–3; hereafter *VHT*. The work describes the friendship as perceived by Petre.

8. De la Bedoyère, p.103.

9. O'Connell, p.282.

10. Both sides of the correspondence between vH to T are in the BL, Add. MSS 44927–44931. vH's first letter was written 20 September 1897, BL, Add. MS 44927. vH noted in his diary that Fr. George Tyrrell, S.J. had visited him for the first time on 9 October 1897.

11. Barmann, pp.140–41. See also O'Connell, *Critics on Trial,* pp.169–74, for a description of Tyrrell's meeting and subsequent friendship with vH.

12. T to vH, 6 December 1897, BL, Add. MS 44927; published in *VHT,* pp.15–19.

13. Ibid. Four letters from Tyrrell to Gertrud are in the vH Papers at Downside Abbey Archives, MS 1272 (29 December 1997, undated, 17 May 1898, 27 May 1898). They reveal a wise director who encouraged Gertrud to explain her situation to her Father: "It will be a great grief to him to hear, and to you to tell but it must be done."

14. vH to T, 26 January 1898; BL, Add. MS 44927.

15. Ibid.

16. 29 December 1897; Downside Abbey Archives, MS 1272.

17. vH to Gertrud, 6 January 1898, written from Rome; Downside Abbey Archives, MS 1272.

18. T to vH, 5 December 1902; BL, Add. MS 44928; quoted in *Life* 2, p.96.

19. "A Perverted Devotion," *Weekly Register* 100 (16 December 1899), pp.797–800; reprinted in *Essays on Faith and Immortality,* arranged by M. D. Petre (London: Edward Arnold, 1914), pp.158–71.

20. Although the Joint Pastoral was signed by the English bishops, David Schultenover in *A View from Rome: On the Eve of the Modernist Crisis* (New York: Fordham University Press, 1992), p.151, identifies Merry del Val as its principal fabricator with editorial assistance from Luis Martin, General of the Society of Jesus who shared Merry del Val's concern about liberalism among England Catholics. The text was published in *Tablet* 97 (5 January 1901), pp.8–12 and was endorsed by Leo XIII whose letter of congratulations to the bishops was printed in *Tablet* 97 (23 March 1901), p.441.

21. *The Church and the Future* was reprinted under Tyrrell's name with an Introduction by M.D. Petre (London: Priory Press, 1910).

22. "Official Authority and Living Religion," *EA* 2, pp.3–23. For details of how this work evolved, see Barmann, pp.158–60. In a letter to Hildegard, vH's second daughter, 24 April 1926, Edmund Gardner, vH's literary executor, expressed some reservations about including this essay in the collection. He added: "Being the earliest of them, it will stand first in the volume, and therefore will not be taken as your Father's final and matured utterance on the subject." Downside Abbey Archives, vHP, MS 1272 (uncatalogued).

23. vH to T, 9 October 1905; BL, Add. MS 44929; published in *SL,* pp.132–34; quote from p.134.

24. Baroness Pauline von Hügel, *The Price of the Pearl and Other Stories* (London, 1895); *Carmen's Secret* (London: Catholic Truth Society, 1897); *A Royal Son and Mother* (Notre Dame: Ave Maria Press, 1902).

25. Father De Lapasture, S.J. preached a sermon on "Self-Sacrifice" at Corpus Christi Church, Boscombe, Bournemouth, 13 September 1908, the twelfth anniversary of the blessing of the church which Pauline von Hügel had founded. This sermon, in which he described her generosity, may be found in *Downside Pamphlets* 187. There is also a brief outline of her "Life and Works" by J. A. Young in the Downside Abbey Archives, MS 1272.

26. 2 April 1901, vH to Hildegard (Hillie), Downside Abbey Archives, MS 1272 (uncatalogued). vH's diary is missing for 1901.

27. For a careful study of the controversy between Loisy and Blondel and vH's response to it, see John A. McGrath, *Baron Friedrich von Hügel and the Debate on Historical Christianity (1902–1905)* (San Francisco: Mellen Research University Press, 1993); also O'Connell, pp.257–62, 296–98.

28. *La Quinzaine* 58 (June 1904), pp.285–312; this article is included in McGrath's *Von Hügel and the Debate on Historical Christianity*, Appendix, pp. 241–80.

29. Diary, 16 July to 27 July 1904.

30. Diary, 22, 24 June 1906; 2 June 1907.

31. For a study of the relationship between vH and Bishop, see Nigel Abercrombie, "Friedrich von Hügel's Letters to Edmund Bishop," *Dublin Review* 227 (1953), pp.68–78, 179–89, 285–98, 419–38. For vH's friendship with Butler, see J. J. Kelly, "On the Fringe of the Modernist Crisis: The Correspondence of Baron Friedrich von Hügel and Abbot Cuthbert Butler," *Downside Review* 97 (1979), pp.275–301. Seventy letters of Alfred L. Lilley, Vicar of St Mary's Paddington Green to vH are at SAUL, Lilley Papers, MSS 30513–30580. For vH's relationship with the Anglican theologian, philosopher and historian Clement Webb see John D. Root, "The Correspondence of Friedrich von Hügel and Clement C. J. Webb, *Downside Review* 99 (1981), pp.288–98.

32. vH to T, 1 April 1905; PP, BL, Add. MS 44929.

33. The Gardner Letters are in the Bodleian Library (hereafter Bodl), Oxford, MS Eng. Misc. a.8. See also James J. Kelly, "The Modernist Controversy in England: The Correspondence between Friedrich von Hügel and Percy Gardner," *Downside Review* 99 (1981), pp.40–58, 119–36.

34. Letter marked confidential, 2 December 1902, Bodl, MS Eng. letters c.55, 199.

35. 5 December 1906, Bodl MS Eng. Letters c.55, 218.

36. Among the Edward Caird Papers at Balliol College, Oxford is a letter written by vH, 21 November 1902; Modern MSS Collections, Box 2. There is a draft of Caird's reply to vH.

37. vH to MP, 19 June 1906; PP, BL, Add. MS 45361.

38. Ibid.

39. vH to MP, 3 July 1906; PP, BL, Add. MS 45361.

40. vH to MP, 23 May 1907; PP, BL, Add. MS 45261.

41. vH to MP, 17 April 1906; PP, BL, Add. MS 45361.

42. Lawrence Barmann, "Confronting Secularization: Origins of the London Society for the Study of Religion," *Church History* 62 (1993), pp.22–40; quote from p.24.

43. 27 April 1904, WWP, SAUL, MS 38347, vii (143); quoted by Barman, Ibid., p.25.

44. *Dublin Review* 138 (1906), pp.357–79.

45. See Barmann, pp.129–32 for a description of this unsuccessful attempt to get signatures of Roman Catholic laymen who were concerned about Loisy's condemnation.

46. vH to T, 18 December 1906, BL, Add. MS 44929; published in *SL*, pp.136–37.

47. Holland quotes Cardinal Steinhuber in his Memoir of vH, *SL*, p.21.

48. Barmann, p.197.

49. vH to T, 1 October 1907, BL, Add. MS 44930; published in *VHT*, pp.162–63.

50. vH to T, 21 October 1907, BL, Add. MS 44930; published in *VHT*, p.164.

51. Diary, 26–29 August, 1907.

52. vH to WW, 5 June 1908, WWP, SAUL MS 38347, vii (143); quoted by Barman, p.215.

53. vH to T, 5 February 1904, BL, Add. MS 44928; published in *VHT*, p.143.

54. Diary 1906 notes on 3 January "M saw Pope about Loisy" and on 8 January: "Letter from M describing her audience with the Pope and speaking up for Loisy."

55. Diary, 6 April 1907 and 7, 8 August 1907 refer to Thekla's entrance into Carmel; De la Bedoyère, p.205 and Loisy, *Mémoires*, 2, p.570 describe difficulties around Gertrud's wedding.

56. vH to T, 30 December 1905, BL, Add. MS 44929; published in *VHT*, pp.186–87.

57. T to vH, 22 June 1908, BL, Add. MS 44931.

58. vH to T, 23 June 1908, BL, Add. MS 44931.

MAKING HISTORY (1908-1912)

4

T he short period between 1908 and 1912 was a turning point for von Hügel. His two-volume work, *The Mystical Element of Religion*, was published in November 1908 and *Eternal Life* appeared in 1912. His friend Tyrrell died in 1909 and his own dreams for a church in which there would be freedom to pursue modern questions also died. But for von Hügel death was not the end. He maintained his faith in God's action in the world and in the Church.

"The Mystical Element"

The theoretical base for this deep faith is worked out in *The Mystical Element of Religion as Studied in Saint Catherine of Genoa and her Friends*, von Hügel's first book, published when the author was fifty-six. What had begun as a short paper had grown "like an out branching tree in every direction" into a two-volume work of 888 pages.[1] When von Hügel first read Catherine's life in 1878 he certainly would not have imagined the work which he finally produced thirty years later and which was the fruit of ten years of research. In this mammoth work we meet von Hügel, the student of religion, the man who wanted to discover how things worked, and particularly how the human person responds to life.

We have seen that von Hügel took seriously his vocation to live the Christian life fully and to help others to do the same. He saw himself as "*making* history" as he explained in a letter to Tyrrell in 1901:

And I am having the strange, very sobering impression that

God is deigning somehow to use me,—me, in my measure, along with others who can and do more, and much more—towards *making*, not simply registering, history. And, dear me, *what* a costing process *that* is![2]

Von Hügel was involved in making history in a number of ways as we have seen, but he himself considered *The Mystical Element* as his major contribution. In the same letter to Tyrrell he expressed his hopes for the fruitfulness of this work:

I can't help hoping now, more strongly than at first, that the result of the whole will be a living organism, something that will be able to enter into other minds and hearts, and grow and bring fruit there. Certainly the effect upon myself is being considerable: I have become a good bit more of a person, please God, of the right, the spiritual-humble sort, by battling and toiling with and in and over these great realities and problems.[3]

In a letter to William James, von Hügel described the impetus that motivated his work: "I have loved its subject-matters for some thirty years, and I had to do the thing *tant bien que mal*, for my own interior growth's sake: *viola tout*."[4]

The Mystical Element offers the patient reader von Hügel's observations and reflections drawn from a rich variety of sources, beginning with ancient Greek philosophy and moving through the centuries to contemporary studies of psychology and religion. The focus is on life, for although "no amount of talk or theory can, otherwise than harmfully, take the place of life, yet observation and reflection can help us to see where and how life acts."[5] As a focus for these reflections he turned to Catherine of Genoa, a fifteenth-century mystic.

Choice of Catherine

Von Hügel's deep commitment to the Roman Catholic Church did not blind him to the restraints of post-Tridentine Catholicism "with its regimental Seminarism, its predominantly controversial spirit, its suspiciousness and timidity."[6] This was why he turned to "one of those large-souled pre-Protestant, post-Mediaeval Catholics," Catherine of Genoa. Newman had taught him to glory in his "appurtenance to the

Catholic and Roman Church, and to conceive this my inheritance in a large and historical manner, as a slow growth across the centuries."[7] Catherine provided a position from which to study that growth.

The choice of Catherine, a lay woman with family responsibilities, is in itself significant, as von Hügel emphasized, for among formally canonized saints, Catherine is "a rare example of a contemplative and mystic who, from first to last, leads at the same time the common life of marriage and of widowhood in the world."[8]

> The very ordinariness of her external lot, a simple wife and widow, at no time belonging to any Religious Order or Congregation; the apparently complete failure of her earthly life, which gives occasion to the birth within her of the heavenly one . . . all this, even if it were all, helps to give an extraordinary richness and instructiveness to her life.[9]

In the preface of the second edition von Hügel defended his choice of Catherine to Dr. Gore who had suggested that St. Teresa would have provided a more useful example for his purposes. Von Hügel's answer was simple: "I happened first to learn to love, and to live in, the world of Caterinetta Fiesca Adorna, and was slowly brought, by such a love and life, to various questions made thus vivid for my own mind and practice."[10] For von Hügel it was indeed a love affair. He visited Genoa over twenty times, lovingly gathering material on Catherine and her friends. But Catherine was not only someone whom he loved. She became the vehicle for bringing together "a treble interest and spirit: historico-critical, philosophical, religious."[11]

Von Hügel believed that "a biographical study can hope to arouse interest and attention in the living facts of religion, in a manner in which no simple theory or generalization can do."[12] His biographical work on Catherine provided a focus for his critical study of religion itself. This was his method in writing the book, although in the completed work Catherine seems more a recurring thread that weaves in and out throughout the various sections, rather than the actual focus for the study. He acknowledged this development in the Preface to the first edition:

> Having begun to write a biography of St. Catherine, with some philosophical elucidations, I have finished by writing an essay on the philosophy of Mysticism, illustrated by the life of Caterinetta Fiesca Adorna and her friends.[13]

Three Elements of Religion

Central to this massive work, and to von Hügel's life and activities, no matter what form they took, was his understanding of the three elements of religion: 1) the external, authoritative, historical, traditional, institutional; 2) the critical, speculative, philosophical; 3) the intuitive, volitional, mystical. Von Hügel insisted that all three must always be present in a mature religious person, although one or another may predominate in a particular individual and at different times in a person's life.

Von Hügel's sensitivity to human development is obvious in his invitation to his readers to reflect on their own religious life in order to discern how the three elements successively appeared. While recognizing variations, he traced the child's apprehension of religion through sense and memory, the youth's through question and argument, the adult's through intuition, feeling, and volition. The transition from one stage to the next is both necessary and difficult; it is a time of crisis. In the first the person moves from an external religion to an intellectual one. In the second an emotional-experiential dimension is added to the external, intellectual religion.[14] The mature religious person thus can say: "I believe because I am told, because it is true, because it answers my deepest interior experiences and needs."[15]

At times von Hügel's insistence on the three elements seems to be overdone. Everything, even God, must fit into the threefold pattern. Using the analogy of the three powers of the soul, God the Father and Creator corresponds to the sense perception and imagination; God the Son, the Logos, to our reason; and God the Holy Spirit to the volitional force. Yet God is one, as is the human personality.[16] In Christ and in the saints we find both the greatest possible multiplicity as well as the deepest unity.

Life of Catherine

After setting the framework of the three elements and providing some background material, von Hügel introduced Catherine, born in Genoa in 1447. As a young girl she wanted to become an Augustinian Canoness like her sister but instead was married to Giuliano Adorno, a man who "did not deserve the rare woman who had been sold to him."[17] At the end of the first ten years of her childless and unhappy married life she was "sadder than ever, with apparently no escape of any kind from out of the dull oppression, the living death of her existence."[18] Then in March 1473, at the age of twenty-six, she experienced her conversion—a sudden and immense love of God which changed her life. For the next twenty-five years "she was guided and taught interiorly by her tender Love alone."[19] Catherine's unfaithful and extravagant husband, Giuliano, also changed. The couple moved into a small home near a hospital where they cared for the sick and in 1479 they moved into two small rooms in the hospital itself. From 1490 to 1496 Catherine served as the matron of the hospital, responsible for its administration and finances. Giuliano died in October 1494 while Catherine continued her ministry to the sick poor until prevented by poor health.

In the midst of the demanding care of the sick, Catherine entered into deep prayer of quiet, receiving the Eucharist daily, a practice which was unusual during that period. The *Vita* described a colorful scene when a friar insisted that he, as a religious, was more free to love God than Catherine who was "married to the world." Catherine responded with "such force and fervor that all her hair came undone, and falling down, was scattered upon her shoulders."

> That you should merit more than myself, is a matter that I concede and do not seek, I leave it in your hands; but that I cannot love Him as much as you, is a thing that you will never by any means be able to make me understand.[20]

For the first twenty-five years following her conversion Catherine had no spiritual director but was "guided and taught by Love." During the last eleven years of her life Don Cattaneo Marabotto, a secular priest and rector of the hospital, was her confessor, and most of Catherine's sayings were transmitted through him. Von Hügel offered his description of the confessor's role:

> Marabotto's Direction consists, then, in giving her the human support of human understanding and sympathy, and, no doubt, in reminding her, in times of darkness, of the lights and truths received and communicated by her in times of consolation.[21]

Even when she was no longer able to work in the hospital because of ill health, Catherine maintained her interest in the care of the sick. Her death occurred in 1510.

Catherine's Doctrine

Von Hügel undertook a critical study of the various sources of Catherine's life and doctrine, Catherine herself having written nothing. As he stated in the original Preface, his critical work on classical and scriptural texts had "whetted (his) appetite" to try to bring order out of the various texts and glosses of the saint's life and legend.[22] The most important text on which all subsequent studies are based was the *Vita e Dottrina* published in Genoa in 1551, over forty years after Catherine's death. It was mainly the work of her confessor, Cattaneo Marabotto, and of her friend and disciple, Ettore Vernazza, who was a lawyer. Von Hügel used a reprint of the thirteenth edition published in 1847.[23]

If Catherine's doctrine could be summed up in one word it would be love. She expressed her immersion in love: "My *Me* is God, nor do I recognize any other *Me*, except my God." "God is my Being, my *Me*, my Strength, my Beatitude, my Good, my Delight."[24] For her, love of God and love of Christ were the same thing. She did not dwell on the historical Jesus but focused on the Christ present in the Eucharist as her food. Von Hügel commented on how Catherine managed to join "a universal love for Love Transcendent, with a particularism of attachment to individual souls, in which that Love is immanent."[25] It was a love that embraced her friends, the sick with whom she worked, and all of creation as the *Vita* noted: "She was most compassionate towards all creatures; so that, if an animal were killed or a tree cut down, she could hardly bear to see them lose that being which God had given them."[26]

Catherine was convinced, and so was von Hügel, that her intimacy with God was not the privilege of a few chosen souls. Two sentences quoted from the *Vita* emphasize this point: "I see every one to be capable of my tender Love." "Truth being, by its very nature, communicable to all, cannot be the exclusive property of any one."[27]

In describing God, and the soul's relationship to God, Catherine used spatial images: "in, within, into" to describe recollection; "out, outside, outwards" to portray liberation and ecstasy; "over, above, upwards" to refer to elevation.[28] Love was Catherine's favorite way of speaking about God, but she also drew on other images such as sun, light, fire, air, ocean, beauty, truth, and goodness. She did not refer to God as Father, Friend, Bridegroom, or Lover, a fact which von Hügel imputed to her lack of the experience of maternity or what he described as "the soul-entrancing power of full conjugal union."[29] This comment may reveal more about von Hügel than about Catherine, for he was convinced that our image of God is "formed out of the seemingly shifting, shrinking flux, and the apparently shapeless mass of our actual, bewildering human manifold; our flesh and sweat, and tears and blood, our joy and laughter, our passions and petty revolts, our weariness and isolations."[30]

Von Hügel insisted upon the primacy of experience but recognized that the language to describe that experience comes from one's tradition. The main literary sources of Catherine's doctrine, according to von Hügel, were the Pauline and Johannine writings from the New Testament, the Christian Neo-Platonist Areopagite writings, and the teachings of the Franciscan, Jacopone da Todi.

For both Paul and Catherine the experience of personal conversion was a focus for their teaching. Everything led up to or looked back upon the conversion experience. All their doctrine was "an attempt to articulate and universalize this original experience." In both "there is the same insistence upon the life-giving Spirit, the eternal Christ, manifesting His inexhaustible power in the transformation of souls, on and on, here and now, into the likeness of Himself."[31] For Catherine and Paul, God and love, Christ and Spirit are one.

An area where Catherine did not follow Paul was in his teaching on women, a fact noted by von Hügel:

> Indeed, in her whole general and unconscious position as to how a woman should hold herself in religious things it is interesting to note the absence of all influence from those Pauline sayings which, herein like Philo (and indeed the whole ancient world) treat man alone as "the (direct) image and glory (reflex) of God," and the woman as but "the glory (reflex) of the man."[32]

Nor did Catherine share the Pauline emphasis on baptism. For Paul, baptism was connected with his conversion experience, whereas for Catherine, baptized as an infant, "the event lay far back in that pre-conversion time, which was all but completely ousted from her memory by the great experience of some twenty-five years later."[33] For her the Eucharist was the key sacramental reality, and it was from John, rather than from Paul or the synoptics, that she drew her Eucharistic doctrine. God is the bread of life for which she hungered. In her reflection on the woman at the well she concentrated on the "living water" which promises spiritual sustenance.

The Johannine influence on Catherine is strong with its emphasis on God as light and love, its invitation to abide in love, its presentation of God as spiritual energy, its focus on life, and its stress on the present enjoyment of eternal life. From John, Catherine (and through her von Hügel) learned to think of religion as "an experience of eternity," a direct touch by God leading to the certainty that God is love.[34]

A third source for Catherine's doctrine is the Areopagite writings from which she drew a number of symbols, including the chain or rope that binds the soul to God, and God as the Sun which gives light, and the Fire which gives heat. Unlike Dionysius who referred to three ways of the inner life, purgative, illuminative, and unitive, Catherine knew only two, the purgative and unitive, and these two were mostly in close combination. Both Catherine and Dionysius spoke of deification, and of the Eucharist as the chief means and the culmination of deification.[35] Von Hügel noted the neo-Platonic influence on Catherine's God-language "derived from extended or diffusive material substances or conditions, Light, Fire, Fountain, Ocean; and from that pervasive emotion, Love, strictly speaking Desire, Eros."[36]

Finally, von Hügel considered the influence of Jacopone da Todi's "Lode" on Catherine's doctrine. Again it is the language of love which characterized both. For Catherine and the sources upon which she drew, there is a tendency described by von Hügel "to find the Then and There of History still at work, in various degrees, Here and Now, throughout Time and Space, and in the last resort, above and behind both these categories, in a spaceless timeless Present."[37] For this reason the historical Jesus and the teaching of the synoptic gospels are somewhat neglected.

Von Hügel returned to the neo-Platonic influence on Catherine's spirituality, reflected in her dualistic attitude toward the body as a prison house of the spirit, a true purgatory, but he pointed out that this view began with the suffering of the last part of her life when her body did indeed seem a prison. For Catherine the conflict was between two dispositions of the soul which either accepted or rejected love, rather than between body and soul.

Whereas the neo-Platonists treated the body and the visible creation as an obstacle to the spirit, von Hügel reminded his readers that Christianity maintains the substantial goodness of the body and matter. For von Hügel, true Christianity is always both attachment and detachment from the visible, concrete world. He insisted that even the mystic needs the material, drawing on the example of the spiritual writer, Père Jean Nicolas Grou, who alternated his prayer of quiet with critical work on the Graeco-Latin classics.[38] Genuine Christianity is always incarnational. In spite of the neo-Platonic strain in Catherine's teaching, she was generally positive in her attitudes. For her, "holiness consists primarily, not in the absence of faults, but in the presence of spiritual force, in Love creative, Love triumphant—the soul becoming flame rather than snow, and dwelling upon what to do, give and be, rather than what to shun."[39] Von Hügel pointed out to his readers that:

> In her greatest sayings, and in her actual life, Purity is found to be Love, and this Love is exercised, not only in the inward, home-coming, recollective movements—in the purifying of the soul's dispositions, but also in the outgoing, world-visiting, dispersive movement—in action toward fellow-souls.[40]

While insisting on Catherine's concern for her neighbor, von Hügel had to admit that in her doctrine more than in her life she was individualistic, noting:

> her strongly ecstatic, body-ignoring, body-escaping type of religion; and how, even in her case, it tended to starve the corporate, institutional conceptions and affections.[41]

This tendency to individualism was particularly evident in her teaching on afterlife, the area in which von Hügel found her most original contribution.

Catherine's teaching on afterlife was based on the analogy with her deepest this-life experience. Her teaching on purgatory was built on a projection of her conversion experience "when a short span of clock-time held acts of love received and acts of love returned, which transformed all her previous condition, and initiated a whole series of states more expressive of her truest self." Purgatory, like her conversion experience, is a plunge into love which transforms the soul.[42] Heaven is the continuation of her total immersion in love whereas hell is the absence of love, for "a little drop of Love" would turn hell into heaven. For Catherine it is the "one God who is the Fire of Pain and the Light of Joy to souls, according as they resist Him or will Him, either here or hereafter."[43]

Catherine's central idea is "the soul's voluntary plunge into a painful yet joyous purgation, into a state, and as it were an element, which purges away (since the soul itself freely accepts the process) all that defects, stunts, or weakens the realization of the soul's deepest longings—the hard self-centeredness, petty self-mirrorings, and jealous claimfulness, above all."[44] She often used the image of nakedness to express the fullness of love. "True love wills to stand naked, without any kind of cover, in heaven and on earth, since it has not anything shameful to conceal."[45] Love embraces all.

The Cult of Catherine

Von Hügel studied the growth of Catherine's cult, indicating how redactors had "mutilated, as far as in them lay, the immensely spontaneous and rich personality of Catherine, in their determination to find her ever all-perfect, and perfect after their own fixed pattern."[46] For von Hügel the spiritual life was a continuous process. In a letter to Tyrrell he commented on the difference between the struggles that he perceived in Catherine's life and the static understanding of holiness of her biographer.

> It is simply *comical* to note the divergence between the *facts* of her continuous struggle, effort, and changing, growing achievements and horizons, and her biographer's emphatic insistence, at every halt in her life, or even of his narrative, that *now* at last (he has said so, as absolutely as language permits, of even the first moment of her conversion) she is at the very summit of perfection.[47]

Von Hügel wanted to present a critical study of Catherine which was faithful to her life. From the time that he was preparing a short sketch of her life for *The Hampstead Annual* (1898) he was concerned about how he should present her illness which he diagnosed as hysteria, but which the *Vita* described as miraculous.[48] A recent author, Baring-Gould, had declared that Catherine was rightly canonized as an instance of what heroism can do in surmounting such an illness. Von Hügel, in a letter seeking Tyrrell's advice on how to present Catherine's health, wrote that his certainty of the nature of her illness had increased his own admiration for her, not only for her work as a nurse but also for the breadth of her spiritual doctrine. He could not simply ignore her illness, and yet hysteria, in the popular mind, was often connected with impurity, and its presence would make everything about the saint uncertain and fantastic.[49] Tyrrell replied with characteristic bluntness that the difficulty was to know "what is expedient to put before the muddle-headed public."[50]

It was one matter to treat Catherine's illness in the *Hampstead Annual.* It was even more important in a critical study of mysticism to understand the nature of Catherine's illness and to insist that the various aspects of that illness, which her confessor, doctors, and disciples saw as proofs of the supernatural, were purely physical phenomena. And yet von Hügel recognized the interaction between soul and body. He devoted the first chapter of Part III, which is the section entitled "Critical," to "psycho-physical and temperamental questions." In it he described Catherine's illness as "of a predominantly psychical type, and concerns more the psychologist than the physician, being closely connected with her particular temperament and type of spirituality, a temperament and type to be found again and again among the Saints."[51] He proceeded to study carefully Catherine's health during the different periods of her life, neither minimizing nor exaggerating its impact on her teaching. It was his conviction

> that she became a saint because she had to; that she became it, to prevent herself going to pieces: she literally had to save, and actually did save, the fruitful life of reason and love, by ceaselessly fighting her immensely sensitive, absolute, and claimful self.[52]

Von Hügel, who had himself suffered periods of poor health, including depression and insomnia, which made it impossible for him to work, appreciated the importance of health but insisted that physical health is not the end of human life although it is one of its conditions. In the matter of health, von Hügel returned to the need to balance the three constituents of religion as the "safeguard of our deepest life and of its sanity."[53]

The Place of Science

One does not expect a book about mysticism and saints to include a defense for the pursuit of science, the term von Hügel used for critical scholarship in all academic disciplines, but this is an underlying theme of von Hügel's work. When Tyrrell offered his final suggestions on the manuscript before its publication he raised a question about this aspect.[54] Von Hügel's reply indicates how important his insights concerning the place of science in one's religious life were, not only for the book, but for his own life.

> I am sure that you must be right as to the persistent obscurity of my view concerning the purificatory function of Science. Yet I live this principle, more and more, and find that it gives sincerity to my scientific work and reality and tenderness to my religion. Hence I cannot but feel that I have got hold of something true and important. May I succeed, if not in the book, then elsewhere, in putting it sufficiently well to induce men to try it in practice. *That* is about the full height of my ambition.[55]

For von Hügel science (or the pursuit of critical scholarship) offered a new discipline and asceticism to the contemporary believer. In the early days of Christianity the expectation of the parousia had provided motivation for detachment. Then the teaching of Augustine on the effects of original sin encouraged detachment and other-worldliness. Neither the parousia nor the teaching on original sin "exercise their old, poignantly detaching power upon us." Yet contemporary men and women also need "some special channel and instrument for the preservation and acquisition of the absolutely essential temper of Detachment and Other-Worldliness." For von Hügel science now offered this channel of purification.[56]

Von Hügel included both historical-cultural and mathematical-physical sciences as means of purification. While his interest was primarily in historical criticism, especially as applied to the New Testament, he included it with the other sciences in justifying, from a religious point of view, the task of the scientist or scholar. All scholarship requires "a slow, orderly, disinterested procedure, capable of fruitfulness only by the recurring sacrifice of endless petty self-seekings and obstinate fancies, and this in face of natural eagerness and absoluteness of mind."[57]

For von Hügel the process of allowing science its function within the spiritual life was redemptive.

> For thus is Man purified and saved—if he already possesses the dominant religious motive and conviction—by a close contact with Matter; and the Cross is plunged into the very center of his soul's life, operating there a sure division between the perishing animal Individual and the abiding

spiritual Personality: the deathless Incarnational and Redemptive religion become thus truly operative there.[58]

Von Hügel drew an analogy with Catherine's teaching on purgatory where the soul voluntarily plunges itself into a state which purges away all selfishness. Through the pursuit of scholarship a similar process can take place as one explores the laws of science and through this purgation enters more deeply into God, the source and sustainer of all reality.[59] For this transformation to occur science must not be absorbed by religion, but must maintain its own autonomy.

> Science and Wisdom can each prosper and help and supplement the other, only if each possesses a certain real autonomy, a power fully to become and to remain itself, and, in various degrees and ways, to stimulate, check and thwart the other.[60]

This autonomy of the various sciences adds to the complexity of life and is often a source of friction.

As von Hügel pointed out, science shifts our self-centeredness and makes us aware that we are part of the world and the cosmos. We recognize that we are "one amongst thousands of similar constituents in a system expressive of the thoughts of God."[61] Von Hügel's awareness of human beings as part of the immensity of God's world and his insistence on the autonomy of matter is an important aspect of his spiritual legacy which will be considered in a later chapter. It can contribute to a theology of creation which supports ecological concerns.[62]

Having reached the end of over 800 pages of *The Mystical Element* the patient reader may be somewhat disappointed in von Hügel's closing statement about Catherine:

> And amongst these Mystics, Caterinetta Fiesca Adorna, the Saint of Genoa, has appeared to us as one who, in spite of not a little obscurity and uncertainty and vagueness in the historical evidences for her life and teaching, of not a few limitations of natural character and of opportunity, and of several peculiarities which, wonderful to her *entourage*, can but perplex or repel us now, shines forth . . . with a penetrating attractiveness, rarely matched, hardly surpassed, by Saints and

Heroes of far more varied, humorous, readily understandable, massive gifts and actions.[63]

Catherine may not have been the greatest among saints and heroes but von Hügel learned from her the ways that God is present in our lives and the costliness involved in becoming the person whom God calls each of us to be.

Von Hügel believed that God offers us a choice between "the noble pangs of spiritual child-birth, of painful-joyous expansion and growth and the shameful ache of spiritual death, of dreary contraction and decay."[64] He found in Catherine inspiration for his own growth. He also discovered the limitations of a mysticism which did not give sufficient attention to the social and the institutional.

In the work itself, Catherine became somewhat submerged by a wealth of related material, a fact that Tyrrell pointed out in his review:

> What was originally intended for a critical life of St. Catherine of Genoa grew so over weighed with *scholia* and discussions that eventually the plan of the book was inverted, and the biography from being the substance became an appendage—an illustration of the theory of mysticism.[65]

For von Hügel himself, Catherine was much more than just an illustration of his theory. She was the focus for years of devoted work in the midst of very trying circumstances. He commented on the impact of the work on his spiritual life in a letter written just a few weeks before he died: "I gained through my much toiling a knowledge of the Saint and of her friends which helped me greatly on to God."[66]

Although the anti-modernist campaign caused a certain cautiousness among Catholics, *The Mystical Element* was generally well received.[67] An example of caution may be seen in Abbot Butler's review of books on mysticism. He did not include von Hügel's book in his review but in the last paragraph he summarized his impression of *The Mystical Element*, referring to the work in a footnote:

> Though this is in a region in which I have not walked, and in an atmosphere in which I find it hard to breathe, still the message that comes from these realms of high philosophy, if I interpret its import aright, is simple and homely enough, and pre-eminently practical."[68]

O'Connell comments that "the Teutonic discipline and thoroughness on display in *The Mystical Element* was not matched by readability, and one wonders if its prose would have been intelligible at all had not that superb stylist George Tyrrell gone over the manuscript word by word."[69] In spite of the difficulties of the text, *The Mystical Element* was reprinted four months after publication, and a new edition appeared in 1923. Von Hügel was grateful to Tyrrell for his contribution to the work but cautious in his public acknowledgment of this collaboration. In the first edition von Hügel expressed his indebtedness "to the Reverend George Tyrrell's *Hard Sayings*, 1898, and *The Faith of the Millions*, 2 vols, 1901, so full of insight into Mysticism."[70] He was more outspoken in his preface to the second edition in 1923, but still cautious: "Father Tyrrell has gone, who had been so generously helpful, especially as to the mystical states, as to Aquinas and as to the form of the whole book, for so many years, long before the storms beat upon him and his own vehemence overclouded, in part, the force and completeness of that born mystic."[71]

Tyrrell's Death and Aftermath

During the less than two years between *Pascendi* and Tyrrell's death the friendship between von Hügel and Tyrrell was strained. The two men reacted differently to the storm that raged after the condemnation of modernism. Von Hügel was determined to avoid anything which would look like a conspiracy and for this reason was unwilling to associate with ex-Roman Catholics, a caution that seemed cowardly to those who had looked to him for leadership. He was uncomfortable with Tyrrell's polemical statements, particularly his reply to Cardinal Mercier which took the form of a book entitled *Medievalism*.[72] While appreciating the work itself, von Hügel expressed his concern for his friend:

> I ever feel that (brilliant as are your controversial, polemical hits) God has made you for something deeper and greater, and that not *there*, but in mystical intuition, love, *position*, do you give and get your full, most real self.[73]

When von Hügel sent Tyrrell his manuscript for revisions, Tyrrell's letter to Petre expressed his frustration both with the book and its author:

A hopeless book; a battery of heavy artillery to bring down a flea. He never asks himself: will this interest people who have *not* spent 10 years on the subject, and to whom S. Catherine will seem a very mediocre personage?[74]

But Tyrrell's criticism went deeper and beneath the irony is hurt and disappointment:

Von Hügel with all his preaching of stress and strain and friction, a coward! It only remains to discover that Christ kept a mistress, and that you have been deleting me to Rome. The man who has been a sort of conscience to me never existed.[75]

In a letter to von Hügel the following week he pointed out that *The Mystical Element* could "never be anything but a difficult book, for the few and not for the many." In the same letter he insisted that he did not wish his friend to "sacrifice his work or sacraments."[76] It was a stressful time for both men, and the fact that they continued to be friends in spite of growing differences between them indicates the depth of their friendship.

In July 1909 von Hügel was called by Maude Petre to Tyrrell's deathbed. Von Hügel and Petre were determined that their friend should have spiritual support but not at the expense of his life's work. Thus they made sure that he received the sacraments without being required to make a retraction, but they were unable, in spite of their best efforts, to provide for a Catholic funeral. Requests were made to both Bishop Amigo of Southwark and Archbishop Bourne of Westminster.[77] When all efforts for a Catholic burial failed, the decision was made to have Tyrrell buried in the parish churchyard of St. Mary's Anglican Church in Storrington. Tyrrell's friend, Abbé Henri Bremond, conducted a simple service at the graveside.

Following Tyrrell's funeral Bishop Amigo suspended Bremond, who had presided at what was considered a "schismatic ceremony," from his right to say mass in the diocese of Southwark, a prohibition later extended to other dioceses by Cardinal Merry del Val, Secretary of State to Pius X. Amigo also sent a list of those who had attended Tyrrell's funeral to Merry del Val. The Cardinal replied with a confidential letter in which he approved the Bishop's action, offered him sympathy in his difficult task, and deplored the behavior of Petre, von Hügel, and the others who had been involved in the funeral. The Cardinal raised the question, whether in view of the real and public scandal, they ought not to be refused the sacraments in their respective dioceses. He urged Amigo to discuss the matter with the Archbishop and some of the other bishops.[78]

In his letter to Merry del Val, Archbishop Bourne communicated the opinion of the senior bishop, Hedley of Newport, that no charges could be proved against von Hügel or Petre. Bourne also reminded Merry del Val that "it is always dangerous to arouse in England the morbid unreasonable sympathy which people so readily give to every wrong-doer whatever the nature of his crime." Bourne did not want to provide an opportunity for such persons to pose "as martyrs for a cause."[79] Both Hedley and Bourne were friends of Lady Mary and Friedrich von Hügel. Less than a month before Tyrrell's death in July, their youngest daughter Thekla had received the black veil, blessed by Archbishop Bourne, which marked her as a professed Carmelite.[80] As one who knew the family well it would have been very difficult for the Archbishop to censure von Hügel. The fact that he avoided doing so, in spite of pressure from Rome, shows his pastoral sensitivity and courage.

Bishop Amigo of Southwark diocese was less restrained in his approach than Archbishop Bourne, but agreed to wait, suggesting that the best time for action might be "when poor Tyrrell's book is published."[81] This was also the approach suggested by the Bishop of Birmingham: "In dealing with Miss Petre and von Hügel and that set the prudent course, it seems to me, is to wait until they have completely committed themselves before inflicting penalties on them. The publication of F. T.'s book will be evidence there is no gainsaying."[82]

Ecclesiastical action was not taken against von Hügel, probably because of the support of Archbishop Bourne. As the historian E. I. Watkin noted:

> Cardinal Bourne has not received the recognition he deserves for his wise and charitable attitude during these difficult years. He refused to be a party to heresy hunting and took under his protection Catholic scholars and thinkers suspected by the zealots.[83]

In spite of Bourne's support, fear of a possible condemnation continued to cast its shadow over von Hügel and his family for the rest of his life, and even after his death. Anatole von Hügel disapproved of his older brother's involvement in Tyrrell's funeral and the controversy which it provoked. In his diary von Hügel noted that he "managed to keep temper and yet (remain) firm." He accepted the fact that they differed, adding "but love him and his Cambridge work."[84]   Maude Petre, whose family also disapproved of her involvement with Tyrrell, was treated less kindly than von Hügel by Bishop Amigo who ordered that she be deprived of the sacraments in his diocese.[85]

Living with Tension

Von Hügel was a man with that rare gift of friendship which reflects God's love and fidelity.   While he did not approve of everything Tyrrell wrote or did, and was particularly upset when he discovered that Tyrrell had been in contact with some bishops of the Old Catholic Church, his love for his friend endured.   In a letter to Maude Petre on the first anniversary of Tyrrell's death he wrote:

> How additionally rare and precious his deep, delicate, massive sense of and witness to Religion, the reality of God and of the World Unseen, appears now, on looking back.   My very difficult, utterly fundamental subject of study, reflection and prayer is bringing this much home to me, and I pray at least as much to him as for him—to him for light and love, gentleness and strength.[86]

It was not easy for von Hügel to express his affection and admiration for Tyrrell while distancing himself from what he saw as his friend's excesses.   In a letter to Edmund Gardner requesting him to attend Tyrrell's funeral one senses von Hügel's dilemma.

> I now think that this fundamental physical ruin largely accounts for the violence which sometimes marred the force of his work, and for the extraordinary recklessness which marked much of his correspondence—both as to what he wrote and as to the persons whom he selected for such outpourings.

Then he added:

> What a great mind, pure, tender heart, strong will, suffering life, soul full of faith and hope!   May God help us to learn, on and on, from him![87]

The problem of how to be faithful to the memory of this remarkable friend, while not identifying with everything he had written and done, continued to challenge von Hügel. In January 1910 his article, "Father Tyrrell: Some Memorials of the Last Twelve Years of His Life," appeared in the *Hibbert Journal*. In a letter to Malcolm Quin, von Hügel acknowledged how difficult the task had been "for one within, and determined to remain within, the Roman Church" for it had meant, "under the present regime, the achieving, as well as may be, the most difficult combinations of qualities."[88]

In a review of *The Mystical Element*, which appeared the month that he died, Tyrrell had written: "All life, according to the author, consists in a patient struggle with irreconcilables—a progressive unifying of parts that will never fit perfectly."[89] Von Hügel's friendship with Tyrrell included elements which von Hügel found irreconcilable. His experience of the Church in the anti-modernist period also included irreconcilable elements. His response was to struggle to live peacefully with the tension.

Von Hügel tried to maintain some influence on those who were committed to change within the Church. He was deeply upset when he learned that the Italian publication, *Il Rinnovamento*, would cease publication for he saw it as "the only really independent, solidly scientific Catholic organ . . . the *one* institution (which) by its very existence proved the possibility of a dignified, thoroughly Catholic limitation to this . . . curialist absolutism."[90] He was willing to try to raise money to keep it publishing and even offered to become its anonymous editor for a three-year period (1910–12). He was concerned that if it should cease it would be "a *huge* encouragement to absolutism and a *profound* discouragement to all our group throughout the world."[91] But in spite of von Hügel's best efforts, absolutism won out. Those whom he called "our group" were scattered. Von Hügel sadly noted the "destructive effects of embitterment in Houtin's case, and that of a large part of the Geneva group."[92] In 1910 Pius X issued a Motu Proprio, "Sacrorum Antistitum," demanding that all priests take the anti-modernist oath or give up their ministry. As a layman von Hügel was not faced with this dilemma but many of his friends and co-workers struggled with this difficult requirement. Some seemed to von Hügel to lack the patience that was required to wait for God's time.

Following Tyrrell's death in 1909, Maude Petre's relationship with von Hügel changed although they remained friends. She identified closely with Tyrrell and was committed to the continuation of his work by editing his writings and by publishing his life. Von Hügel, on the other hand, seemed to Petre to distance himself from Tyrrell. When she asked whether he wished her to acknowledge the help she had received from him in preparing Tyrrell's *Christianity at the Cross-Roads* for publication, he declined, sharing with her the attitude which he believed they should adopt:

> It is then not necessarily cowardice or trimming, but may come from the deepest, wisest love of souls, if we look well around us before each step, if we plant our feet, very deliberately and slowly, alternately on the stepping-stones, between and around which roars a raging, deep, drowning stream.

He suggested that they should "very largely mark time, and when we do act, act with an almost provocative reticence."[93] This was not Maude Petre's style.

In spite of their differences, von Hügel continued to offer his support and advice to Petre during the difficult anti-modernist period.[94] In November 1910 he wrote:

> Just as we do not allow ourselves to be driven by anyone or anything into the camp of simple negation or scepticism, but, on the contrary, we watchfully work and pray to turn the very stress and strain into so many occasions of deeper faith and constructive love, so also *we do not allow ourselves to be insincere even against the insincere* or try and build up the Future upon casuistical *échappatoires* of the Past.[95]

It was this spiritual freedom that von Hügel sought for himself and his friends. His reluctance to incur excommunication, a price which Petre was willing to pay for her convictions, proceeded from his strong commitment to the institutional aspect of Catholicism. He willingly endured its limitations in order to share in the richness of the tradition. It was his way of maintaining the external historical element of religion which he considered essential for his own spiritual life and for his work as a director of others.

Von Hügel's correspondence during this period reveals a man who was often not well, unable to work, crushed by the triumph of absolutist forces within the church and disappointed in a number of his friends. Only his strong faith enabled him to maintain hope and to live creatively with the tension.

Eternal Life

Von Hügel's second book, *Eternal Life*, grew out of what was to have been an article prepared for the *Encyclopedia of Religion and Ethics*. The editor had told him "to make the paper as long as the subject-matter might seem to deserve or require."[96] The result, much too long for the encyclopedia, was published as a book with over 400 pages in 1912 at the same time as Petre's *Autobiography and Life of George Tyrrell*.[97] Von Hügel described in the Preface how his book seemed to grow and flow readily from his pen, probably because it was a subject which had been occupying his mind and life for many years.[98] When he sent the work to his niece, Gwendolen Greene, he advised her to read it twice, adding: "I wrote the thing praying; read it as written, child!"[99]

The work begins with a definition of what von Hügel meant by "eternal life":

> an experience, requirement, force, conception, ideal which is, in endless degrees and ways, latent or patent in every specifically human life and act; which, in its fullest operativeness and its most vivid recognition, is specifically religious; and which, in proportion to such fulness and recognition, is found to involve the consciousness, or possession, of all the highest realities and goods sought after or found by man, and the sense (more or less) of non-succession, of a complete Present and Presence, of an utterly abiding Here and Now.[100]

The author proceeded to study the chief types and stages of "eternal life" revealed in the religions and philosophies of the past and present. In describing the present he focused on institutional religion, taking as representative of religious institutions the Roman Catholic Church. Drawing on the insight of Troeltsch concerning social psychology, von Hügel insisted that the essence of religion is common worship.[101] Both the strengths and weaknesses that he observed within the Catholic Church were critically analyzed. But it was in holy persons that he caught a glimpse of "eternal life," men and women such as Damien with the lepers, the Curé of Ars Jean Baptiste Vianney, Eugénie Smet who founded a missionary order, and his own spiritual father, Abbé Huvelin.[102]

Von Hügel insisted that religion is social both horizontally as regards the rest of the human family, and vertically as regards God. Our little span of earthly life is not enough for religion to reach its fullest development. It is but the necessary beginning of a life in God which will continue in a life beyond. Only "eternal life" will satisfy our deepest longings.

Von Hügel, through his involvement in the modernist crisis and even more by his writing, had indeed made history. He had learned from his own experience as well as from his friends. Through his books he was becoming more widely known. During the remaining twelve years of his life he shared the fruit of his labor through lectures, publications, and individual guidance.

NOTES

1. Bernard Holland, Memoir in *SL*, p.32. See Appendix for Chapter II of *ME* 1.

2. vH to T, 18–20 December 1901, BL, Add. MS. 44927; emphasis is vH's; published in *SL*, pp.102–3; quote from p.103.

3. *Ibid.*

4. James Luther Adams, "Letter from Friedrich von Hügel to William James," *Downside Review* 98 (1980), pp.214–36; quote from p.228. The letter was written 10 May 1909.

5. *ME* 1, p.30; references are to the 2nd ed. (1923) unless noted.

6. *ME* 1, p.xxi.

7. *ME* 1, p.xxxi.

8. *ME* 1, p.248.

9. *ME* 1, pp.86–87.

10. *ME* 1, pp.viii–ix.

11. *ME* 1, p.xxiii.

12. *ME* 1, p.86.

13. *ME* 1, vii (1908 ed.)

14. *ME* 1, pp.50–55.

15. *ME* 1, p.54.

16. *ME* 1, p.66.

17. *ME* 1, p.102.

18. *ME* 1, p.104.

19. *ME* 1, p.118.

20. *ME* 1, p.141.

21. *ME* 1, p.158.

22. *ME* 1, vi (1908).

23. *ME* 1, pp.90–91.

24. *ME* 1, pp.265–66.

25. *ME* 1, p.167.

26. *ME* 1, p.163.

27. *ME* 1, p.268.

28. *ME* 1, p.273.

29. *ME* 1, p.229.

30. *ME* 1, p.368.

31. *ME* 2, p.79.

32. *ME* 2, p.75

33. *ME* 2, p.76.

34. *ME* 2, p.90.

35. *ME* 2, p.99. Devotion to the Eucharist was also characteristic of vH's spirituality. He was a frequent communicant and often visited churches in order to pray in the presence of the reserved sacrament.

36. *ME* 2, p.101.

37. *ME* 2, p.110.

38. *ME* 2, p.138.

39. *ME* 2, p.238.

40. *ME* 2, p.239.

41. *ME* 2, p.201.

42. *ME* 2, p.246.

43. *ME* 2, p.218.

44. *ME* 2, pp.385–86.

45. *ME* 1, p.268; quote from *Vita*.

46. *ME* 1, p.184.

47. vH to T, 7 July 1900; BL, Add. MS 44927; emphasis is vH's; published in *SL*, pp.85–87; quote from pp. 86–87.

48. "Caterina Fiesca Adorna, the Saint of Genoa, 1447–1510," *The Hampstead Annual* (1898):70–85.

49. vH to T, 3 October 1898; BL, Add. MS 44927; published in *VHT*, pp.41–47; quote from p.43.

50. T to vH, 5 October 1898; BL, Add. MS 44927; published in *VHT*, pp.48–50; quote from p.48.

51. *ME* 2, p.7.

52. *ME* 1, p.223. vH used similar language to describe his own conversion. See Chapter 1 above.

53. *ME* 2, p.60.

54. T to vH, 8 April 1908; BL, Add. MS 44931.

55. vH to T, 16 April 1908, BL, Add. MS 44931; published in *SL*, pp.148–51; quote from p.148.

56. *ME* 2, p.380.

57. *ME* 2, p.383.

58. *ME* 2, p.331; vH's spirituality of scholarship will be discussed in Chapter 7 below..

59. *ME* 2, pp.385–86.

60. *ME* 2, p.371.

61. *ME* 2, p.331.

62. See chapter 8 below.

63. *ME* 2, pp.395–96.

64. *ME* 2, p.395.

65. "The Mystical Element of Religion," *Quarterly Review* 211 (1909): p.105.

66. vH to Butler, 15 December 1924, Downside Abbey Archives.

67. Barmann, p.222.

68. "Mystical Books and Books on Mysticism," by the Abbot of Downside, Edward Cuthbert Butler, *Downside Review* 30 (1911), pp.3–20; reference to vH is on pp.18–19. vH notes in his diary a visit from Abbot Butler on 5 February 1909. Butler is described as "friendly but seemed to want to find out how the book had been reviewed by the officials and to get me not to count on his reviewing it."

69. O'Connell, p.372.

70. *ME* 1, p.xv (1908). In September 1908 vH wrote to T: "And it is such a deep consolation to me to find page upon page of my book given up to very respectful learning from or discussion with you. This consoles me for not having any special mention of you in the Preface." BL, Add. MS. 44931; published in *SL*, p.155.

71. *ME* 1, p.vii.

72. *Medievalism: A Reply to Cardinal Mercier* (London: Longmans, Green & Co., 1908).

73. vH to T, 27 June 1908, BL, Add. MS 44931; published in *SL*, pp.152–53, quote p.153.

74. GT to MP, 1 April 1908; PP, BL, Add. MS. 52367.

75. Ibid.

76. T to vH, 8 April 1908, PP, BL, Add. MS 44931.

77. Francis Bourne had succeeded Vaughan as Archbishop of Westminster in 1903, a post he held until 1935. Bourne was in Rheims, taking part in ceremonies connected with Joan of Arc's canonization, a fact commented on by Wilfrid Scawen Blunt: "It is also curious that Bourne should be just now away in Rheims, officiating at Joan of Arc's canonization; Joan of Arc, who was refused by the Bishops of her day burial at all, her ashes being scattered to the winds lest any relic of her should be preserved, and over the place of whose martyrdom were ecclesiastically inscribed the words 'Heretic and Sorceress,' yet she is to-day being worshiped on all Catholic altars. The same might happen, who knows, to Father Tyrrell." Wilfrid Scawen Blunt, *My Diaries: Being a Personal Narrative of Events, 1888–1914, Part II, 1900–1914* (London: Martin Secker, 1919), p.267.

78. Archives of the Diocese of Southwark Vigilance Committee (VC) MS 71, Merry del Val to Amigo, July 30, 1909. Merry del Val had also written to Amigo on July 25 in support of Amigo's actions. VC, MS 61.

79. AAW, Bo.124/5, Bourne to Merry del Val, 15 August 1909. Hedley's letter to Bourne, 12 August 1909, is in Bo.124/5, as well as in VC, MS 128 where it has been incorrectly dated 12 August 1919.

80. Diary, 26 June 1909. On 29 June vH notes a visit with Thekla, "delightfully well and happy at feeling herself finally settled."

81. AAW, Bo.124/5, Amigo to Bourne, 13 August 1909.

82. VC, MS 79.

83. E. I. Watkin, *Roman Catholicism in England from the Reformation to 1950* (London: Oxford University Press, 1957), p.218.

84. Diary, 15 September, 28 October 1909.

85. Michael Clifton, in his biography of Amigo, notes: "There is a certain stubbornness about his attitude which he showed to good effect on other issues but which was surely out of place here. Baron von Hügel was in a similar position in the Diocese of Westminster and no action was taken against him." *Amigo—Friend of the Poor: Bishop of Southwark, 1904–1949* (Leonminster, Herefordshire: Fowler Wright Books, 1987), p.34.

86. vH to MP, 16 July 1910, PP, BL, Add. MS 45361.

87. vH to Edmund Gardner, 17 July 1909; *SL*, pp.165–66.

88. vH to Malcolm Quin, 17 November 1909, *SL*, pp.172–75; quote from p.173. vH's article appeared in *Hibbert Journal* 8 (January 1910), pp.233–52.

89. Tyrrell, "Review of *The Mystical Element of Religion* by Baron F. von Hügel," *Hibbert Journal* 7 (July 1909), p.689.

90. vH to MP, 15 October 1909; PP, BL, Add. MS 45361.

91. vH to MP, 18 October 1909, PP, BL, Add. MS 45361.

92. vH to MP, 15 October 1912, PP, BL, Add. MS 45362.

93. vH to MP, 14 September 1909, PP, BL, Add. MS 45361; published in *SL*, pp 168–70. vH had discussed the matter with his friend, Edmund Bishop.

94. There are long letters written by von Hügel and references to frequent visits both in Petre's diary and in vH's. vH carefully read and commented on Petre's works, including the *Autobiography and Life of George Tyrrell*. PP, BL, Add. MSS 45361, 45362.

95. vH to MP, 17 November 1910, PP, BL, Add. MS 45362; emphasis vH's; published in *SL*, pp.183–85; quote from p.184.

96. Friedrich von Hügel, *Eternal Life: A Study of Its Implications and Applications* (Edinburgh: T. T. Clark, 1912), p.v; hereafter *EL*.

97. vH had hoped that his book would come out first. He wrote to Petre on 15 October 1912 stating that he had explained to his publisher that if his book came out first it "might help somewhat to deflect and to break such blows as may be leveled at your publication." However his letter of 28 October 1912 thanked Petre for the "two striking *distingués* volumes." PP, BL, Add. MS 45362.

98. *EL*, p.vi.

99. *LTN*, p.72.

100. *EL*, pp.1–2.

101. *EL*, pp.326–27. vH who seldom used footnotes here provided reference to Troeltsch, *Die Bedeutung der Geschichtlichkeit Jesu für den Glauben*, 1911.

102. *EL*, pp.372–78.

SHARING THE FRUIT (1913-1925)

5

N ew opportunities opened up for von Hügel as his scholarship was gradually recognized by the academic world and his gifts attracted a number of persons seeking his spiritual direction.

Following the publication of *The Mystical Element* and the death of Tyrrell, Barmann suggests that von Hügel took a positive lesson from the historical events in which he had played a key role and moved into the future. "He did not become embittered, nor did he give up working and struggling for what he always considered to be the goals of his life's endeavor."[1]

The memory of the events which Maude Petre cherished as "the most sacred portion" of her life,[2] and which she continued to recount, were for von Hügel extremely painful. In many cases silence seemed to him to be the best response. When asked by Professor Clement Webb to address the Oxford Society of Historical Theology in the summer of 1920 on the work of Roman Catholics during the past twenty years, he refused because of poor health but also because it would include speaking of "the dreariness of the Modernist involvement, at a date still too early . . . to do much good." The subject was for him "largely a depressing one."[3]

As the years passed von Hügel found himself torn by conflicting demands on his time and energy. He was anxious to complete certain works before it was too late. Ill health, probably aggravated by this anxiety, often prevented him from doing more than a couple of hours of scholarly work each day. But he resolutely continued to do whatever his strength allowed until the end of his life. While struggling to write even when he was not well, von Hügel maintained an extensive correspondence, much of it in the form of spiritual direction or accompaniment of others on their spiritual journey.

This chapter will consider the last twelve years of von Hügel's life with special emphasis on his work as teacher, scholar, and spiritual counselor. These were ways in which he shared the fruit of his life of study and prayer.

A Time of Suffering

After weathering the storm of the condemnation of modernism and its aftermath, von Hügel might have hoped to enjoy his work in peace and quiet, but the next few years brought their own difficulties. His mother died 4 February 1913.[4] In 1914 he made his will which began with the statement: "I desire to die as I have striven to live a devoted member of the Catholic and Roman Church."[5] When England declared a state of war with Austria in August 1914 von Hügel found himself a "hostile alien." He went immediately to the Home Office and applied for naturalization which he received the following December.[6] During the global crisis von Hügel underwent his own personal crisis as he watched his eldest daughter, Gertrud, die and as he himself suffered poor health.

Early in March 1915 he traveled to Rome for the first time in ten years in order to be with Gertrud whose health was deteriorating and whom he had not seen for three years.[7] He stayed with her until her death on 12 August 1915. This loss of his eldest daughter at the age of thirty-eight affected von Hügel deeply. As he wrote to his Anglican friend, Bishop Talbot, Gertrud was his "darling help and sympathizer."[8] To another friend he described her as "the soul closest to me upon earth in all my intellectual work, plans and trials."[9]

The depth of von Hügel's pain is evident in his letter to Bishop Talbot whose youngest son had been killed in the war.

> Yesterday I fulfilled a six months term of really unbroken anxiety, sadness and sacrifice, yet, thank God, of light and love, not my own, but His—the time of watching the dearly loved life of our first-born disappearing from this our earthly scene.[10]

In the midst of his pain, von Hügel, always the student, added, "I have been learning much."

One of the lessons von Hügel learned from Gertrud was the

transformation that suffering can effect. In a letter to Wilfrid Ward, who was terminally ill, he described this transformation which he had observed in his daughter.

> The Cross became, not simply a fact, to bear somehow as patiently as we can, but a source and channel of help, of purification, and of humble power—of a permanent deepening, widening, sweetening of the soul.[11]

Von Hügel knew that suffering in itself was not good, but through Gertrud he learned a lesson which he would never forget: that God can and does give "opportunities and graces and growths to the sufferer" who is receptive.[12]

Von Hügel had his share of suffering through the years. Even as a young man he had a series of nervous breakdowns which made it difficult for him to work. Eventually he was able to see God's loving providence in all the events of his life, including his struggles with illness. In a letter to his niece, written just a couple of years before his death, he described what he called "a very distinct nervous breakdown—such an old acquaintance that!" Looking back on these difficult periods in his life he could write:

> They are very salutary for one, I find—they make one feel one's utter dependence upon God, even for getting away from utter self-absorption, which then seizes one all round.[13]

His deafness had been a source of frustration throughout his entire adult life. Old age brought its own losses. Von Hügel learned to integrate these negative experiences and to help those who turned to him for help to do the same.

"The German Soul"

Von Hügel's focus had been almost exclusively with church politics, but during the war he was drawn into the larger political arena. He was concerned about what Christianity had to say about war and presented a paper on that topic to the London Society for the Study of Religion at its first meeting after the outbreak of the war.[14] In this paper, later published as "Christianity in the Face of War: Its Strength and Difficulty," he began with the leading sayings and practice of Jesus and the primitive Christians, and then traced the history of attitudes toward war.[15] With his German name, and many German friends, he considered that he was in a position to explain some of the differences between the German and the English mentality, a task which he undertook in "The German Soul and the Great War."[16] Although his sympathies were with the English, he tried to reduce some of the tension and anti-German sentiment that prevailed in England. The two essays were published together as a book.[17] The work was a combination of learning and practical examples drawn from his own and others' experiences.

The Teacher

Von Hügel considered it a privilege and a duty to hand on the rich Christian tradition. We have seen that the education of his daughters was a priority for him. Even when the family was in Rome, there were regular lessons, prepared and taught with vigor—and carefully noted in the diary. In his long letter of advice to Margaret Clutton on the instruction of her son Arthur, von Hügel revealed his own approach to religious education:

> *There is no Religious Doctrine* Book such (as) you, most naturally, dream of. *What* a good thing for you! *You*, as I had to do, *will have to make up your own book.* And thus your teaching of him will make you grow, and will make him grow with your growth, in a far more real degree.

He explained how he divided up the half-hour's lesson in such a way that it was "*a bracing alive, richly varied, attractive time,*" adding, "But such a lesson takes time to prepare."[18] For von Hügel this was time well spent for the teacher as well as for the students. To assist Margaret Clutton in her rightful role von Hügel recommended a number of books so that she would be able to instruct her son in religious doctrine and in the area of sexuality. As with others, von Hügel sought to empower Margaret Clutton so that she might assume her own responsibilities as a parent.

Von Hügel provided the same kind of assistance to Mme Garceau with her two sons.[19] The Garceau family were neighbors whose father was in the army serving in France. In 1916 von Hügel undertook the religious education of Henri and later his younger brother Gilbert, preparing both boys for the reception of the sacraments and instructing them as he had his daughters, first with the catechism and then with a more advanced study of the bible. He also made arrangements for

Henri to attend St. Paul's School, providing the necessary tuition, bus money and pocket money. When told of the arrangements Henri was "deeply moved, but shy and silent."[20] Von Hügel immediately began to teach him Latin. The diaries reveal a fatherly affection, and a delight in Henri's accomplishments, whether it was making the cricket team or admission to Cambridge University. Von Hügel notes his last lesson with Henri on the synoptic gospels just before the young man left for Cambridge, taking with him a Douay-Rheims English Bible as a gift from his mentor.[21]

Von Hügel was always the teacher, encouraging and supporting others in their pursuit of knowledge. During 1917 he noted in his diary that he had sent letters to German War prisoners, two of them seminarians studying Catholic theology and one a student of medieval history.[22] He also provided books for these young men.

Von Hügel's role as teacher included groups as well as private tuition. As he became more recognized as a scholar he was asked to lecture to an ever wider audience. He participated in a Summer School at Birmingham organized by Francis Sydney Marvin in 1916, speaking on "Progress in Religion," and was asked to take part in 1918 and 1920. He had to refuse the second invitation because of ill health and the third because of his desire to finish his own work. The experience seems to have been good for von Hügel who particularly enjoyed the informal discussions.[23]

Although involved ecumenically, von Hügel maintained a certain caution as to when and how he participated. For instance, when Albert Dawson invited him to contribute answers to questions related to "The Clergy and the Creeds," von Hügel carefully weighed the advantages and disadvantages "at least as regards collaboration on the part of a Roman Catholic—a practicing member of that great Church" and discerned "that this is not the form and method in which at least I myself can hope to do good—more good than harm." Robert Hugh Benson did participate, stating definitively in his response: "A Catholic does not 'pursue' truth; he claims to possess it."[24] Benson's answer helps one to appreciate the problems facing von Hügel as he struggled to be a faithful Catholic and at the same time to remain open to the truth he recognized among other churches and religions.

Von Hügel enjoyed addressing young people. At the request of Leo Ward, Wilfrid's son, von Hügel spoke to a group of fifty at Oxford on 19 May 1917 on the topic "The Teaching of Jesus, a Doctrine of Immense Alternatives and Abiding Consciousness." In March 1920 he spoke on "Responsibility in Religious Belief," to the secretaries of the British branches of the Student Christian Movement.[25] On 16 May 1920 he addressed about 1000 Oxford undergraduates on "Christianity and the Supernatural."[26] Von Hügel was also involved in what is now called "Continuing Education," speaking to various groups of clergy and to the general public. In 1921 von Hügel gathered some of his essays and addresses into one volume for publication.[27] A second series was collected after his death by Edmund G. Gardner and published in 1926.

The Scholar

Von Hügel had become recognized not only as a teacher but as a scholar. In 1914 he received his first academic honor, an honorary degree from Saint Andrews University. This recognition by the ancient Scottish university brought joy to the son of a Scottish mother. He saw it as a affirmation of his *Mystical Element*. On his way to receive the degree he stopped in Edinburgh where he gave an address entitled: "On Certain Central Needs of Religion, and the Difficulties of Liberal Movements in Face of the Needs: As Experienced within the Roman Catholic Church During the Last Forty Years."[28] These years had brought much personal pain as well as joy to the scholar.

Although, he did not belong to the academy, von Hügel maintained close ties with both Cambridge and Oxford. Cambridge had been home for his mother in her later years as well as for his brother, Anatole, who was curator of the University Museum. On his frequent visits to his mother and brother at Croft Cottage he often participated in academic events in the colleges. His family connections provided valuable opportunities for scholarly conversation. He shared Anatole's keen interest in and support for St. Edmund's House, a residence for priests who were studying at Cambridge, which eventually evolved into a college of the university.

Von Hügel wrote three entries for the eleventh edition of the *Encyclopedia Britannica* (Cambridge University Press, 1911), two of these on biblical topics, the third on Loisy.[29] In the list of contributors he is described as "Member of Cambridge Philological Society, Member of Hellenic Society, and Author of the *Mystical Element of Religion*, etc."

Von Hügel also had close friends in Oxford, especially Professor Clement Webb. He was a frequent visitor to the university and often was invited to give lectures. In 1920, when the restriction limiting the

Oxford Doctor of Divinity degree to Anglican clerics was removed, von Hügel was granted the degree of Doctor of Divinity from the University of Oxford, the first Roman Catholic to be so honored since the Reformation.[30]

The London Society for the Study of Religion continued to provide von Hügel with intellectual stimulation and a forum for scholarly discourse. E. R. Bevan described him in action at these gatherings:

> Those who heard the Baron speak at one of these meetings will never forget it—the grey hair standing up from his forehead, the large dark eyes in a face of fine ivory, the divine fire which seemed to fill him, the passionate sense of the reality of God, which broke forth in volcanic utterance, strange bits of slang and colloquialisms mingling with magnificent phrases, and left him when he ended, exhausted and trembling.[31]

Each meeting of the LSSR is noted in the diary with names of those present. A number of the addresses in *Essays and Addresses* were given to this society.

Von Hügel's later years were enriched by his friendship with Norman Kemp Smith, Professor of Philosophy in Princeton from 1906 to 1916 and then in Edinburgh where he held the Chair of Metaphysics. On 29 November 1917 Kemp Smith, twenty years younger than von Hügel, attended his lecture at Kensington Town Hall on the topic of "Religion and Illusion." The young philosopher initiated the relationship which would grow into friendship by sending von Hügel a pre-publication copy of his work, *A Commentary to Kant's Critique of Pure Reason.* Von Hügel responded by inviting Kemp Smith to his home for lunch or tea. The friendship which developed is documented by their correspondence which began in 1917 and continued until von Hügel's death in January 1925.[32]

Barmann points out that at this time in his life the older man needed "support, inspiration, and stimulus to persevere in the intellectual work which had been the main thrust of his whole life," and these Norman Kemp Smith was able to provide.[33] In an early letter von Hügel wrote: "And, if I am taken soon, may you live to do far better, far more influential, work than I have done, or could still hope to do!"[34] When he received the news of Kemp Smith's appointment to the Chair at the University of Edinburgh, he wrote: "I weigh my words when I say that this fact ranks with hardly a dozen as pure and as full joys granted me during my now long life."[35] In a letter dictated toward the end of his life von Hügel commented: "What a pleasure it is to have friends whom one can admire, nothing makes one grow like that."[36] Von Hügel's friendship with Kemp Smith also allowed the older man to share in the fruitful activities of his friend: "*That* is one of the joys of friendship—by sympathy born from such friendship, one quadruples, or more, one's own interests, indeed even influence."[37]

The University of Edinburgh invited von Hügel to give the Gifford Lectures in 1924–26, accompanied by the offer of a Doctor of Divinity degree. This honor was deeply appreciated by von Hügel as a recognition of his scholarly contribution. He wrote to Kemp Smith who had been influential in obtaining the invitation: ". . . unless someone had cared and watched and pressed, as occasion offered, and had worked with both wisdom and devotion for it—someone, too, in a position to render his action strongly effectual: I should never have attained to this biggest chance for doing something abiding."[38] Unfortunately poor health prevented von Hügel from delivering the Gifford Lectures, but his study in their preparation contributed to his last book, *The Reality of God*, published after his death.[39] The support of Kemp Smith, in the form of weekly letters, gave von Hügel the feeling that he had an audience as he struggled with what was to be his final work.[40]

Von Hügel had hoped that his friend Ernst Troeltsch, whom he had met in 1901, would be able to lecture in England and had made the preliminary arrangements, not without considerable difficulties, caused both by anti-German feeling and by concern for Troeltsch's orthodoxy.[41] When all seemed finally settled Troeltsch died suddenly in January 1923. This premature death was a great blow to von Hügel who immediately arranged to read Troeltsch's paper in Oxford but was prevented from doing so by ill health. Although he was anxious to finish his own book, he interrupted this work to edit Troeltsch's lectures for publication. In his introduction to Troeltsch's papers he wrote:

> Surely, in all times and places, the most ready, yet also the most costly way of learning deeply, that is, of growing in our very questions and in our whole temper of mind, is to learn in admiration of some other living fellow-man, recognized by us

as more gifted, or more trained, or more experienced than ourselves. Thus did Providence give Dr. Troeltsch also to myself to learn from.[42]

For von Hügel learning was a religious passion.

The Spiritual Counselor

Von Hügel was convinced of our interconnectedness and for this reason he took seriously his responsibility to share with others the wisdom which he had acquired through personal experience and study. At the same time his experience with others became a source for his own theological reflections on religion. His writing was an extension of his personal direction of individuals and his direction a more personal application of his writing to particular individuals. In response to a request for a copy of *The Mystical Element* for St. Deiniol's Library, he graciously wrote: "Long, grateful intercourse and sympathy with souls of a rare depth and delicacy of faith and love must, I think, have given some abiding substance to some of these many pages."[43]

Letters were an important vehicle through which von Hügel carried out this mutual accompaniment for a variety of persons of different ages and backgrounds. Many letters begin with an apology for not replying sooner, often because of illness and pressure of work. The spirit of prayerful reflection with which he responded to requests for guidance is evident in his reply to Margaret Clutton:

> I have purposely given myself two full days, in which to ruminate the contents of your very important and deeply interesting letter. And I have also offered my Sunday Holy Communion, very specially, for the gaining of light in this matter.

He then proceeded to write thirty-five closely written pages in response to her questions.[44]

The diaries record a steady stream of visitors for lunch or tea at the von Hügel home, often followed by long walks and talks in Kensington Gardens. However, written correspondence was probably a more effective way than conversation for von Hügel to communicate with those who sought his advice. Letters also had the advantage of providing a permanent record which could be reread.[45] Von Hügel himself had carefully recorded the advice which he had received from Abbé Huvelin, often referring to it in his lectures and in his letters.

Von Hügel's letters reveal his personal struggle to live the dynamic religious life described in *The Mystical Element*, as well as his advice to others on how they might enjoy a full religious life. In the preface of *Essays and Addresses* he recommended his work "especially to those who attempt to combine a faithful practice of religion with an historical analysis and a philosophical presentation of it."[46] Von Hügel believed that these elements could and must be held together in a creative tension.

At a time when "winning converts" to the Catholic Church was encouraged, von Hügel counseled those whom he directed to remain faithful to their own tradition as we shall see in his advice to Evelyn Underhill and Gwendolen Greene which will be discussed in the following chapter. In a letter to Greene he stated that he did not "aim at making R.C.s: that would be odious presumption." He added his convictions:

> That God and His grace are (in various degrees, no doubt) everywhere—but specially, very especially, in Christianity. That the presumption is always in favor of souls remaining, as to institutional appurtenance, where they are—it being God's affair to make it clear to them if, doing their best where they are, He wants them elsewhere.[47]

These reflections arose from von Hügel's encounter with Frances Lillie, a woman from Chicago who had read *The Mystical Element* and felt drawn to the Catholic Church. She visited von Hügel, who described her as "an M.D., a humorous, shrewd, self-knowing woman, drawn by just one thing to Rome—the crowd, the praying poor in our Churches."[48] In her case von Hügel recognized the authenticity of her desire to become a Roman Catholic and arranged for her reception at the Carmelite Church, with Lady Mary as her godmother.[49] As spiritual director von Hügel encouraged those whom he accompanied to respond to their own deepest desires for this was how he understood God to act in our lives.

Later Years

Von Hügel continued his life of study and writing, lecturing to various groups, and directing a number of persons, encouraged in these tasks by the recognition of scholars such as Kemp Smith. He also experienced periods of illness, something which he had had to endure throughout his life but which became more serious in his later years. In October 1918 he had surgery followed by a year's recuperation when he was unable to do much intellectual work.

In November 1923 Friedrich and Mary von Hügel celebrated their golden wedding anniversary. In March 1924 von Hügel was very sick and received Extreme Unction. He recovered and in spite of bad health continued to work as much as he was able, dictating to his secretary, Miss Adrienne Tuck, the evening before he died on 27 January 1925. Lady Mary described his death to Canon Lilley:

> The end was so peaceful and quiet. He passed away in his sleep. A slight flicker was all that told of the passing. No struggle of any kind. He was not afraid of death. He had had the last sacraments in March, and he told our Carmelite daughter that he thought it would come like that.[50]

Friedrich von Hügel is buried in the cemetery of the parish church at Downside Abbey, beside his mother and sister. In a letter to a friend written in 1919 he noted that he and his brother intended to be buried at the Abbey: "We all loved and love that fine Abbey Church, and the genial, scholarly, very English Benedictines there—the lineal descendants of the Monks of Westminster Abbey and with the history of the Order going back to A.D. 520."[51] Their commitment to prayer and scholarship was reflected in von Hügel's own life. The inscription on his tombstone is from Psalm 85: "For what have I in heaven but Thee, and besides Thee do I desire on earth?"

Notices in journals and personal letters of sympathy to Lady Mary indicate the esteem in which von Hügel was held.[52] Yet even in his obituary the *Tablet* felt it necessary to remind its readers that it was "to be regretted that some writers who have failed to understand and to give proper weight to *nuances* of thought have not hesitated to claim that Baron Friedrich was in religious matters a Modernist."[53] *The Times* remarked that although his writings were never censured, "his views were generally regarded in his own communion as somewhat risky and eccentric." However, *The Times* also assured its readers that it would be "an error to identify Baron von Hügel with the movement called 'Modernism.' "[54]

Von Hügel's deep spirituality, evident in his writings and in his correspondence, was appreciated by persons from many traditions. We have followed von Hügel's spiritual journey and observed how he integrated in a creative tension the historical, intellectual, and mystical elements of religion in his own life, and how he shared his wisdom with others as teacher, scholar, and spiritual counselor, or perhaps simply as friend. The following chapters focus on his contribution as a spiritual guide not only during his lifetime but as a resource for a contemporary spirituality. Chapter Six observes the spiritual guide in action by studying his relationships with Wilfrid Ward, Juliet Mansel, Evelyn Underhill, and Gwendolen Greene.

NOTES

1. Barmann, p. 243.

2. Maude Petre, "George Tyrrell and Alfred Fawkes," *Modern Churchman* 20 (December 1930), p.542.

3. vH to Professor Webb, 3 December 1919, *SL*, pp.297–98.

4. Diary, 4 February 1913.

5. vHP, SAUL, MS B3280.H8. The will was made on 7 July 1914 and was not changed. Its administration was granted to Baroness Hildegard von Hügel on 21 April 1925.

6. Diary, 12 August, 9 December 1914.

7. Diary, 8 March to 14 August 1915. Italy declared a state of war on 11 March. In June, Gertrud's husband, Count Francesco Salimei, began his military service.

8. vH to Edward Talbot, 6 September 1915; *SL*, pp.221. Talbot (1844–1934) was then Bishop of Winchester, having served as Bishop of Rochester and of Southwark.

9. vH to Canon Newson, 2 October 1915; *SL*, p.225.

10. vH to Edward Talbot, 6 September 1915; *SL*, pp.220–221.

11. vH to WW, 17 February 1916, WWP, SAUL, MS 38347 vii 143 (194); *SL*, p.227.

12. Ibid.

13. *LTN*, pp.187–88.

14. Barmann, "Confronting Secularization: Origins of the London Society for the Study of Religion," *Church History* 62 (1993), p.37.

15. *The Church Quarterly Review* 79 (January 1915), pp.257–88.

16. *The Quest* 6 (April 1915), pp.401–29; 7 (January 1916), pp.257–88.

17. *The German Soul in its Attitude towards Ethics and Christianity. The State and War* (London, Paris, Toronto: J. M. Dent & Sons, 1916).

18. vHP, SAUL MS 30994; published by Joseph P. Whelan, "The Parent as Spiritual Director: A Newly Published Letter of Friedrich von Hügel," *The Month* n.s.2 (1970),

pp.52–57; 84–87; quotation from published letter, p.56; emphasis is vH's. Margaret Mary Petre Clutton was Maude Petre's youngest sister.

19. Diary, January 1918.

20. Diary, 21 October 1917.

21. Diary, 9 October 1923.

22. Diary, April 1917.

23. A number of letters from von Hügel to F. S. Marvin in the Bodl, MS. Eng. lett. c. 263–267 concern the summer schools. The diary for 8 to 11 August 1916 described the experience.

24. A number of letters in which various scholars responded to set questions as well as vH's refusal to participate are in Bodl, MS Eng. lett. c.196. vH's letter is dated 17 March 1914 (f.62); R.H. Benson's reply is f.65.

25. EA 1, pp.3–19.

26. "Christianity and the Supernatural," was published in The Modern Churchman 10 (June 1920), pp.101–21; included in EA 1, pp.278–98.

27. Essays and Addresses on the Philosophy of Religion (London: J. M. Dent and Sons, 1921). One reason for vH's decision to publish these essays was his financial position. In an unpublished letter to Hildegard, 3 September 1920, he refers to selling jewelry and clocks in order to pay off a deficit, his unwillingness to accrue debts, and his decision to publish his essays. Downside Abbey Archives, MS 1272 (uncatalogued). In a letter to Kemp Smith (20 September 1920) vH mentioned his experience of "financial anxieties" for the first time in his life. The letters of vH to Kemp Smith as well as Kemp Smith's to vH are at SAUL, vHP MS 30420, MSS 2977–3066. They were edited by Lawrence F. Barmann, The Letters of Baron Friedrich von Hügel and Professor Norman Kemp Smith (New York: Fordham University Press, 1981); hereafter Letters KS, p.104.

28. EA 2, pp. 89–131.

29. "John, The Apostle," The Encyclopedia Britannica, 11th ed., v. 15 (1911), pp.432–33; John, Gospel of St.," v. 15 (1911), pp.452–58; "Loisy, Alfred Firmin," v. 16 (1911), pp.926–28.

30. The Oxford Doctor of Divinity degree had been limited to Anglican clerics from the time of the Protestant Reformation. This restriction was removed and the degree granted to six non-Anglican clerics, including von Hügel, on 24 June 1920. Friedrich's father, Carl von Hügel, had also been honored by the University of Oxford which conferred on him the degree D.C.L. honoris causa in 1848. Charles von Hügel, p. 27.

31. Obituary notice from The Times (28 January 1925); reprinted in Some Letters of Baron von Hügel, privately printed, Chicago, 1925, p.7.

32. Letters KS. For a description of the meeting of the two friends, see Introduction, p.4. The importance of friendship in vH's spirituality is discussed in Chapter 7 below.

33. Letters KS, p.9.

34. 19 April 1919, Letters KS, p.25.

35. 1 July 1919; Letters KS, p. 36.

36. April 1924, *Letters KS*, p.219. Barmann uses this sentence, which sums up vH's appreciation for the gift of friendship, as an epithet for the book.

37. 30 July 1920, *Letters KS*, p. 92.

38. 3 June 1922, *Letters KS*, pp.169–70.

39. Edmund G. Gardner, ed., *The Reality of God and Religion and Agnosticism* (London, 1931). The book is composed of two works: what were to have been his Gifford lectures and an unfinished study of Alfred Lyall begun in 1912. The material was put into publishable form by his literary executor.

40. 17 December 1924, vH to KS, *Letters KS*, p. 281.

41. For a description of these difficulties, see Hans Rollmann, "Ernst Troeltsch, Friedrich von Hügel and the Student Christian Movement," *Downside Review* 101 (July 1983), pp.216–26.

42. Ernst Troeltsch, *Christian Thought: Its History and Application*, lectures written for delivery in England during March 1923, translated into English by various hands and edited with an Introduction and Index by Baron F. von Hügel (London: University of London Press, 1923), p.xxxi. In a letter to the Editor of *The Times Literary Supplement* (29 March 1923), p.216, vH described his relationship with Troeltsch and his deep appreciation for him. See Appendix vi, Barmann, *Letters KS*, pp.341–45. This letter was translated into German in *Christliche Welt*, to the annoyance of Frau Troeltsch, who objected to "the intimate bits" which vH had included to soften his English readers "out of their militant anti-Germanisms." vH to KS, 4 July 1923, *Letters KS*, p.197.

43. vH to Mrs. Drew, 25 September 1909, *SL*, p.170.

44. "The Parent as Spiritual Director," *Month* n.s.2 (1970), p.52.

45. E. Glenn Hinson in "Letters for Spiritual Guidance," *Spirituality in Ecumenical Perspective* (Louisville, KY: Westminster/John Knox, 1993), pp.161–76, notes this advantage of letters as a means of spiritual guidance and lists vulnerability, acceptance, expectancy, and constancy as principles for spiritual guidance through letters. Hinson presents vH as an example of one who used letters effectively for spiritual guidance.

46. *EA* 1, p.xviii.

47. 4 October 1920, *SL*, p.312.

48. 8 January 1921, *Letters KS*, pp.111–12.

49. vH's letters to Mrs. Lillie were privately printed as *Some Letters of Baron von Hügel* in 1925. All but one are included in *SL* (pp.300, 312, 341, 352, 354, 356, 369). vH recounts Mrs. Lillie's visits and her entrance into the Church in his diary for 3 to 11 November 1920.

50. Baroness Mary von Hügel to A. L. Lilley, 30 January [1925], Lilley Papers, SAUL, MS 30628.

51. vH to Professor Sonnenschein, 3 January 1919, *SL*, p.262.

52. Holland includes quotations from letters received by Lady Mary in *SL*, pp.52–57.

53. *Tablet* 145 (31 January 1925), p.140.

54. *Times* (25 January 1925); reprint in *Some Letters of vH*, p.2.

PART II

A GUIDE FOR THE JOURNEY

THE SPIRITUAL GUIDE

6

Although he was a lay person without any formal training, we have seen that von Hügel became recognized as a spiritual guide. He was convinced that God acted in our lives through others. For this reason he generously responded to requests for his direction. This time-consuming work, seen as a distraction by some of his family, was for von Hügel a sacred responsibility.

In order to observe von Hügel as spiritual counselor, I have chosen four persons from among those of different ages and backgrounds whom von Hügel directed: Wilfrid Ward, Juliet Mansel, Evelyn Underhill, and Gwendolen Greene.[1] Wilfrid Ward was an old friend who turned to von Hügel for help in 1916 when faced with a terminal illness, although the association between the two men went back to 1873 when von Hügel became a neighbor and friend of Wilfrid's father, W. G. Ward.[2] The three women, Juliet Mansel, Evelyn Underhill, and Gwendolen Greene, were Anglicans, although Greene became a Roman Catholic after von Hügel's death. Juliet Mansel was a schoolgirl, granddaughter of a friend, Adeline Chapman, when von Hügel first undertook her direction in 1910. Evelyn Underhill was already a distinguished author when she met von Hügel in 1911, although she did not formally choose him as her director until 1921, a relationship which continued until von Hügel's death in 1925, and one which profoundly influenced her writing and her own guidance of others. Gwendolen Greene was a "spiritual child" of von Hügel who remembered him from her earliest years but her formal relationship with him as her "spiritual father" began in 1918 when she was thirty-eight and the mother of three children.

99

Wilfrid Ward

Although Wilfrid Ward was only four years younger than Friedrich, the latter seems to have served as a mentor for Wilfrid, offering him encouragement and advice. Their friendship was severely strained during the difficult period following *Pascendi* when Ward, as editor of the *Dublin Review* for the crucial years 1906–16, upheld the official Catholic position. Ward described his ambiguous relationship with von Hügel to Bernard Holland:

> As to von Hügel, I owed him a great deal all my life and I do not know whom I admire more, but our relations have been most curious, as, on the combined theological and political matters that divide Catholics (I mean perhaps rather the politics of theology) we have never agreed, and at times strongly disagreed, so that my admiration has never been exactly that of a follower.[3]

Ward was in the process of writing his memoirs when he became terminally ill. The figure of von Hügel loomed large in these reminiscences. Wilfrid's daughter, Maisie Ward, included in her book on her father excerpts from his fragmentary notes which describe how he saw von Hügel:

> His learning and enthusiasm and his picturesque mentality carried one away. He had a deep sense of the worth-whileness of the religious controversies of the day, and a moral elevation in the conduct of them which reminded me of my father. The approval and encouragement of my work was invaluable to me as an incentive. He was a saint and a mystic as well as a scholar and thinker. His general position was that, provided you have the spirit of the saints, intellectual freedom is as safe for a Christian as it is desirable. Sanctity and freedom of mind agree well together, he maintained.[4]

In spite of personal differences over the years it was to von Hügel that Ward, who had just celebrated his sixtieth birthday, turned in February 1916. Faced with cancer of the stomach he wrote to his old friend: "You can probably help me more than anyone else." Von Hügel, whose daughter Gertrud had died six months earlier, was not well himself at the time but he promised to write to Ward each Monday.

The letters between the two old friends, Ward's dictated because of his weakness, von Hügel's proceeding from his recent experience of suffering and death, are a moving testimony of faith. Ward, who knew that he was dying, desired to make the best possible use of the time that remained. While others pretended that he was getting better, with von Hügel he could acknowledge what was happening to him. He was helped by von Hügel's description of Gertrud's dying and recognized something "truly providential" occurring in his own life. "At these moments one says in one's heart what one has always read in one's prayer books, that God alone can do it and that one must trust Him."[5] Von Hügel suggested that Ward not ask how to endure the pain but "count on God's grace for the day, hour, even minute," assuring him that "God, the essentially timeless will thus and then help His poor timeful creature to contract time to a point of most fruitful faith and love."[6]

In response to a request for suggested reading von Hügel advised fifteen minutes of spiritual reading each day, a practice which he himself had carried out for forty years. Such reading was not for information but for spiritual nourishment, like sucking a lozenge. He also sent Ward an art book and a book of *Selected English Letters*. In response to questions about past sins, von Hügel urged his friend to focus more on the present than on the past.

Von Hügel shared with his dying friend his insights into the mystery of suffering which philosophers had tried to fathom. Von Hügel was convinced that the apparent sterility of suffering added to our pains, and that suffering, while not good in itself, can be an occasion of grace and growth, a reality which he had seen in his beloved Gertrud. He reflected with Ward on the fact that only Christianity has taught us the true function of suffering.

> But Christ came, and He did not really explain it; He did far more, He met it, willed it, transformed it, and taught us how to do all this, or rather He Himself does it within us, if we do not hinder the all-healing hands.[7]

He added a request that Ward pray for him for "in suffering, we are very near to God." For von Hügel pain and prayer came together.[8]

Von Hügel did not hesitate to assume the role of guide for the dying Ward, seeing his contribution as "God's touch and not mine."

Ward's deceased sister Margaret, before entering a cloistered convent, had asked von Hügel to help her brother. At the time von Hügel answered that it was not his way to act as a spiritual guide for anyone. The fact that he was able to offer this service to the dying Ward seemed to von Hügel a reflection of God's gracious love.[9] Von Hügel's letters to Ward during the last weeks of his life show a sensitivity to the dying man. They also reveal the writer's Christocentric spirituality in which Christ brings life in the midst of suffering. Wilfrid Ward died in April 1916.

Juliet Mansel

A marked contrast to von Hügel's sensitive accompaniment of the dying Ward is his eager direction of the adolescent struggles of Juliet Mansel. Von Hügel's letters to Juliet as well as his letters about her to her mother, Mildred Mansel, and her grandmother, Adeline Chapman, express the love of a father whose daughters have grown up and who had no grandchildren. However, they are more than letters from an indulgent grandparent for they present a demanding invitation to enter deeply into the Christian life.

As a young girl Juliet stayed in the von Hügel home during vacation periods and while she attended a day school in London. In letters to both her mother and her grandmother, von Hügel expressed his gratitude for the presence of "that sweet little strong-charactered" young girl who brought "brightness and delight" to his home.[10] Years later Juliet Mansel described the von Hügel household as she recalled it:

> No people could have been so different as the Baron, his eccentric and lovable wife, the daughter of Sidney Herbert, and their handsome daughter, Hildegard.[11]

She recounted the memories of a fifteen-year-old in that household:

> Every evening, after school hours, he read aloud to her and he allowed nothing to interfere with these readings, though he was engaged on one of his great books at the time. He took her to art galleries, museums and sometimes to films, which were silent in those days and in which he took a boyish delight.[12]

Twenty-eight letters from von Hügel to Juliet Mansel are preserved among the von Hügel papers at St Andrews University. One of the earliest of these letters, written in February 1910, offered sympathy to Juliet on the death of a friend and illustrates his affection for her.

> And since all that affects you, for joy or sorrow, good or evil, passes through my old heart dearie, with and for you, I want just to write you a little letter of truest and deepest fatherly sympathy. . . . May this trouble too help you to develop into a soul full of faith and love, and of a deep sense of God's presence. . . . Pray for this poor old father who loves you as truly and dearly somehow, as if he were your physical Father.[13]

In another letter he referred to his "*previous* three girls, Gertrud, Hildegard, and Thekla."[14] She is his "sweet little Benjamen, my youngest abiding life."[15] Another letter ends by asking her to "pray for your old devoted fatherly thing as I never forget my youngest daughter before God."[16]

In a lengthy letter written at the time when Juliet was preparing for her confirmation the Baron laid out a program which sums up his views of spirituality.[17] His comments on the social aspect of religion explain how he understood spiritual interdependence and his own role as spiritual guide: "We shall never learn much about it (the spiritual life), except souls more experienced than ourselves are touched by God to come and start us and help us on our way." But this can act "*only in and through the unforced insight of our own, docilely inclined, minds and the free, loving self-dedication of our wills.*" Juliet should accept from his advice only what appealed to her mind, heart and conscience.[18]

Von Hügel recommended a balance between the explicitly religious and other areas of life:

> You will then, Child, even for the sake of religion itself, ever eagerly love your games, your dancing, your hunting, and such other physical pleasures and activities as suit your health and social circumstance; you will enter delightedly into your music, poetry and other art; you will devote yourself to your studies of history or science; you will wholeheartedly care for, and help (in proportion to your special gifts and *attraits*) in social, political, moral questions and necessities.[19]

"*Attrait*" was a favorite term used by von Hügel for the particular way in which God leads an individual. He insisted that each person should follow his or her own particular *attrait*.

In the same letter, addressed to the young Juliet, von Hügel laid out four great religious principles and practices. He began with the reality and practice of the presence of God. Accompanying this sense of God's presence is the practice of contingency, of creatureliness, a reality that requires the institutional aspect of religion, an aspect rooted for von Hügel in the incarnation. The third reality and practice is the sense of our human weakness, error and sin. Von Hügel opposed any exaggerated preoccupation with sin but recommended a daily examination of conscience. Rather than focusing on self, von Hügel encouraged his young friend to occupy herself with God and others in a spirit of "joy, expansion, admiration, adoration, gratitude." The final principle was the reality and sense of the true function of suffering. Von Hügel believed that Christianity alone faced the mysterious depth of suffering, not as a theory but "as a force and a fact," leading with the help of Christ's spirit, to "purification, acceptance, expansion, intimate union with God and man, spiritual power, joy overflowing." Juliet should work on these principles "with simplicity, perseverance, and above all, *with love, and love, AND LOVE.*" The observance of these practices will bring her an "unshakable, because creaturely strength, a deep joy, and a steady homely heroism, a gently flowing love and service of your fellow-creatures, in, with and for God, the Infinite, our Home." This beautiful letter to the seventeen-year-old Juliet expressed not only his hopes for her, but the characteristics of his own spirituality.

In Holy Week of the same year von Hügel suggested that Juliet read John 13:1–17: "I should like you to read and pray over them *very* carefully—thinking how *you* are called to wash your neighbors' feet—the feet of those God has specially given you."[20] He included practical advice on how to get the most out of her time at school, suggesting to the reluctant student that she adopt a positive attitude toward school rather than *"sulking through the inevitable."*[21]

The depth of von Hügel's affection for Juliet is evident in his reflections which he shared with her:

> And as part of this abiding life, which, please God, will never go, I saw and see you, my child, who have just simply become part of my true self, and whom, I feel spontaneously, I must

and will cherish and help to grow as part of that life and soul which God has given me to live and be in and for Him.[22]

In the same letter he told her about his mother-in-law, Lady Herbert's death, and then encouraged her to respond to her own *attrait* even as Lady Herbert had responded to hers.

The seriousness with which von Hügel wrote to Juliet is apparent:

I should like you to take all I am going to write as *very deliberately meant*, as, I do humbly believe, *coming from God*, through me unworthy, to you, little old Daughter mine.

He shared with her his own struggles as a young man when religion saved him from himself. Juliet also belonged "*to that needing religion type*."[23]

It was not only Juliet's spiritual life but her intellectual life which occupied von Hügel's attention. In preparation for a proposed trip to Italy he gathered extensive material "In Aid of a Fruitful Visit to Rome."[24] He encouraged her study of Latin, commenting on how Augustine never learned Greek because of disagreeable memories of his early experience. This evoked a favorite insight: "*We never get to know or do properly except what we love.*"[25]

Two days after Gertrud died the Baron wrote to tell Juliet the sad news.

I want to add that, tho' no one affection ever can or does simply take the place of another, yet that, the going of my dearest first born makes me more than ever feel my love for you, child—the youngest of those so kindly given me by God. I more than ever love to watch your work and service, and to rejoice in any and all good and happiness and pleasure that may come to you.[26]

By this time Juliet was no longer a school girl but a young woman who had gone to Dieppe to help with the war effort. Von Hügel's love for Juliet continued but it seems that she did not respond as he wished, although she continued to visit him when she was in London and often read with him. From Juliet's perspective, von Hügel seemed to have been unaffected by the war and unable to appreciate how she had dramatically changed through her experience as a nurse on the front and the death of her fiancé.[27] When she visited him in February 1919 he described her as "strained, overwrought underneath," and referred to his own loss of temper.[28]

A final letter of von Hügel written in January 1921 referred to the need for physical and spiritual healing to come together. He assured Juliet of his prayers and suggested that she attend a communion service. Just as salmon jump upstream, he urged her to "jump, Child, jump; I jump with you, look we can manage."[29] His diary notes that she did go to communion.[30] A year later he commented on lunch with Juliet and a visit to the Tate Gallery during which "she was in a very pleasant gentle mood, but no sign of religion."[31]

The letters of von Hügel to Juliet Mansel raise the question whether the relationship may have been more a response to von Hügel's needs than to Juliet's. Unlike his direction of Evelyn Underhill and of Gwendolen Greene which was initiated by them, von Hügel's guidance of Juliet seems to have been assumed by him as a parental figure. There is no doubt of his affection for Juliet but at times the suitability of his advice to a schoolgirl may be questioned. He related to her as to a daughter. Like many daughters, she returned his affection but needed to find her own way.

Evelyn Underhill

Von Hügel's direction of Evelyn Underhill was very different from that of the young Juliet Mansel. For Evelyn Underhill, von Hügel was a great teacher, the one whose "power of holding, and practicing together (in all their fullness and variety), the pastoral and the philosophic sides of the spiritual life" made him "the most influential religious personality of our times."[32] She credited him with leading her from a disembodied mysticism to a more integrated spirituality. His enduring influence on her life and on her writing may be seen in her many references to him in her published works. Her debt to him was expressed in a brief tribute, first published anonymously, in the *Guardian* the week following his death, "Baron von Hügel as Spiritual Teacher," and in her essay, "Finite and Infinite: A Study of the Philosophy of Baron Friedrich von Hügel."[33] For his part, meeting Evelyn Underhill and engaging in a serious dialogue with her during the last three years of his life must have helped him to clarify his own thinking about religion and the place of the mystical element within the Christian life.

Von Hügel's relationship with Evelyn Underhill began, as did many of his friendships, when he read her book and then contacted the author. His diary notes that three days after he began Underhill's *Mysticism* she visited him for the first time to discuss it.[34] Von Hügel offered a number of suggestions which Underhill incorporated into her subsequent writing. Even before this meeting she had noted the influence of his classic *The Mystical Element* on her *Mysticism*. "This book, which only came into my hands when my own was planned and partly written, has since been a constant source of stimulus and encouragement."[35] In her preface to the twelfth edition written in 1930 she spelled out how she would plan the book if she were writing it again, making reference to the "twin doctrines emphasized in all von Hügel's work":

> First, that while mysticism is an essential element in full human religion, it can never be the whole content of such religion. It requires to be embodied in some degree in history, dogma and institutions if it is to reach the sense-conditioned human mind. Secondly, that the antithesis between the religions of "authority" and of "spirit", the "Church" and the "mystic," is false. Each requires the other.[36]

She had learned these important lessons from von Hügel. Although they had known each other for ten years it was not until 1921 that Evelyn Underhill requested that von Hügel formally undertake her spiritual direction.[37]

Underhill had been baptized as an Anglican but was for many years non-practicing. As a young woman she had been strongly attracted to the Roman Catholic Church, especially to its liturgical life, but she had been discouraged from becoming a Roman Catholic by the condemnation of modernism in 1907, and also by her future husband's opposition to such a move. Stuart Moore feared that if Evelyn became a Catholic her confessor would come between himself and his wife. Underhill herself had recognized the need for personal religion "to attach itself to a traditional church," and as she acknowledged in *Mysticism*, she appreciated the example of all the great saints who had been deeply committed to the church.[38] But her intellectual integrity would not allow her to join the Roman Catholic Church and no other church seemed to meet her need.

Underhill's return to the Anglican Church in which she had been baptized was the occasion for von Hügel to write and express his joy that she had taken this step, noting:

I quite realize how difficult (how dangerous unless definitely called) such a change to the Roman Catholic Obedience has become for many educated minds. And though I certainly should love to see you simply and completely one of us; and though again I am not going to be sure that you will never be given that special call, I mean *that* was not what so far made me wistful at the thought of you.[39]

Von Hügel believed that Underhill needed to root her mysticism in a visible sacramental religion and he was pleased that she had recognized this and acted on her need for an institutional grounding. He added an assurance of his willingness to help her in whatever way he could. Realistically he added:

We are *both* very busy, so we have each the guarantee that we will not take up each other's time without good cause.[40]

In a second letter he made some practical suggestions for institutional practices, recognizing that she would find the "institutional" difficult but that it would be beneficial for her. In response to what he perceived as her need for "de-intellectualizing, or at least developing homely, human sense and spirit dispositions and activities," he suggested music, painting, and gardening.[41]

While respecting the way that the spirit was guiding her, von Hügel nevertheless insisted on his role as director, chiding her for making a retreat without consulting him.[42] She was not to have two directors at the same time. His directions to her were carefully thought out and clearly presented, and he expected them to be followed.

In response to questions raised by Underhill in December 1921 von Hügel laid out concrete answers in a letter which she was to read once a month and then report to him after six months.[43] Underhill summarized von Hügel's directives into her "Rule Christmas 1921." The advice that von Hügel offered to Underhill affirmed her own religious experience and built on it. He encouraged her to get herself, "gently and gradually, interested *in the poor*," suggesting that she visit them two afternoons a week, "very quietly and unostentatiously." Such a practice would help her and eventually might also help the poor. He supported her work of directing others but told her not to take on new cases until after Easter. "I believe this (practiced only on the unsolicited invitation of the persons concerned) is distinctly good for you."[44] Von Hügel understood Underhill's difficulties with Roman Catholicism, but urged her to acquire a "Catholic mind."

Not only did von Hügel invite Underhill to root her spiritual life in the church, but he also led her to a greater Christocentric faith. He encouraged her to develop an incarnational spirituality which would complement her mystical theism. Rather bluntly he told her to either develop a Christocentricism or join the Unitarians. To Underhill's objection that she did not feel the need for a "half-way house" between herself and God, he replied that the infant does not feel its mother's breast "a half-way house" between itself and its mother. "The infant feels that breast as the self-giving of that mother." Von Hügel helped Underhill to discover the self-revelation of God in the person and life of Jesus Christ, insisting that both currents are needed, the "sensible, contingent, historical, incarnational current and the mystical God unincarnate."

Underhill's report on her observance of von Hügel's advice is detailed and direct as is his reply given in Midsummer 1922 in which he included his "religious advice for the year to end June 30, 1923." Underhill reported a loss of the prayer of quiet, but her "old religious life now looks too thin and solitary." She liked the retreat, Holy Communion, but not confession. Her visiting of the poor had been a "complete success." She was visiting eight families whose names she had received from a friend. "The women are perfectly wonderful," although visiting them made her feel pampered. "However jangled one may be when one goes to them, one always comes away mysteriously filled with peace and nearer God." She was involved in giving instructions to various groups, including "collections of clergymen!", a work which she saw as "direct, inconspicuous and needed." Von Hügel gave his blessing to this work, adding "I particularly like the collections of clergymen." To Underhill's statement: "Unless I can leave *all* professional vanity at the foot of the cross I may as well give up altogether," von Hügel wisely commented: "This, of course, is excessive." He urged her not to struggle against various desires directly since this led to "strain, scruple, self-occupation." Rather she should "try gently, to get thoroughly at home with, saturated by, your joy."

Underhill noted that she found intercessory prayer difficult but recognized the need for "some redemptive and social character to devotional life" if her prayer were not to be "too thin and vertical." Von Hügel encouraged her in her own form of prayer with no formal meditation, assuring her that intercessory prayer would come. He described prayer as a "dim background," an "over-againstness" so that "the doing of your studies, composition, speaking, etc.," is done with "a sense that all you are doing is, in its perfection, always beyond you." In this statement one senses that von Hügel is describing his own experience of prayer.   In reply to Underhill's report that she was still mainly theocentric, although she now recognized the value of the Christocentric but she was unable to accept the dogmatic "language of Nicene," von Hügel told her not to "throw overboard" anything here. His words throw light on his own approach:

> Your and my chances of genuine growth depend very largely upon our persistent refusal to identify the ultimate truth, or even our own ultimate capacity, with what we actually see or even what we here and now are capable of.

His advice is to "neither force adhesion nor allow rejection, but let it alone, as possible food for others, and indeed for yourself later on."

In response to Underhill's reference to Holy Communion as the historical link with other Christians back to the beginning, von Hügel, reflecting the Roman Catholic understanding of sacrament, commented that "covenanted graces" are attached to valid orders, but that God supplies "by a pure Grace the absence of the covenanted grace." Underhill recognized the need for a church but could not "conceive of submission to Rome." She assured von Hügel that she was satisfied as an Anglican: "having discovered a corner I can fit into and people with whom I can sympathize and work." Von Hügel urged her to make "no exceptions to readiness to follow God's clear commands." He wanted her to remain open to wherever God might lead her, even to Rome if that should be God's will for her.

A further directive written in September 1922 offered advice for "times of spiritual dryness." She should keep up or revive "activities and interests of a not directly religious kind" while dropping her rule and religious activity.

> We live quite abnormal lives, all of us, in these feverish times and our nerves are on edge and require attention. Treat your soul as the captains in the pre-steam days treated their crew. These men had always to be busy, but not always sailing. Weeks of no wind or of wrong wind would keep them from sailing. What then? They would at once, as *part of their work*

and life, drop the sailing and take to mending and making sails and nets, etc. So do you.

In June 1923 Underhill sent her annual report and von Hügel replied. The Christocentric side of her faith had become deeper and stronger. Although she had "blank times," she had "never known such deep and real happiness." She expressed her gratitude to von Hügel: "All this, humanly speaking, I owe entirely to you. Gratitude is a poor, dry word for what I feel about it." In response to her fear that her "invisible experience" was only subjective consolation and desolation closely related to her "nervous and even bodily life," causing her to question not only her own experience but "the whole spiritual scheme," von Hügel asked her simply, "These experiences of yours are not articles of faith, are they?" She should use what helped her, realizing that there would be changes as she matured.

Underhill was experiencing a number of different pressures, including family claims, as well as more and more demands on her time. She felt that she was "turning into a sort of fluid clergyman!" Von Hügel's reply shows how he himself had learned to cope with the same problem:

> *As to helping others,* I find a great relief in what I have now practiced only these last two years. I now know, roughly, how much I can try to help others without getting markedly empty myself. So now, when I have got to that point, I politely refuse to answer any fresh correspondents. I tell them frankly how matters stand and that God will find them, if really necessary, some helper with sufficient leisure for the purpose.

He suggested that she increase the quality (not quantity) of her visits to her aging parents. He concluded by proposing two rules, "a maximum rule for fair weather and a minimum rule for foul."

> For foul weather, morning and night prayer (with examen) all quite short—and the two Holy Communions a week. For the rest, some extra needlework or gardening or what not.

There was to be no report until the end of June 1924, but he added realistically "supposing I am still alive then."

Von Hügel was opposed to Underhill joining guilds, although she might encourage others who find them helpful to do so for "there are many such ways to God." When Underhill asked about joining the Order of the Holy Dove, von Hügel, who placed great emphasis on personal freedom and attentiveness to the way God was guiding each person, raised two questions: Did she feel that it would in no way complicate or trap her, but only gently support and steady her? Were the personnel "solid, simple, sober souls?" If her answer to these two questions was yes, she might join. Underhill did join the Order of the Holy Dove, a lay order of contemplatives who did not live in community. She was a member until the chief anchoress died and the order quietly ceased.[45]

Underhill's report of June 1924 is missing but not von Hügel's reply to her on 9 August 1924, six weeks late, with the explanation that he had "just regained, after a year of brain-weakness, something of a spring in my work, and did not dare answer such letters till my holiday from composition work." He offered two suggestions for Underhill to pray over quietly "without strain or rush of any kind." She should drop her "*vivacious irritated or confusing attention*" to her spiritual misery "by a quiet turning to God and Christ and the poor." She should restrict her literary religious labors to perhaps two-thirds of her output over the last ten years.

Von Hügel met Evelyn Underhill's need for intellectual integrity while supporting her mysticism, and encouraging her to develop an institutional foundation. He not only offered very concrete suggestions for her spiritual life but provided a philosophical framework which allowed her to move from her earlier monistic world view to one in which the spiritual was rooted in the material, the mystical in the historical and institutional. For this she was grateful to von Hügel with his insistence on the concrete as the "sacramental utterance of God." In spite of its shortcomings, von Hügel believed that the church was a necessary base for a religion which was to avoid individualism and be rooted in the community, past and present. Along with church membership went corporate worship, an important element of religious response. Through external practice one joined the communion of saints past and present. Von Hügel viewed church affiliation and external practices as a necessary expression of religion. Rather than being oppressive, he experienced them as supportive of faith and encouraged Underhill and others to discover this for themselves.

Gwendolen Greene

"I sat beside him, always on the same little low chair. . . . I always felt like a child with my uncle, and I never attempted to be anything else."[46] Thus Gwendolen Greene described her formal talks with her uncle which began in 1918, shortly after the death of her father, Sir Hubert Parry, who had, like von Hügel, married into the Herbert family. No doubt one reason for this seating arrangement was the Baron's deafness which made conversation difficult.

If von Hügel led Evelyn Underhill toward the institutional element of religion, he acted as guide for Gwendolen Greene in the development of the intellectual element. His direction of his niece included suggested reading and discussion of the classics, in order that she might become a "sober, persevering, balanced, genial, historical Christian."[47] For von Hügel history was a way of enlarging one's personal experience by entering into contact with the past and thus learning about the human heart. Few people would have been willing to undertake the rigorous program of reading and study carried on for six years by Gwendolen Greene under her uncle's direction.

The letters of von Hügel to his niece provide an opportunity to watch the perceptive director at work. He gently led her step by step, responding to her questions, making suggestions, sharing his own journey with her. As with Evelyn Underhill, von Hügel led Greene to a recognition of the need for a church and he encouraged her to be faithful to her own Anglican communion. For him the church was the form of our interconnectedness with one another and with all Christians past and present.

> And, *it is the Church* (which, imperfectly understood, "dumbs" my bewildered Child)—it is the Church which, at its best and deepest, is just *that*—that inter-dependence of all the broken and the meek, all the self-oblivious, all the reaching out to God and souls, which certainly "pins down" neither my child nor this her old groping Father—which, if it "pins down" at all, does so, really only—even taken simply intellectually—as the skeleton "pins down" the flesh.[48]

Although von Hügel emphasized the historical, social, institutional aspect of religion, he also encouraged Greene in her own form of prayer and warned her against being "churchy."[49]

Von Hügel was conscious of the need to respect God's action in his niece's life. This was particularly the case as she became interested in joining the Roman Catholic Church. In a long letter he shared with her the problem which he had experienced with his eldest daughter

Gertrud, one which made him cautious in his relationship with this spiritual daughter. He himself had educated Gertrud in the faith but in a way that "so strained and perplexed that very sensitive young soul that her very love of me and her natural openness to all impressions from me, bereft her for years of all faith." In his colorful language he accused himself of "having *put out my True's spiritual eyes.*"[50] After this painful experience with his daughter, von Hügel did not want to make a similar mistake with his niece. "My chief prayer has been that I might never strain, never complicate, never perplex you. . . . I might just simply help and feed and carry you, if and when and where you require it—to let God lead."[51] Their discussion had centered on liberty and freedom in the Roman Catholic Church. Von Hügel admitted that he had been thinking of his own case rather than hers. With characteristic honesty he wrote:

> I deliberately admit *some* difficulty, *some* complication for such as myself; but I do not cease, thank God, to see and experience that the gain of my Roman Catholic appurtenance is, even simply for the solidity of my freedom, for the balance and reality of my outlook—*just simply even to my life of scholarship and thinking IMMENSE.*[52]

Gwendolen was not to understand this as a plea for her to enter the Roman Catholic Church. "Only deep, strong, most clear calls of conscience would make it right for you to think of such a change."[53]

For Gwendolen Greene this change did not occur until after her uncle's death. In her Introduction to *Letters to a Niece*, she blamed herself for not saying with greater certainty that she had found her home in the Catholic Church.

> He knew I had never seen the need for any Church till I knew him, nor did I know the possibility of loving any Church till I found his. But this was not enough. I had to show him more—and this I could not do. I was so used to listening and accepting, not explaining.[54]

The last sentence points to one of the limitations of von Hügel's direction. In spite of his insistence that each person follow her own *attrait*, his strong personality and possibly his deafness sometimes made it difficult for those whom he was directing to articulate their own position.

Von Hügel's advice to his niece has continued to inspire Christians who are seeking to deepen their spiritual life.[55] He encouraged her "to see things in the large and upon the whole, and at their best."[56] All her activities were ways of loving God:

> At one moment packing; at another silent adoration in church; at another, dreariness and unwilling drift; at another, the joys of human affections given and received; at another, keen, keen suffering of soul, of mind, in an apparent utter loneliness; at another, external acts of religion; at another, death itself.[57]

He added: "But it is for God to choose these things, their degrees, combinations, successions; and it is for Gwen, just simply, very humbly, very gently and peacefully, to follow that leading."[58] It was advice that von Hügel strove to follow in his own life.

The Spiritual Companion

We have seen how von Hügel skillfully guided those who turned to him for help on their spiritual journey. For Wilfrid Ward he was a spiritual companion during the last months of Ward's life. For Evelyn Underhill, who had a strong intellectual and mystical understanding of religion, he provided encouragement to form an institutional base on which to ground her mysticism. For Gwendolen Greene, who had a mystical sense, he opened up the intellectual and the institutional elements of religion. His efforts with Juliet Mansel do not seem to have borne fruit in the way that von Hügel hoped. This may be because his advice to her was premature and proceeded more from his need than from hers.

Von Hügel was respectful of those whom he directed, urging them to accept only what was helpful for them. His words to Greene in his very first letter, 25 April 1918, were to accept only what fitted her, although he added:

> Such things ought always to feel, at first, as just a size or two too big for us—as what gently stimulates us to a further growth and expansion; but they should always be quietly ignored, if, and in so far as they come before our quiet look at them as conundrums simply imposed on us from without.[59]

In his reply to another correspondent he wrote concerning his advice:

"If they find a place in your heart and conscience, good, get them to grow there; if they don't fit, well, again, I will have meant well and you will forgive!"[60]

Von Hügel saw his task as one of facilitating the spiritual growth of others by directing them to embrace the tradition with all its richness in a spirit of freedom. He lived his own *attrait* while encouraging fellow travelers to be faithful to theirs. The following two chapters present in a more systematic way the spirituality which von Hügel shared not only with those whose religious development he fostered during his lifetime, but with succeeding generations.

NOTES

1. The correspondence between Wilfrid Ward and vH is in SAUL, vHP, MSS 3157–3166; WWP, MS 38347 vii 143. The letters of von Hügel to Mansel written between 1910 and 1921 are in SAUL, MS 37194. A number are published in *SL*. The letters to Underhill written between 1921 and 1924 are in SAUL, MS 5552. These are included in Margaret Cropper's *Evelyn Underhill* (London: Green and Co., 1958); hereafter *EU*. For letters to Greene, see *Letters from Baron Friedrich Von Hügel to a Niece* (London: Dent & Sons, 1928); hereafter *LTN*.

2. See Chapter 2 above for vH's relationship with W. G. Ward. After his death Ward collected a number of his father's articles into a book, *Essays on the Philosophy of Theism*, which he dedicated to vH.

3. Maisie Ward, *The Wilfrid Wards and the Transition: Insurrection versus Resurrection* (London: Sheed & Ward, 1937), p.479.

4. Ibid., p.300.

5. WW to vH, 17 February 1916, vHP, SAUL, MS 3158.

6. vH to WW, 6 March 1916, WWP SAUL, MS 38347 vii 143 (196).

7. 28 February 1916, WWP, SAUL, MS 38347 vii 143 (195); published in *SL*, p.228.

8. 27 March 1916; WWP, SAUL, MS 38347 vii 143 (!98); *SL*, p.231.

9. 20 March 1916; WWP, SAUL, MS 38347 vii 143 (197).

10. vH to Adeline Chapman, May 1909, vHP, SAUL, MS 37194/3; vH to Mildred Mansel, 21 December 1909, SAUL, MS 37194/4.

11. "A Letter from Baron von Hügel," *Dublin Review* 225 (April 1951), pp.1–11; quote p.1; published anonymously with a prefatory note. The original letter written 11 March 1910 is in vHP, SAUL, MS 37194/8.

12. Ibid., p.2.

13. vHP, SAUL, MS 37194/7.

14. 4 April 1910, vHP, SAUL, MS 37194/10.

15. 30 October 1911, vHP, SAUL, MS 37194/29.

16. 9 May 1911, vHP, SAUL, MS 37194/24.

17. 11 March 1910, vHP, SAUL, MS 37194/8. See n.11 above. Joseph Whelan considered this letter to be perhaps vH's finest letter of spiritual direction. He used it as the conclusion of his book, *The Spirituality of Friedrich von Hügel*, pp.226–36.

18. Ibid., p.226. The emphasis is vH's.

19. Ibid., p.228.

20. 23 March 1910, vHP, SAUL, MS 37194/9; *SL*, pp.175–76.

21. 28 September 1910, vHP, SAUL, MS 37194/17; *SL*, pp.180–81.

22. 30 October 1911, vHP, SAUL, MS 37194/29; incorrectly dated in *SL*, pp.193–94 as 13 October 1911. Lady Herbert died 30 October 1911 (Diary 1911).

23. 12 May 1911, vHP, SAUL, MS 37194/25; emphasis is vH's.

24. A thirty-six-page typed MS, "Letters in Aid of a Fruitful Visit to Rome," is at SAUL, vHP, MS 37194/23 dated 20 April 1911.

25. 8 September 1911, vHP, SAUL, MS 37194/28.

26. 14 August 1915, vHP, SAUL, MS 37194/36.

27. James J. Kelly, *Baron Friedrich von Hügel's Philosophy of Religion* (Leuven University Press, 1983), p.211; account of a conversation with Juliet Mansel.

28. Diary, 21 February 1919.

29. 6 January 1921, vHP, SAUL, MS 37194/50.

30. Diary, 9 January 1921.

31. Diary, 7 January 1922.

32. "Baron Von Hügel as a Spiritual Teacher," *Mixed Pastures: Twelve Essays and Addresses* (Freeport, NY: Books for Libraries, 1933), p.230.

33. "Finite and Infinite: A Study of the Philosophy of Baron Friedrich von Hügel," followed by an additional note, "Baron von Hügel as a Spiritual Teacher," *Mixed Pastures*, pp.217–33.

34. Diary, 16 July 1911, notes: "Mrs. Stuart Moore came, my first sight of her; discussed with her first four chapters of her 'Mysticism.' " Evelyn Underhill was married to Stuart Moore.

35. *Mysticism: A Study of the Nature and Development of Man's Spiritual Consciousness* (London: Methuen and Co., 1911; reprinted 1930), p.xiv.

36. Ibid., pp.ix–x.

37. Underhill's association with vH previous to her request for his direction is indicated in vH's diary for 13 February 1916 which notes a request from Mrs. Stuart Moore to address the "Religious Thought Circle" on "What do we mean by heaven and hell?" vH gave the paper 12 December 1916 to 120 people, including Underhill. On 14 December he noted having received a "charming letter about my address from Mrs. Stuart Moore."

38. *Mysticism*, p.8.

39. This first letter is dated 29 October 1921; vHP, SAUL, MS 5552.

40. Ibid.; emphasis is vH's.

41. 5 November 1921, vHP, SAUL, MS 5552.

42. *EU*, p.94.

43. vHP, SAUL, MS 5552. EU wrote to vH 21 December 1921; vH replied with a lengthy letter which became the basis for his direction and her response.

44. vH to EU, vHP, SAUL, MS 5552; material that follows is from these papers; emphases are vH's.

45. vHP, SAUL, MS 5552 includes the discussion concerning joining the Order of the Holy Dove. Information about the Order is in MS 5553/3, a copy of the unfinished draft of Lucy Menzies' Life of Evelyn Underhill.

46. *LTN*, p.xi.

47. *LTN*, p.xii. Greene describes how parcels of books arrived regularly along with a letter explaining their significance. These included not only Christian classics but works on other religions.

48. *LTN*, p.25; emphasis is vH's.

49. *LTN*, pp.62–63.

50. 22 February 1921, *LTN*, p.122. See Chapter 3 above for details concerning this crisis. True was an affectionate name for Gertrud.

51. *LTN*, p.123.

52. *LTN*, p.128; emphasis is vH's.

53. *LTN*, p.129.

54. *LTN*, p.xl.

55. *LTN* has been reissued by Fount (Harper Collins, 1995).

56. *LTN*, p.134.

57. *LTN*, p.59.

58. *LTN*, pp.59–60.

59. *LTN*, p.3.

60. To Mrs. Frances Lillie, 13 March 1920; *SL*, p.300.

A LAY
SPIRITUALITY

7

Von Hügel's strong sense of his vocation as a lay person in the Catholic Church convinced him that "God's calls, within our one great common vocation, are many and various."[1] Although he lived many years before Vatican II and its teaching on the "universal call to holiness," his life and writings reflect his response to that call. His study of Catherine of Genoa, a lay woman who believed "everyone to be capable of (her) tender love," was formative for his lay spirituality.[2] As Nicholas Lash points out, there is "in von Hügel's scheme of things, no place for distinctions between first-class and second-class Christians—between an elite corps of geniuses and pattern setters and the slaves of habit who live their religion simply at secondhand."[3] All are called by God to live a full religious life using the gifts that they have received.

Life itself was the source of von Hügel's philosophy of religion and spirituality. In the Introduction to his last book, he wrote:

> The starting-point for us, the arsenal of materials, the test and final tribunal of our knowledge, is not any theory, however brilliant and captivating, but that tough, bewildering, yet immensely inspiring and truthfully testing thing, life as it is and as it surrounds us from the first.[4]

In the "givenness" of his own life von Hügel discovered the reality of God present in all persons and in all creation, but especially in his relationships with family and friends. As a lay Catholic, a husband and father, he developed a rich spirituality, deeply rooted in the historical realities of his life.

This chapter considers von Hügel's relationship with his family and

119

friends as a privileged revelation of God and an expression of his lay spirituality. It also studies the ecclesial and ecumenical spirituality which he was able to develop as a lay person in the Roman Catholic Church. An underlying theme that binds these strands together is hospitality. Von Hügel's heart and mind were open to people and ideas. This hospitality found concrete expression in the stream of visitors to 13 Vicarage Gate, his home from 1903 until his death. Here members of the executive committee of the London Society for the Study of Religion met, friends from Europe and North America found welcome, and persons seeking advice on their spiritual journey received help.

A Spirituality of Relationships

At a time when theology and spiritual writing within the Roman Catholic Church was done almost exclusively by clerics, the rootedness of von Hügel in family relationships is a significant aspect of his spirituality. As William Thompson emphasized, "The Baron did theology out of the narrative of his life and the lives of those he pondered."[5] He recognized the need to be grounded in the concrete, an insight that he shared with those who looked to him for guidance. As a source for von Hügel's lay spirituality it is helpful to look at the lives of those who were closest to him.

Von Hügel embraced the "givenness" of his life which included not only his deafness and his health problems, but his relationships with family and friends. In a letter to Maude Petre, expressing concern for Tyrrell if he should leave the Society of Jesus, von Hügel wrote these telling sentences concerning his own situation: "I feel so strongly what an *immense* help it is to my own soul's health and growth, that I am *not* free to fix the degree and kind of my relations with my fellows, but that the chief of them are all determined for me—as son, brother, husband, father."[6]

His father's death, when he was only eighteen, left Friedrich as the oldest son with a sense of responsibility for his family. His letters reveal his concern for his mother who lived her last years in Cambridge where she died in 1913. He also had great admiration for his mother-in-law, Lady Herbert. He seems to have been close to his sister Pauline who died in 1901. The fact that his brother Anatole and his sister-in-law did not share his theological views and had been upset by his involvement in Tyrrell's funeral created some tensions in their relationship but this was also part of the "givenness" of his life.

Von Hügel's relationship with his wife seems to have been a source of great joy as well as stress. His comment on Saint Catherine's lack of an experience of "the soul-entrancing power of full conjugal union" suggests that von Hügel himself enjoyed this reality.[7] His early letters to his wife reveal a passionate young man who was trying to integrate this love into his spiritual life. He found few models of conjugal spirituality within the Catholic Church. The twenty-two-year-old Friedrich wrote to his young wife who was visiting her mother:

> I've just come from Mass, and a talk with Fr. Bulbeck. He was very nice. I asked him about my scruples as to goings on after our marriage. He said that touches, kisses, etc., of a kind that would be wrong towards anyone else, would if from affection, be good and commendable when applied to the wife. Also that one should keep distinct the idea of a better, and the notion that the—possibly—less good is bad. I don't think I'd have those scruples, much, if I was with you, and well—that's a comfort. Fr. B. seemed to think so too for he said, as chief answer, that we must find it a hard trial being separated, and talked of Saints Elezear and Delphina who were separated too for a time. Do read their life, old 'un; it's in Butler's *Lives of the Saints*, Sept. 27th. Fr. B. says that quite as a young man he read the life and he has ever remembered and often thinks of this bit: Writing out of Italy to St. Delphina, St. Elezear said: "You desire to hear of me. Go often to visit our amiable Lord J. Ch. in the holy Sacrament. Enter in spirit his Sacred Heart. You will always find me there." St. Delphina lived to see her husband canonized![8]

Friedrich did not expect to be canonized but he did desire to be a saint.

Von Hügel's later writings reflect a positive attitude toward sexuality which was not characteristic of Catholic teaching in the late nineteenth and early twentieth centuries, a period when marital sex was often considered a substitute for adultery and its sole purpose to be procreation. In his letter to Margaret Clutton he encouraged her to help her son to appreciate "how normal and healthy, how pure and God-loved, is the social sex-life of marriage, and how rich it is in a joy which englobes and spiritualizes the strongest sensible pleasures."[9]

This positive appreciation for conjugal love must have come from his own experience as spouse.

Friedrich and Lady Mary, who had different interests, seem to have provided mutual support for one another and respected each other's various activities. Lady Mary had her own income which would have given her a certain independence. The fact that both were often ill added stress to their relationship. Von Hügel in his diaries expressed his concern for "Molly" and noted their walks and talks together. His letters to his daughter commented on her health: "Mama is pretty well, but with many ups and downs, and great depressions and sickness off and on."[10] In spite of periods of illness throughout her life, Lady Mary lived almost eleven years longer than her husband, dying 2 December 1935 at the age of 86.

Von Hügel's experience as a parent profoundly marked his spirituality. These words to a married woman capture the spirit with which he embraced his vocation as parent:

> Ever since I have had, ever since I *could* have children, I have felt myself a creature enriched with the noble duty of giving on the largest scale—with the obligation to possess a reserve of light and life and love—a reserve for dearest little beings who would not have existed but for myself. I have not, it is true, created these beings; yet it was because I chose to marry, to be and to act as a husband and a possible father, that these particular beings became possible, and that, when they actually came, they possessed many a physical and temperamental peculiarity of my own, good, bad and mixed.[11]

His three daughters were very precious to him. We have seen his active participation in their education, especially their religious education which he considered the right and duty of parents. While respectful of the clergy, he insisted that parents are the best teachers of their children, a point that he emphasized in his response to questions posed by Margaret Clutton.[12]

Not only did von Hügel guide his daughters as children but he remained a devoted parent, supporting them in their vocational choices. As an aristocratic Victorian father he considered it his duty to provide for his three daughters. He drew up Gertrud's marriage settlement, provided an income for Hildegard, and made the financial arrangements for Thekla with the Prioress of the Carmelite Monastery.

He also ensured that Thekla would have an income in the unlikely event that she should leave Carmel. His love and concern for each of them is evident in his diaries and letters.

Gertrud shared her father's literary and religious interests and was very close to her father. Her translation of Thureau-Dangin's life of St. Bernardine of Siena from French to English was published in 1906. Her father worried about her health and was concerned about the marriage settlement with Count Francesco Salimei which was complicated by Italian law. He spent considerable time in working with lawyers on this during 1907, that trying year when he was finishing *The Mystical Element* and living in the strained ecclesiastical atmosphere.[13] We have seen how deeply he experienced Gertrud's death in 1915 and how his attitudes toward suffering were profoundly affected by this painful experience.[14]

Von Hügel's letters to Hildegard, his middle daughter (or Hillie as her father called her), are affectionate and full of fatherly concern. When he received his half year's profit of 13 pounds from Dent for *The Mystical Element* he immediately sent half of it to her.[15] Hildegard was the one who accompanied her father to Rome when Gertrud was ill and stayed with him until her sister's death. Describing her own relationship with her father she wrote:

> All through my life he took the very greatest interest in anything that interested *me*, though it was probably quite other and outside any interests of his own. But his wonderful sympathy, and humble, keen wish to learn from anyone, made him such a marvelous companion and friend all through my childhood as well as in mature life.[16]

Hildegard, who served as the executor of her father's will, survived him by only one year, dying in 1926.

His youngest daughter, Thekla, entered the Carmelite Monastery in 1907 at the age of 21. Von Hügel considered celibacy "a choice gift of God" while opposing "the idea that marriage was something nasty and impure." In a letter to Maude Petre he expressed his happiness in Thekla's vocation and her *complete* freedom from any negative attitudes toward marriage.[17] In more detail than usual, his diary described Thekla's clothing day. He led his daughter up the chapel aisle and to the entrance of the convent dressed in her bridal gown and then saw her reappear in her novice's dress behind the grating.[18] In spite of this dramatic parting, Thekla remained close to her father. To Bernard Holland, whose daughter was considering joining a religious order, von Hügel wrote:

> The daughter that I specially gave to God remains, quite accessible to us all still; whereas the daughter that seemed left to us in the ordinary life has already been called home.[19]

Visits to Sister Thekla were important for von Hügel, although speaking through a grill must have been particularly difficult for him, because of his deafness. Each visit to the monastery is carefully noted in his diary with comments on Thekla's health and happiness. Her father usually walked there and back, accompanied by his dog. In October 1923, one of his last visits to the monastery, he noted that they talked about Thérèse of Lisieux, the young Carmelite who had been beatified on 29 April 1923. A few days previously he had met Cardinal Bourne at a special lunch with the Carmelites and had enjoyed "a charming talk with the cardinal" about the "Little Flower." The Cardinal had commented on how hidden is the life of most holy souls, pointing out that Thérèse became known only because she had been ordered to write her story. Thekla told her father that this was most unusual and would not happen in her monastery.[20]

Thekla lived a full and active life as a contemplative nun. Between 1907 and 1938 thirty-three new Carmelite foundations were established in England at the request of the bishops. In her role as bursar and later as sub-prioress, Thekla packed trunks and boxes for the new communities as well as making the necessary financial arrangements for them. She was the longest survivor of her family, dying in 1970 at the age of 84, in the monastery infirmary where her sister Gertrud's crucifix hung on the wall.[21]

A Spirituality of Friendship

In addition to his family von Hügel was enriched by his many friends. We have seen the importance of his friendships with George Tyrrell and with Norman Kemp Smith.[22] The list of manuscripts preserved at St Andrews University Library reflects the variety of those with whom he corresponded and the constancy with which he maintained these relationships over the years. Just the month before he died he described letter writing as "the divinely intended and specially blest means and price of such most precious touch with our friends."[23] His diary notes the flow of visitors to his home, including women and men, young and old, scholars, clerics, and agnostics. Von Hügel, who recognized the significance of our interdependence, learned from all his relationships and valued each friend as a precious gift and revelation of God. In the words of Abbot Butler, "never was there a loyaler or more enthusiastic friend."[24]

An Ecclesial Spirituality

Perhaps even more foundational than family relationships and friendship was the all embracing love for the church which characterized von Hügel's spirituality. In one of his letters he referred to the church as "the Beloved Community, the world-wide congregation of believers."[25] The vocation of the Christian was to be a saint and one learned how to become a saint from other faithful persons. Von Hügel believed that this could best be done within the Catholic Church, although he recognized God's grace active in other churches and religious traditions. In a letter to Kemp Smith, who had asked whether von Hügel really believed that the Roman Catholic Church could assimilate the best in the modern world as it had once assimilated the best in the Graeco-Roman world, he pointed out a number of Roman Catholics who had achieved this assimilation and he expressed his hope that there might be a future triumph of such an approach. His conclusion reveals von Hügel's deepest conviction that "the essential, the most indispensable of the dimensions of religion is *not breadth, but depth*, and above all, *the insight into sanctity and the power to produce saints.*"[26] He firmly believed that this was the real power of the Roman Catholic Church, before which all other achievements fade.

While von Hügel recognized the role of "officials" within the church, he resolutely refused to limit the Church to its "officials." When Tyrrell was experiencing difficulties with Cardinal Ferrata, the Prefect of the Sacred Congregation for Religious, von Hügel reminded him:

> The Church is more and other than just these Churchmen; and religion is more, and largely other, than even the best theology: and we, i.e. he, L (Loisy), you, M.D.P. (Petre), I—our housemaids too, are true, integral portions of the Church, which in none of its members is simply teaching, in none of its members is simply learning.[27]

Von Hügel, who described himself as "a lay lover of religion," understood his vocation to be that of a lay scholar within the Catholic Church.[28] He carefully explained in the Preface of *The Mystical Element*, dated Easter 1908, just a few months after the condemnation of modernism, how he understood his contribution to the life of the Church. Describing himself as "a proudly devoted and grateful son of the Roman Church," he recognized the many different kinds and degrees of light both within and without the Christian and Catholic Church.[29] He then situated his work as a lay person within the Church, acknowledging that the official Church has "the exclusive right and duty to formulate successively, for the Church's successive periods . . . normative forms and expressions of the Church's deepest consciousness and mind." But this articulation does not take place in a vacuum. It is the role of what he called "the Church's unofficial members" to do the "tentative and preliminary work" that is necessary if the Church is to express its deepest consciousness.[30]

As a lay person von Hügel was freer to speak the truth as he perceived it than were clergy who were bound by rules of censorship.

> I am a layman, who, just because he speaks with no kind of official authority, can the more easily say simply what he knows.[31]

This freedom which he claimed as a lay person must have been especially precious to him when he saw many of his friends who were priests deprived of their professorships, among them Tyrrell, Loisy, Semeria, and Genocchi. But von Hügel believed that the independence and freedom which he enjoyed as a lay person carried responsibilities. In discharging his scholarly work, he strove for "a layman's special virtues and function: complete candor, courage, sensitiveness to the present and future."[32]

We have seen that von Hügel's loyalty to the Catholic Church included critique. He acknowledged the centralizing process that had occurred within the Catholic Church which placed all "doctrinal and disciplinary powers in the hands of the Monarch Pope." His hope was that just as laymen, including W. G. Ward, had pressed this policy on Rome, "zealous believers, perhaps again mostly laymen and non-Italians, may arise who will successfully aid the return to a wider and richer, a truly Catholic, action."[33] Writing in 1912, von Hügel hoped that the Church would eventually work out a fruitful relationship between authority and freedom. He was convinced that:

> The curialist presentation of the situation, as a simple alternative between anarchy or autocracy, revolt or self-stultification, will not for ever terrify into nonentity or goad into scepticism the freely docile children of Jesus Christ and of his Vicar, the Servant of the servants of God.[34]

The wider, richer Catholicism that von Hügel envisioned was more concerned with truth than with orthodoxy. His refusal to pass judgment on orthodoxy was a consistent attitude throughout his life. In a letter to Tyrrell in December 1901 he indicated his attitude toward condemnations:

> I love so much to leave to the dear Christ-Master, to Love Infinite, all dividing off of the goats from the sheep. And all, even indirect, exclusion on the score of orthodoxy—how painful it is always, and how little Christian the temper, where this predominates.[35]

In an article on the occasion of Archbishop Mignot's death in 1918, von Hügel noted again the position which was his as a layman, "one whose primary instinct and business is not with any personal delimitation of orthodoxy at all."[36] Yet he had to admit that "the Archbishop represents a temperament, gifts, outlooks and affinities markedly different from those of Pope Pius X." He added a list of others who had not always enjoyed favor in Rome: J. H. Newman, H. E. Manning, Bossuet, Fénelon, Mabillon, and even Saint Paul who was reproved by Saint Peter. He wisely concluded:

> The list would only illustrate how ruinous is the refusal to see suns where there are spots, or spots where there are suns; and how little in keeping with the complex facts of actual history is an orthodoxy pressed without patience or discrimination.

A religion of "sheer correctness alone" would not be the religion of Jesus Christ who was rejected by the officials of his day.[37]

Although von Hügel carried out his work as an independent scholar, he insisted on the importance of being part of a community. In a revealing letter to his daughter Hildegard he referred to his own requirement of "a large liberty, of much initiative and great activity," and his consciousness of "a strong tendency to fall out of the ranks; to break away from the *corporate*, the belonging, as a part, to any one body as a whole."[38] This tendency, perhaps intensified by his deafness, was one against which von Hügel struggled. He was convinced that Christianity was a social or corporate reality. This was the reason it was so important to maintain active church membership. For him communion with the Catholic Church, in spite of its restrictions, was an expression of interconnectedness, not only with God but with the saints throughout the ages. It was also communion with persons of every class, including the poor, a characteristic of the Roman Catholic Church that was valued by von Hügel who referred to "the crowd, the praying poor in our Churches."[39]

An Ecumenical Spirituality

Von Hügel was an ecumenical Roman Catholic Christian before his church entered into the ecumenical movement.[40] While the theology of the time was confessional and controversial, often fueled by anti-Catholic sentiment, he was able to see beyond these boundaries and to address his writings to all Christians.[41] At the same time he was deeply rooted in his own tradition and in his lectures often acted as a self-appointed, unofficial spokesperson for the Catholic Church. For a Catholic writer to combine this openness to other traditions with loyalty to his own tradition was unusual at the time, but as we have seen, von Hügel was unusual. David S. Cairns, Professor of Dogmatics and Apologetics in the United Free Church College, Aberdeen, aptly described von Hügel as "a big Christian, big enough to learn from everybody, and hold his own ground."[42]

We can appreciate the pioneering ecumenical spirit of von Hügel when we reflect on the difficulties experienced by later Catholic scholars who engaged in ecumenical activity. Yves M. J. Congar described the problems he experienced with ecclesiastical authorities between 1939 and 1956 because of his ecumenical work.[43] Prior to Vatican II the Catholic Church not only did not join the ecumenical movement but looked with suspicion on all ecumenical activities.

Von Hügel's ecumenical spirit is evident in his first presentation on St. Catherine of Genoa prepared for the *Hampstead Annual* in 1898. In a letter to Tyrrell he commented on his strongly Protestant audience:

I wanted so much to make them feel how much we have still, so largely unconsciously, in common, and that the difficulties raised by such a life, indeed by mysticism generally, are absolutely interconfessional, indeed inherent to the religious problem generally, and that they are as readily findable in the Bible as in her of Genoa.[44]

In the Preface to Maude Petre's *Von Hügel and Tyrrell: The Story of a Friendship*, published in 1937, the Anglican Canon Lilley commented on the contribution of both von Hügel and Tyrrell to an "English theology."

The chords of a richer theological harmony, for which all had been ineffectually fumbling on their separate instruments, were suddenly heard with a delighted wonder and surprise.[45]

The theological horizon was expanding at the same time that *Pascendi* was imposing its restrictions upon Catholic writers. Within the larger ecumenical horizon von Hügel developed his philosophy of religion but he always insisted that he did so as a Roman Catholic. We have seen how his involvement as a member of the Synthetic Society between 1896 and 1908 and as a founding member of the London Society for the Study of Religion from 1904 until his death provided an ecumenical context for his work.

Von Hügel's scholarly work was fueled by and contributed to ecumenical collaboration. Most of the German scholarship that von Hügel absorbed was the work of Protestant scholars, among them Rudolf Eucken, Ernst Troeltsch and Heinrich Julius Holtzmann. These scholars became personal friends of von Hügel.[46] The Protestant biblical scholar, Charles Augustus Briggs, Professor at Union Theological Seminary, coauthored with von Hügel a work on *The Papal Commission and the Pentateuch*.[47] Briggs, who had been excommunicated from the Presbyterian Church in 1893, shared von Hügel's commitment to the cause of liberty for Christian scholars. Both men believed that the challenges to Christian faith required the concerted effort of Christian scholars from all traditions and considered their critical work on the bible as a means of preparing for Christian unity.

Von Hügel's ecumenical and pastoral sensitivity is apparent in a letter to Canon George Newson about a proposed speaking engagement:

I understood from you that these are not fully settled, cheerily comfortable Church-people. You will understand how much

I would wish to be sure as to the kind of people I was addressing, since nothing is more distressing, I find than, unwittingly, to unsettle settled souls, instead of helping the other way on. You will also readily guess that by this I do not refer to any confessional differences, but to the critical problems and difficulties which, unbeknown to so many, really beset us all.[48]

Von Hügel longed for visible unity among Christians and believed that eventually this would come through Rome. But he added in parentheses "(what is true in the Protestant instincts even more than in the Protestant objections having been fully satisfied)" and suggested that this would occur "in a temper and with applications more elastic than those of the later Middle Ages and especially than those of post-Reformation times."[49] For von Hügel, Christian unity would not be simply a "return to Rome." He saw the Church as leading to God who alone is "the fully adequate home of the supernaturally awakened soul." One great international church would lead Christians to move beyond even "our noblest, national aspirations."[50]

In an article written by invitation for the *Homiletic Review* on the occasion of the four-hundredth centenary of the Protestant Reformation, von Hügel described the convictions common to Catholicism and Protestantism.[51] Following the example of the Benedictines of the Congregation of St. Maur, the chief founders of modern historical criticism, he referred to Protestants as "our separated brethren," a phrase adopted by Vatican II. The spirit with which von Hügel undertook the ecumenical task was the same as that which animated all his work—an honest seeking for the truth, wherever it might be found.

We all greatly require criticism, stimulation, reproof, of our most intimate and cherished convictions; and it is our reciprocal duty, with tact and restraint, to try to serve our fellows similarly.[52]

With his usual directness he examined Catholic positions at work within Protestantism, not hesitating to acknowledge sin on both sides. Drawing on Cardinal Juan de Lugo he argued that "truth, great or little, is usually mediated to the soul, neither by a spiritual miracle nor by the sheer efforts of individuals, but by traditions, schools and churches."

And he concluded that "we thus attain an outlook, generous, rich, elastic; yet also graduated, positive, unitary, and truly Catholic."[53]

In the Preface to his collection of *Essays and Addresses*, published just four years before his death, von Hügel laid out a number of basic convictions which underlie his work. Among them he stated his belief that there are "many fragments of truth and goodness and few wholes."

> The fragments of truth and goodness, where they subsist in good faith with regard to fuller truth and goodness, can already, in their degree and way, be of touching beauty and of real worth—of value, also to the opponents of those who hold these fragments.[54]

Within this framework von Hügel situated Christians who were not in communion with the Roman Catholic Church as well as non-Christians. In his recognition of the truth and goodness to be found in other traditions von Hügel cited the attitude of such authoritative figures as the missionary archbishop, Cardinal de Lavigerie toward Moslems and of Cardinal Manning toward his Anglican friends.[55] One senses the caution of the author who wrote as a Catholic layman within an ecumenical context at a time when the Roman Catholic Church was suspicious of the ecumenical movement.

In an address to Junior Members of the University of Oxford in May 1920 on "Christianity and the Supernatural," von Hügel indicated that he would draw his examples and analysis from what he knew best and loved very dearly, the Roman Catholic Church, but he added:

> This does not mean that noble, truly supernatural devotedness does not occur elsewhere in other Christian bodies, indeed also amongst Jews and Mohammedans, or amongst Parsees, Hindoos and Buddhists, even amongst that apparently increasing mass of men who would be puzzled to say where they stand theologically at all.

Having acknowledged God's action among all persons of goodwill, he expressed his

> . . . very deliberate, now long tested conviction that, be the sins of commission or of omission chargeable against the Roman Catholic authorities or people what they may, in the faith and practice is to be found a massiveness of the

supernatural, a sense of the World Invisible, of God as the souls's true home, such as exists elsewhere more in fragments and approximations and more intermittently.[56]

Von Hügel's ecumenical spirit of openness to other denominations and other religions was not common among either Protestants or Catholics in the 1920s. When von Hügel tried to arrange for Ernst Troeltsch to address the Student Christian Movement conference at Swanwick, Professor David Cairns expressed his reservations to the secretary of SCM, Tissington Tatlow. While he respected von Hügel whose letter had been "like himself, candid, humble and generous," Cairns feared that exposure to Troeltsch's ideas would be detrimental to the faith of the young people.[57] This cautious approach contrasts with von Hügel's confident faith that God is present in all human searching.

Von Hügel's respect for other denominations was appreciated by Christians from a variety of backgrounds. Among the many who wrote to Lady Mary after her husband's death was the Lutheran Archbishop Nathan Söderblom of Upsala who described von Hügel as "that lay-Bishop in the Church of God" who had "become a teacher and an initiator to seeking and believing souls in all the chief sections of the entire Church and communion of Christ."[58]

The question might be asked, if during this period the Roman Catholic Church was opposed to ecumenical activity, how did von Hügel avoid being censured for his involvement. His friend, Dom Butler, writing after von Hügel's death, suggested a possible explanation:

> The Authorities no doubt knew the religious influence he was wielding in circles outside the Catholic Church, and did not think it advisable that that influence should be weakened, or that work impeded, especially as the writings were of a kind little likely to be read by many beyond those for whom they were intended; and also the Authorities well knew the man himself.[59]

Von Hügel's ecumenical spirit was an integral expression of his lay spirituality. As a layman he carried out the "tentative and preliminary work" which prepared the way for the Catholic Church's recognition of God's action in other ecclesial communions and in other religions. In the area of ecumenism von Hügel practiced those virtues which he had described as belonging explicitly to the layman: "complete candor, courage, sensitiveness to the present and future."[60] When he met in March 1914 with a small group who were planning an ecumenical congress in Paris he advised them on procedures "best calculated to conciliate and secure Catholic cooperation." They should "work, not for official approbation but official toleration—not by direct and formal approach but by wise and balanced selection of committees," suggesting that they choose not clerics but laymen, at least at first. He warned that there should be "no advertising for most of this pontificate."[61] Although Benedict XV succeeded Pius X in August 1914, it would take the Catholic Church five more decades before it officially entered into the ecumenical movement and embraced a position in the decrees of Vatican II which was similar to that articulated by Friedrich von Hügel.

Not only was von Hügel's ecumenical vision accepted by the Roman Catholic Church but the method that he used is also widely followed within the ecumenical movement. He recognized the need for all Christians to work together for the renewal of the Church and appreciated the need for dialogue, often beginning with what was held in common by both parties before considering the differences between them. Friendship was the foundation on which von Hügel developed his dialogue with persons from many traditions. Many of these ongoing friendships were nourished by his involvement in the London Society for the Study of Religion, a structure which provided opportunities for serious interreligious dialogue and an atmosphere in which this could take place. Subsequent ecumenists have discovered that it is only in such an atmosphere of mutual trust and friendship that fruitful dialogue occurs.

Von Hügel's pioneering efforts, as well as those of many other ecumenically minded Christians, prepared the way for a more ecumenical church. Patrick Ruddle describes von Hügel as a "prophetic ecumenist." He suggests that rather than call him a forerunner of Vatican II it would be more exact to refer to him as "a prophet in the sense that he helps us to discover the full richness, the multiplicity in the unity and the unity in the multiplicity of God's authentic message."[62]

This chapter has considered the lay spirituality of von Hügel as it found expression in his relationships with family, friends, and church as well as with the larger ecumenical family. It was a spirituality characterized by hospitality. In the following chapter we will examine the philosophical foundation for his lay spirituality drawing once again on his three elements of religion.

NOTES

1. *EA* 2, p.241.

2. *ME* 1, p.268. See Chapter 4 above.

3. Lash, *Easter in Ordinary*, p.165.

4. *RG*, p. 29.

5. *Christology and Spirituality* (New York: Crossroad, 1991), p.102.

6. vH to MP, 5 September 1905; PP, BL, Add. MS 45361; quoted by de la Bedoyère, p.175.

7. *ME* 1, p.229.

8. De la Bedoyère, pp.4–5; see also Chapter 2 above. De la Bedoyère quotes from vH's early letters to Molly written in 1871, 1873, and 1875–76.

9. 11 June 1912, vHP, SAUL, MS 30994; published by Joseph P. Whelan, "The Parent as Spiritual Director: A Newly Published Letter of Friedrich von Hügel," *The Month* n.s.2 (1970), pp.52–57; 84–87; quotation from published letter, p.86.

10. vH to Hildegard, 5 July 1895; vHP, Downside Abbey Archives, MS 1272 (uncatalogued).

11. *EA* 1, p.105; emphasis vH's.

12. "The Parent as Spiritual Director," p.86.

13. Diary, 1907.

14. See Chapter 5 above.

15. vH's letters to Hildegard are in the Downside Abbey Archives, VHP, MS 1272 (uncatalogued). Letter concerning payment by Dent is 6 November 1911.

16. "Rough Notes by Baroness Hildegard von Hügel," *SL*, Appendix 3, p.66.

17. vH to MP, 15 December 1910, PP, BL, Add. MS 45362.

18. Diary, 29 February 1908.

19. 9 June 1921, *SL*, p.332.

20. Diary, October 1923.

21. Information about Sister Thekla was provided by Sister Mary of St. Philip, Prioress of the Carmelite Monastery, London, who as assistant infirmarian cared for Sister Thekla during her last four years; letter of 9 September 1994. The Carmel at Notting Hill Gate where Thekla lived had been founded in 1878 by French Carmelites. In 1883 Madeline Dupont (Mother Mary of Jesus) became prioress, a position which she held until her death in 1942. From 1934 Thekla served for many years as Sub-prioress. E.I. Watkin, *Roman Catholicism in England from the Reformation to 1950* (London:

Oxford University Press, 1957), p.225, described the remarkable expansion of Carmelite monasteries in England during the first half of the twentieth century.

22. See Chapters 3 and 5 above.

23. Letter to his cousin Elizabeth Sharp, 23 December 1924, *SL*, p.374.

24. *Tablet* 145 (14 February 1925), p.201.

25. vH to Mrs. F. R. Lillie, 13 October 1920, *SL*, p.312.

26. 31 Dec. 1921, *Letters KS*, pp.161–62; also Barmann, p.251; emphasis is vH's.

27. vH to T, 18 December 1906, BL, Add. MS 44929; published in *SL*, pp.136–37; quote p.136.

28. *ME* 1, p.x; references in this section are to the 1908 edition.

29. *ME* 1, p.ix.

30. *ME* 1, p.xi.

31. "Father Tyrrell: Some Memorials of the Last Twelve Years of His Life," *Hibbert Journal* 8 (January 1910), p.234.

32. *ME* 1, p.xi.

33. *EL*, p.359.

34. *EL*, p.360.

35. vH to T, 18 December 1901, BL, Add. MS 44927; *vHT*, pp.84–85.

36. "Eudoxe Irenée Mignot," *The Contemporary Review* 108 (May 1918), pp.519–526; quote from p.520.

37. Ibid., p.525.

38. vH to Hildegard (1899), quoted by de la Bedoyère, pp.117.

39. *Letters KS*, p.112

40. *Spirituality in Ecumenical Perspective* (Louisville: Westminster/John Knox, 1994), essays edited by E. Glenn Hinson in honor of Dorothy and Douglas Steere, highlights the influence of vH on an ecumenical spirituality. Douglas Steere, himself a Quaker, wrote his PhD thesis on the religious philosophy of von Hügel (Harvard 1931).

41. See Chapter 1 for a description of English Catholicism during the late nineteenth and early twentieth centuries.

42. Letter of Cairns to Tissington Tatlow, secretary of Student Christian Movement, 22 November 1921; SCM Archives, Selly Oak Colleges Library, Birmingham; quoted by Hans Rollmann in "Ernst Troeltsch, von Hügel and the Student Christian Movement," *Downside Review* 101 (July 1983), p. 221.

43. See "Difficulties: A Time for Patience," Preface to *Dialogue Between Christians: Catholic Contributions to Ecumenism* (Westminster, Maryland: Newman Press, 1966), pp.28–45.

44. vH to T, 27 October 1898; BL, Add. MS 44927; quoted in *vHT*, pp.52–54.

45. *vHT*, p.vi.

46. Hans Rollmann has documented vH's correspondence with these scholars. See "Troeltsch, von Hügel and Modernism," *Downside Review* 96 (1978), pp.35–60; "Holtzmann, von Hügel and Modernism," *Downside Review* 97 (1979), pp.128–43, 221–44.

47. (London, 1906); translated into French and Italian; Italian version published in *Il Rinnovamento*. William J. Hynes in "A Hidden Nexus between Catholic and Protestant Modernism: C. A. Briggs in Correspondence with Loisy, von Hügel and Genocchi," *Downside Review* 105 (July 1987), pp.193–223, documents the relationships among these scholars who saw their critical work on the bible as a means of preparing for Christian unity.

48. 14 December 1909, "Excerpts from Correspondence of Baron Friedrich von Hügel with The Reverend Canon George Newson," in A. Hazard Dakin, *Von Hügel and the Supernatural* (London: SPCK, 1934), p.259.

49. *EA* 1, p.276.

50. *EA* 1, pp.276–77.

51. "The Convictions Common to Catholicism and Protestantism," *Homiletic Review* (1917); reprinted in *EA* 1, pp.242–53.

52. *EA* 1, p.252.

53. *EA* 1, p.253. vH cited de Lugo (1583–1660) on a number of other occasions: *EL*, p.351; *EA* 1, pp.63, 92–93, 234–35.

54. *EA* 1, p.xiii.

55. Ibid.

56. *EA* 1, p.281.

57. Letter of Cairns to Tissington Tatlow, 22 November 1921, SCM Archives, Selly Oak Colleges Library, Birmingham; quoted by Hans Rollmann in "Ernst Troeltsch, von Hügel and the Student Christian Movement," *Downside Review* 101 (July 1983), p. 221.

58. Quoted by Holland in his Memoir of vH, *SL*, p.53.

59. *Tablet* 145 (14 February 1925), p.201.

60. *ME* 1, p.xxvii.

61. Diary, 5 March 1914.

62. Patrick J. Ruddle, "The Ecumenical Dimension in the Work of Baron Friedrich von Hügel," *Ephemerides Theologicae Lovanienses* 50 (December 1974), p.254; see also Michael Hanbury, "Baron von Hügel and the Ecumenical Movement," *Month* n.s.29 (March 1963), pp.140–50.

THREE ELEMENTS OF RELIGION 8

V on Hügel's integration of his philosophy of religion with a living faith, as well as his skill in drawing on the experiences of daily life, make him a valuable resource for a contemporary approach to spirituality. Early in his career he realized that "the greatest and most difficult of all requirements is the practical combination of great intellectual openness and activity with a childlike spirit of faith, simplicity, and love."[1] His ability to combine these characteristics lies at the heart of his spirituality which held together the institutional, the intellectual, and the mystical elements of religion in a creative tension. Just as he struggled to carry out his work as teacher, scholar, and spiritual guide, he maintained a three-fold commitment to the institutional expression of religion, to scholarship, and to personal sanctity.[2]

Von Hügel interpreted the history of religions, including Christianity, as a history of struggle among priests, professors, and prophets representing the institutional, the intellectual, and the mystical. All three elements are necessary in a religion as well as in our personal lives for we are in von Hügel's words "complex creatures" who "do well not to mutilate" ourselves but to "check, supplement, purify, ever anew, each constituent and range" of our religion by the others.[3] This chapter will study von Hügel's spirituality as it reflected the three elements, recognizing that although they belong together they ought not to be collapsed into a single element.

The Historical Element

Von Hügel believed that spirituality must be rooted in the concrete historical realities of life. This was true for all religions but particularly for Christianity as an incarnational religion. He rejected any "purely spiritual spirituality" as not only un-Christian but as impossible and insisted that humans can and do experience "the infinite, the timeless and spaceless, God" but that this experience comes "through the senses of the visible and audible, the resistant and the heavy, and the various combinations that constitute experience of the external world."[4] The Church provided the historical link with Jesus and with the saints and for this reason was precious. The person of Jesus embodied for him how human life was to be lived.

Institutional Religion

Church membership was for von Hügel a way in which he was rooted in the concrete. He was utterly convinced that institutional religions are necessary in order to nourish the spiritual life of the individual. We have seen how he encouraged Evelyn Underhill in this regard.[5] He had less success in his attempt to persuade Kemp Smith to commit himself to membership in some historical church as a means of drawing on an experience which would enhance his qualities as a philosopher.[6] In his insistence on the need for the institutional expression of religion von Hügel disagreed with his friend Ernst Troeltsch who thought that the modern person did not need the Church and that the Church no longer had anything to offer.[7] The necessity of the institutional was also the focus of von Hügel's disagreement with William James. For James religion was exclusively private and personal whereas for von Hügel it was also corporate and social.[8]

The incarnational aspect of all religion, a theme which underlies von Hügel's writing, was developed in his lecture on "The Essentials of Catholicism." A person is saved not by personal efforts and labor alone, but by God working with and in one's own human powers and in "the varyingly rich or poor history, society, institutions which . . . have experienced, articulated, and transmitted, and are at this moment more or less mediating, the touch, the light, the food of God."[9] For von Hügel the fully Catholic understanding of religion was organic and incarnational, and included various Christian, Jewish, and Islam communities. In support of this interpretation von Hügel drew on the teaching of the Spanish Jesuit, Cardinal Juan de Lugo, professor of theology in Rome from 1621–1641. De Lugo taught that God aids those who belong to various groups "to practice those elements in the worship and teaching of their respective sect, communion, school which are true and good and originally revealed by God."[10]

In the same address on "The Essentials of Catholicism" von Hügel drew on the thought of Blondel (although he referred to him simply as "a French lay philosopher") in order to show that "the Jew, indeed the Moslem, the Brahmin, the Buddhist, even the Agnostic and the sincere Atheist, are being secretly solicited by grace within themselves to love and to practice whatsoever is good and true within their present community or position."[11]   To be Catholic is to be open to the overflowing richness of the Supreme Reality revealed to humankind in very human ways and indeed in all creation.

While recognizing God's action in all religions, von Hügel was strongly opposed to reductionism which would make them all the same. Each religion has its own special developments which should be preserved.

> As well deprive a flower of its "mere details" of pistil, stamen, pollen, or an insect of its "superfluous" antennae, as simplify any Historical Religion down to the sorry stump labeled "the religion of every honest man."[12]

Such a rationalistic approach to religion was impoverishing. Von Hügel looked rather to the fullness which he believed to be present within the Catholic tradition but which he also recognized in other traditions.

In the Introduction to his last book he returned to his conviction concerning "the uniqueness of the Christian and Catholic values at their best, with the hospitable, grateful sense of how dear and true and good can be and are the lesser lights, the lesser helps God nowhere forgets to give His children."[13]   The fact that Christianity sprang historically from another historical religion supported this understanding. The Christian acceptance of the Old Testament was a recognition of God's action in Judaism.[14]   Von Hügel was able to combine a sense of Catholicism as universal and inclusive with a profound respect for the truth present in other faiths, seeing in all historical religions the God-given means by which humans experience God's revelation.

A Christocentric Spirituality

The reality of God was the focus of von Hügel's life and study.

But as a Christian this reality was incarnated in the concrete particularity of Jesus Christ.[15] In a beautiful sentence of the *Mystical Element* he described this reality:

> For a Person came, and lived and loved, and did and taught, and died and rose again, and lives on by His Power and His Spirit for ever within us and amongst us, so unspeakably rich and yet so simple, so sublime and yet so homely, so divinely above us precisely in being so divinely near—that His character and teaching require, for an ever fuller yet never complete understanding, the varying study, and different experiments and applications, embodiments and unrollings of all races and civilizations, of all the individual and corporate, the simultaneous and successive experiences of the human race to the end of time.[16]

Von Hügel faced many of the Christological concerns that have provided the agenda for twentieth-century theology. His historical studies, especially his critical study of the New Testament writings, and his openness to other religions led him to a theocentric approach to Christology which brought together creation and incarnation. "God has in various degrees, in various ways, been coming into the world ever since He made it." He insisted that God should not be limited to the incarnation in Jesus Christ although it is this "supreme kind of incarnation (which gives their completion, interpretation, and standard to all those lesser preveniences) that we find and adore in the incarnation of Christ."[17]

Von Hügel recognized the reality of God in all of life, among the ancient philosophers as well as the Jewish prophets, in nature as well as in the reserved sacrament. God was also present in the ordinary lives of ordinary people. During the war, as a member of a committee to inquire into religion in the army, von Hügel emphasized how crucial it was that "Tommy" should "feel the richness that is there, all round him and within him."[18] This was the presence of God incarnate in our humanity. He believed that incarnation "in the widest and most varied, as well as in the most precise and deepest, sense of the word" was the heart of Christianity. Christianity was not a doctrine but "the penetration of spirit into sense, of the spaceless into space, of the eternal into time, of God into man."[19]

Von Hügel accepted as fact that we really can know very little as to what Jesus actually taught and did, or even who he was. This realization did not disturb him for he had faced the difficulties raised by historical criticism early in his career, acknowledging "a view widespread amongst serious scholars," that restricted our information about Jesus' words and actions to the synoptic gospels. Von Hügel considered three features of Jesus' teaching to be characteristic: the *humanities* of Jesus, his experiences of spiritual growth, temptations, and suffering; the exorcisms; and Jesus' belief in and proclamation of a Proximate Second Coming. These were teachings which raised difficulties for the next two generations of Christian theologians who succeeded the gospel writers.[20] Questions concerning all three continue to engage the scripture scholar and theologian.

As a philosopher of religion, who was also an exegete, von Hügel entered into the history and dogma controversy between his two friends Loisy and Blondel.[21] His unsuccessful effort to provide a meeting ground between the historian and the philosopher found expression in his article "Du Christ éternel et de nos christologies successives."[22] Drawing on his own experience, von Hügel was convinced that the rightful demands of history can (and must) be assimilated into faith, a conviction that he maintained throughout his life.

Von Hügel believed that the Council of Chalcedon, with its teaching on the two natures of Christ, had been more satisfactorily attended to as regards the divine nature than the human nature. Theology had largely ignored the limitations, weaknesses, growths, and temptations which were part of Jesus' life.[23] Von Hügel was convinced that these neglected areas had important implications for our own humanity since in the incarnation God entered fully into all aspects of our human lives:

> But with Him, and alone with Him and those who still learn and live from and by Him, there is the union of the clearest, keenest sense of all the mysterious depth and breadth and length and height of human sadness, suffering, and sin, *and,* in spite of this and through this and at the end of this, a note of conquest and triumphant joy.[24]

These words serve as a reminder that although von Hügel's teaching on institutional religion and on Christ have been considered under the historical element of religion, that teaching has a mystical dimension as well as an intellectual one. As William Thompson emphasized, adoration is the heart of von Hügel's theology and christology.[25]

The Intellectual Element

Von Hügel appreciated the intellectual element of religion and devoted his life to the scholarly study of religion. His concern for the proper place for the intellectual element of religion was evident even in his early writings. In a letter to the editor of the *Tablet* in 1894 he referred to the need to avoid both "the unchristian exaltation of the intellect and its deprecation or practical neglect."[26] He rejoiced in the struggle to understand and saw this as a purification of faith.

A Spirituality of Scholarship

Scholarship was the path by which von Hügel responded to his vocation to become a saint. Plagued by poor health, his pursuit of scholarship was a costly discipleship. He strove for what he described as "intellectual virtues": candor, moral courage, intellectual honesty, scrupulous accuracy, chivalrous fairness, endless docility to facts, disinterested collaboration, unconquerable hopefulness and perseverance, manly renunciation of popularity and easy honors, love of bracing labor and strengthening solitude."[27] Poor health might slow him down but it did not prevent him from the persistent pursuit of knowledge. A hostile ecclesiastical environment might temper his writing but it did not discourage him from writing and lecturing to a growing circle of admirers, mostly from outside his own faith tradition.

An attitude that characterized von Hügel's approach to life was "teachableness." He used this term in his early effort to share with his Hampstead neighbors his insights into Catherine, and through her into religion, pointing out to his readers the "need for 'teachableness' which can learn to admire and appropriate, even where it cannot do so altogether."[28] This open attitude, the ability to see different sides of a problem and to learn even from those with whom he disagreed, was an enduring trait in von Hügel's work.

Toward the end of a lifetime of scholarly work, von Hügel described for his friend Norman Kemp Smith the purifying effect of such activity:

Oh, *how* humble, how unworldly, how un-self-occupied, how

pure of heart—pure, not only from all sensuality but from all hate, all jealousy, all rationalist forcing one's poor thinking machine, how passive (in the right sense) one has, I have, to be, to gain any steady, useable light in these deepest facts and burrowings! *That* is one, perhaps the chief encouragement to such toil: it makes one better, smaller in one's own poor eyes![29]

At a time when science was often seen as the enemy of religion, von Hügel upheld the work of the scientist. In *Eternal Life* he presented a sympathetic treatment of Darwin showing how his work contributed to Christianity. During a period when evolution was looked upon with suspicion by church authorities he insisted on the positive aspects of Darwin's teaching, while pointing out problems with "purely genetic" biological studies:

Yet the increase of light furnished by the movement so predominantly initiated by Darwin, concerning the closeness of the relations between man's spirit and man's body, between man and other living beings, and between the whole living world and its inorganic environment, has also brought, as all sincere research cannot fail to bring, much helpful criticism, confirmation, and growth to our apprehension, analysis, and formulation of the facts and requirements constitutive of our religious experience.[30]

In the following description of Darwin one can see that von Hügel shared the great scientist's appreciation for life in all its forms:

Darwin's rapt interest in the interrelated lives of plants and insects, in a bird's coloring and a worm's instincts, are, in their grandly self-oblivious out-going to the humble and little, most genuine flowerings of the delicate Christian spirit in this fierce, rough world of ours.[31]

Many of von Hügel's studies focused upon the place of the physical sciences within the search for truth, an appreciation which he probably received from his father. As a young boy he had studied natural science, particularly entomology and ornithology. When he moved to England in 1867 he studied geology under William Pengelly.

These early studies of insects, birds, and rocks continued throughout his life. In 1909 he wrote to Tyrrell:

> I was fifty-seven yesterday and am giving myself a set of newer geological type books, a geological hammer and a set of geological type specimens. So expect to tramp about with me to gravel-pits and quarries, please. I find the renewal of my first studies and discipline *most* resting and refreshing.[32]

This rootedness in the concrete is characteristic of von Hügel's spirituality.

In his study of mysticism von Hügel became aware that the mystics had neglected the concrete. In 1898, in a long letter to Tyrrell, he summed up what he understood as the teaching of the mystics, noting that they taught that the soul is purified "by turning away from the particularity of the creature to the simplicity of the Creator." Von Hügel went on to add that there was no place in this theory for science and that he wished to add this aspect to their teaching.

> As the body can live only by inhalation and exhalation, nutrition and evacuation, etc., and as the mind can only flourish by looking out for sensible material and then elaborating and spiritualizing it; so the soul can live, to be fully normal in normal circumstances, only by a double process: occupation with the concrete and then abstraction from it.[33]

Von Hügel believed that this occupation with the concrete, which is the task of experimental science and critical scholarship, was a purifying medium and that the study of the concrete should have *"its normal necessary place in the very theory of spirituality."* This being the case, von Hügel maintained that people who are making retreats should be taught that they "must *study or work* at something definite and concrete."[34]

Von Hügel insisted upon the autonomy of science as well as the autonomy of all the other departments of life. Science, art, morals, politics are not religion, nor should they be absorbed into religion. In a colorful metaphor, he suggested that these other departments of life should be "as scrupulously reverenced by religion, as would a levy of young women by some mature man." He admitted that this is *"immensely* difficult to the natural man" who has discovered a deep vivid religion and easily becomes convinced that *"religion is everything."* Under the influence of Eucken, Bergson, and Blondel, von Hügel was able to see the dangers in such an attitude and for this reason insisted upon "the *otherness* of science."[35]

While insisting upon the autonomy of science, von Hügel saw scientific research as possessing a purifying and deepening role in one's religious life, an insight which he developed in *The Mystical Element*.[36] Science is not a department of religion but it can be a dialogue partner with religion and it offers a method within the philosophy of religion that will lead the scholar more deeply into the mystery of God.[37] Von Hügel probably would have agreed with the conviction of a contemporary theologian that "*Methodology, not subject matter*, has kept theology trailing behind in the age of science."[38] In his support of Loisy and in his own work he attempted to develop a scientific approach to the study of the bible and the history of Christianity which would support Christian faith. Such methods "require a slow, orderly, disinterested procedure, capable of fruitfulness only by the recurring sacrifice of endless petty self-seekings and obstinate fancies, and this in the face of that natural eagerness and absoluteness of mind which strong religious emotions will, unless they too be disciplined and purified, only tend to increase and stereotype."[39]

As a scholar von Hügel saw himself building on the work of those who had preceded him: Plato, Plotinus, Augustine, Aquinas, Kant, and Hegel. ". . . standing upon their shoulders, I may be able to see still further than they did, although if I stood on my own feet alone, I should certainly see much less far than any of them saw."[40] He rejoiced in his ability to contribute to the ongoing study of religion through his writing and through contact with other scholars.

A letter to a young Jesuit scholastic, Martin D'Arcy, provides insight into von Hügel's deeply held convictions concerning the requirements for the pursuit of scholarly work. Such work requires "a liberty which is free from every touch of licence, and a scholarship which is not cheap apologetics."[41] But scholarship also demands passion for "only what we can really love do we end by doing well."[42] Such freedom and love can be costly as von Hügel had learned but he was convinced that the spiritual life calls for "severe scientific sincerity."[43]

> Those that try and push matters on must be prepared for more or less of martyrdom. But, oh joy!—things move, things grow, light comes, and souls are helped, for all that . . . and not one pang, or sigh, or tear of the laborers or the self-

purifiers is lost or fails to go directly to help on this increase of life for souls.[44]

Von Hügel was convinced that "at bottom, and in the long run, all is well." In a letter to Tyrrell he explained what he meant by this:

I mean, that it will all be found, in the slow, intermittent, combined and mutually supplementary and corrective devotednesses and patient light-awaitings of us all, to have been occasioned by, and to have a place in, that ever deeper apprehension of the mystery of life and of love, and of the necessity for their continuous, painful deepening within our hearts, which Christianity has indefinitely increased and developed, just because it is life at its most fruitful and most self-conscious point.[45]

Von Hügel acknowledged the loss that the restrictions of ecclesiastical authorities imposed in terms of confidence and productiveness of scholars.

Newman, Duchesne, Blondel—it would be untrue to say that any one of these did not and does not produce differently than they, otherwise, could and would have done.[46]

Of Duchesne, he added: "I fear, the chances of his ever now producing some great and really characteristic book are over and gone, and not likely ever to return. What a pity!"[47]

On another occasion he quoted advice which he had received from Duchesne to Tyrrell:

Work away in utter sincerity and open-mindedness; lead as deep and devoted a spiritual life as you can; renounce, from the first, and every day, every hope or wish for more than toleration; and then, with those three activities and dispositions, trust and wait with indomitable patience and humility, to be tolerated and excused.[48]

Such advice did not fit Tyrrell's personality but von Hügel himself took it to heart.

A number of von Hügel's addresses dealt with the problems faced by the individual scholar within the Church. In an address on "Institutional Christianity," he asked:

How then are we, scholars or scientists, to work or to develop our extant or incipient Churchmanship in the borderlands and mixed territories created for us by the very fact of our earnest scholarship and fervent Churchmanship?[49]

His response to this question included a realistic acceptance of the limitations and costs of belonging to any community or church, balanced by a deep appreciation for the advantages of such belonging:

> It remains true that there can be no Church for us on earth, if we will not or cannot put up with faulty Church officials and faulty Church members; and again, that we shall never put up with such faultiness sufficiently unless we possess or acquire so strong a sense of all we have to gain from Church membership as to counter-balance the repulsiveness of such faults.[50]

Because von Hügel was convinced that the benefits of Church membership outweighed all disadvantages, even in terms of scholarship, he was able to maintain the conviction that "at bottom, and in the long run, all is well." As early as 1900 he referred to the "cross planted right into our intellectual life" but added that like all crosses this cross too brings "the joy of life."[51]

Von Hügel's combination of loyalty to the Roman Catholic Church and spiritual self-determination during a difficult period in the history of the Roman Catholic Church required a balancing act. In 1918 he looked back on his relationship to the Church:

> When at eighteen I made my full and deliberate submission to the Catholic Church, to her as my teacher and trainer throughout my life, it never entered my head—it has never entered my head during the now well-nigh fifty years of my Catholic practice—to ask for permission to think—also to think my religion—any more than it occurred to me to get leave to be hungry and thirsty and to eat and to drink, or to feel the impulsions of sex-life, or to love my family or country. Every one of these things was and is continuously felt to require a continuous purification, correction, supplementation by grace and training within and through the Church; yet, not one of these things but is felt, in its essence, to possess a certain spontaneity, autonomy, right, duty, method and range of its own.[52]

Von Hügel did not deny the oppressive aspects of religion which needed to be critiqued. He courageously undertook this task. As he explained to his niece, he tried to make the Roman Catholic Church "inhabitable *intellectually*"—not because the intellect was the most important thing in religion "but because the old Church already possesses in full the knowledge and aids to *spirituality*, whilst, for various reasons which would fill a volume, it is much less strong as regards the needs, rights and duties of the mental life."[53]

In an article published just the month before he died, von Hügel recalled his "hot battles and difficulties" caused by his membership in the Roman Catholic Church and "a temptation to avoid all such complication through a most possible pure individualism and so enjoy a complete freedom." As he looked back he recognized that church membership had protected him from "scepticism and psychological self-inflation" and that it was "quite compatible with the healthy liberty" needed for his work.[54]

Von Hügel's scholarship nourished his spirituality and provided new ways of looking at religious issues. This was important not only for individuals, including himself and those whom he directed, but he believed that it was important for the Church itself. It was a responsibility which he assumed as a scholar:

> We shall thus be both old and new, derivative and original, supported and supporting—supporting, at the last, in our little measure, not only other souls, but the very institution itself.[55]

Careful intellectual work continues to be a purifying and at times frustrating experience as scholars struggle to articulate "the old Faith and its permanent truths and helps—to interpret it according to what appears the best and the most abiding elements in the philosophy and science of the later and latest times."[56] Only a deep mystical spirit, such as von Hügel had, can support this intellectual effort on behalf of the institution.

The Mystical Element

At the heart of human life von Hügel discovered the experience of "creatureliness," of openness to the mystery of life and to the source of all life.

For reality is more than any and all of our imaginings of it. It is more than truth; it overwhelms whilst it supports us; and it will have produced one of its chief functions and effects if it keeps us thoroughly humbled in its presence—from the presence of the daisy to the presence and reality of God.[57]

Nature, including the human person, provides intimations of God. For von Hügel traces of God are everywhere. Because God is within us we can perceive these intimations of God in all of creation. The appropriate response to God's presence in and around us is adoration.

As he reflected on his own life, von Hügel recognized that the experience comes first, and only later does one develop the theory to explain the experience. He recalled how as a child he delighted in the sense of beauty and harmony in external nature as well as the mysterious divine Presence in the churches of Florence.[58] Even at an early age nature and historical religion had been means through which he had experienced the reality of God. His adult life was devoted to the intellectual pursuit of that reality, a study supported and enlightened by a life of prayerful contemplation. As he struggled to write during his later years he reflected on the process with his friend, Kemp Smith:

> How one grows, how sustained and yet humbled one feels and *is* when thus plunged in work of a modestly creative kind! I always find it to become a sort of prayer.[59]

This contemplative attitude toward all of life was characteristic of von Hügel's spirituality—a spirituality rooted in the concrete realities of his life but open to critical reflection and mystical experience.

Suffering

The experiences of suffering and of joy are special moments of openness to God's presence. Tension, friction, costliness, the cross, were experiences that characterized von Hügel's life and those around him. Abbé Huvelin had told him in 1893: "You will suffer continually from isolation: It is your vocation."[60] His deafness contributed to a sense of isolation and although eventually he found some relief through the use of hearing aids, there are hints in his letters of the difficulties that it caused him: "and deafness means crippledness and a handsome crop of little humiliations during such social attempts."[61] Von Hügel suffered in other ways as well throughout his life. At times he was unable to work, a situation which he found very painful:

> I have had a succession of nervous attacks and prostrations,
> of a kind with which my earlier years were full, and which just
> now have left me two little islets of three or four days each of
> work and balance; jutting out above intervening weeks of
> waiting for the rise in the tide of strength.[62]

For him these difficulties were part of the "givenness" of life, a mark
of his creatureliness. He lived and worked much of his life as a sick
man. Suffering could not be escaped but "the suffering of contraction
and of slow spiritual death" could be avoided and replaced by "the
suffering of expansion equivalent in the spiritual life to the growing
pains of boyhood."[63] Such suffering willingly accepted could lead to
a transformation as he witnessed in his daughter Gertrud. Such a
transformation was the beginning here and now of eternal life.

In a long essay on the topic of "Suffering and God," portions of
which were read as an address to the London Society for the Study of
Religion, von Hügel drew on arguments from Greek philosophy, the
Hebrew scriptures, and Christian theology and concluded that God
does not suffer for suffering is intrinsically evil and God is all goodness
and joy.[64] However he maintained that there is sympathy in God for
the suffering of creation and that Christ, the incarnate God, has shared
our sufferings in his humanity.

Joy

Suffering must give way to joy. For von Hügel only a life
penetrated by joy and spontaneity was truly religious. This joy included
a zest for life. To support his conviction about the centrality of joy he
cited the Roman Catholic Church's requirements for canonization
which included the note of expansive joy.[65] With his usual
concreteness he compared Newman, who had "never succeeded in
surmounting his deeply predestinarian, Puritan, training" with Huvelin
who from boyhood had nourished his soul "on the Catholic spirituality
as it flowered in St. Francis." Although both were naturally melancholy
in temperament, Huvelin radiated "a spiritual joy and expansion" which
Newman seemed to lack. His conclusion was that Newman "could
indeed be beatified, but only Huvelin could be canonized."[66]

At the end of the address on "Suffering and God," von Hügel
recounted a personal experience of joy, inviting his listeners to reflect
on their own lives for similar experiences. On a Good Friday forenoon
in Rome in 1899 he was feeling dejected, "dull and dead, conscious of

nothing but myself." Then he had a sense of the great seekers for God in this "eternal" Rome: Peter, Paul, Cecilia, Agnes, Rabbi Akiba, Marcus Aurelius, Plotinus, Augustine—and behind them all Jesus Christ, "Suffering Love, gently, pathetically triumphant." Out of this "appeared Joy, pure Joy, an Ocean of it, unplumbed, unplumbable, with not one drop of Sin or Suffering or of the possibility of either. . . . And yet this Pure Joy was utterly compassionate, utterly sympathetic." Even the "dear little emerald lizards" at his feet joined in his happiness. He saw the dreariness which had preceded his happiness as "an effect of that contrasting Joy of God, or rather of my very dim but real apprehension of that Joy."[67]

For von Hügel joy was another name for God. "And this love of God, where uninhibited and full, brings Joy—it seeks God, Joy; and it finds Joy, God."[68] "Joy and God are essentially interconnected, indeed the ultimate, alone sufficing joy is God."[69]

Integration

Unlike William James who restricted religious experience to the mystical, von Hügel always insisted that the mystical required and included the historical and intellectual elements. In a letter to James, von Hügel expressed his gratitude for the scholar's work on *The Varieties of Religious Experience* as well as his concern that James "separated religious experience from its institutional-historical occasions and environments and from the analytical and speculative activity of the mind."[70] For von Hügel mysticism was not a rare experience but an element of all genuine religious experience which did not stand alone.

The three elements as they were lived out in his life and reflected in his writings form a rich and vibrant spirituality. It was a spirituality appreciated by those who knew him during his life. The Jewish scholar, Claude Montefiore, wrote of him after his death in the *Jewish Guardian*:

The feeling deepened with each conversation one had with Baron von Hügel that one was in the presence of a very big man, and a man, moreover, who was a peculiar, beautiful and rare combination of scholar and saint. . . . He knew a lot about religion and God from endless books and much thinking, but he also knew a lot about them from experience and from life. . . . The great scholar-saint was much more than any book, and a much greater evidence than any written words of the God in whom he so passionately believed.[71]

The young man who desired to become a scholar and a saint had profoundly influenced many of his contemporaries. Through his writings his influence has continued. We turn in the final chapter to a consideration of that continuing influence, a recognition of the limitations of von Hügel's thought for our times, and some suggestions for ways that his insights may be expanded in the light of contemporary concerns in order to provide a resource for a contemporary spirituality.

NOTES

1. vH, "The Spiritual Writings of Father Grou," *Tablet* 74 (21 December 1889), p.991.

2. Hans Rollman comments on these commitments in "Von Hügel and Scheler," *Downside Review* 101 (1983), p.32.

3. *EA* 2, pp.66–68; from an address delivered to the Religious Thought Society, July 1913, "On the Place and Function, Within Religion, of the Body, of History, and of Institutions." In *RG*, pp.143–44, he referred to "the four stages of the 'p's:, first the priest, then the prophet, then the parson, then the professor."

4. *RG*, pp.139–40.

5. See Chapter 6 above.

6. vH to KS 1 July 1919 and KS's reply, 11 August 1919, *Letters KS*, pp.37, 40. KS promised to consider the matter carefully. See also Barmann's comments in the Introduction, pp.7–9.

7. Troeltsch, *Christian Thought: Its History and Application*, Introduction by von Hügel, p.xxix.

8. James Luther Adams, "Letter from Friedrich von Hügel to William James," *Downside Review* 98 (1980), pp.214–36. This letter, dated 10 May 1909, was found by James Luther Adams in a copy of *Mystical Element* sent by von Hügel to James in 1909.

9. *EA* 1, p.235; from an address to a gathering of young men at Liddon House, London, May 1913.

10. *EA* 1, pp.234–35; also pp. 63, 93 and 252. vH returned to this theme and again used Cardinal de Lugo in support of his position in his last work; *RG*, pp. 149–51.

11. *EA* 1, p.236.

12. *EA* 1, p.92.

13. *RG*, p.21.

14. *RG*, p.150.

15. For a study of vH's christology see Whelan, *The Spirituality of Friedrich von Hügel*, pp. 33–75; also William Thompson, *Christology and Spirituality* (New York: Crossroad, 1991), pp.101–20.

16. *ME* 1, p.26.

17. "Remarks Made by Baron Friedrich von Hügel at a Meeting of the Committee to Inquire into Religion in the Army 1917." *SL*, Appendix 2, pp.65–66.

18. Ibid., p.63.

19. *EA* 2, p.107.

20. *EA* 2, pp.189–90. This reference to the results of biblical criticism was part of an address to the LSSR in May 1921. vH's convictions concerning the results of biblical criticism remained constant throughout his life.

21. See Chapter 3 above.

22. *La Quinzaine* 58 (June 1904), pp.285–312; this article is included in McGrath's *Von Hügel and the Debate on Historical Christianity*, Appendix, pp. 241–80. César Izquierdo, "History and Truth: The Exegetical Position of Baron Von Hügel," *Downside Review* 108 (1990), pp.295–312, discusses vH's distinction between the Christ which history presents to us and the Christ who is the object of faith and love.

23. *EA* 2, p.196.

24. *ME* 1, p.27.

25. William Thompson develops the theme of adoration in vH's theology and christology in *Christology and Spirituality*, pp.101–20.

26. "Fenelon's 'Spiritual Letters'," *Tablet* 83 (2 June 1894), p.858.

27. *ME* 1, p.79.

28. "Caterina Fiesca Adorna, the Saint of Genoa, 1447–1510," *The Hampstead Annual* (1898), p.71.

29. 30 July 1920, *Letters KS*, p. 96.

30. *EL*, p.280.

31. *EL*, p.281.

32. vH to T, 6 May 1909; BL, Add. MS 44931. This is the last letter of vH in the collection. Tyrrell died in July 1909.

33. vH to T, 26 September 1898; BL, Add. MS 44927; quoted in *vHT*, p.32.

34. Ibid., p.34; emphasis is vH's.

35. In a lengthy letter written 26 September 1900 vH replied to a number of questions which Petre had raised from her reading of Eucken's *Kampf*; emphasis is vH's. vH wrote that his words were "an amplification of Eucken by means of Bergson and Blondel." PP, BL, Add. MS 43361.

36. See Chapter 4. Clement C. J. Webb considered vH's teaching on the purifying role of science on religion as his "most original and fruitful" contribution to the philosophy of religion. "Baron Friedrich von Hügel and His Contribution to Religious Philosophy," *Harvard Theological Review* 42 (1949), pp.1–18.

37. For a contemporary analysis of how theology can be pursued as a scientific study see Nancey Murphy, *Theology in the Age of Scientific Reasoning* (Ithaca: Cornell University Press, 1990). Murphy draws on Roman Catholic modernism as an example of the

effect on theology of scientific reasoning replacing medieval epistemology and uses Tyrrell's essays to illustrate theological analogues for the elements of scientific research. See pp.88–129.

38. Murphy, p.127.

39. *ME* 2, p.383.

40. *RG*, p.22.

41. Joseph Whelan, "Friedrich von Hügel's Letters to Martin D'Arcy," *Month* 42 (1969), pp.23–36; quote on p.29. In a letter to Kemp Smith, 12 November 1924, vH noted that he had met D'Arcy at the Jesuit House of Studies in Oxford where he had been invited "as a deliberate proof to me how thoroughly, in spite of all the Tyrrell affair, the younger English S.J.s trusted me." *Letters KS*, p. 270. Martin C. D'Arcy (1888–1977) was the author of several philosophical studies.

42. vH to D'Arcy, Ibid., p.31.

43. *ME* 1, p.viii.

44. vH to T, 4 June 1902, BL, Add. MS 44928; quoted in *vHT*, pp.107–8.

45. vH to T, 4 December 1902; BL, Add. MS 44928; quoted in *vHT*, p. 113.

46. vH to T, 4 March 1900, written from Rome; BL, Add. MS 44927; quoted in *vHT*, p. 124.

47. Ibid.

48. vH to T, 19 August 1900; BL, Add. MS 44927; quoted in *vHT*, pp. 130–31.

49. "Institutional Christianity or The Church, Its Nature and Necessity," *EA* 1, p.266; address delivered in London to the Executive Committee of the British branches of the Student Christian Movement, October 1918.

50. *EA* 1, p.267.

51. vH to MP, 26 September 1900; PP, BL, Add. MS 43361.

52. "Eudoxe Irenée Mignot," *The Contemporary Review* 108 (May 1918), pp.520–21.

53. *LTN*, pp. 165–66; emphasis is vH's.

54. "Der Mystiker und die Kirche aus Anlass des Sâdhu," *Das Hochland* 22 (December 1924), pp.320–30. This work is cited by John J. Heaney in "The Enigma of the Later von Hügel," *Heythrop Journal* 6 (1965), pp.145–59; quote from p.150.

55. *EA* 1, p.16.

56. vH to MP, 13 March 1918, PP, BL, Add. MS 45362; *SL*, p.248.

57. *RG*, p. 33.

58. *RG*, p.80.

59. All Saints 1923, *Letters KS*, p.205.

60. James J. Kelly, "Counseling von Hügel," *Tablet* 228 (July 1974), p.695.

61. vH to T, 30 June 1904, BL, Add. MS 44929; quoted in *SL*, pp.127–29; the occasion was Archbishop Mignot's visit to vH.

62. vH to T, 12 June 1905, BL, Add. MS 44929; quoted in *SL*, pp.129–30.

63. *RG*, p.132.

64. *EA* 2, pp.167–213. This address was presented in May 1921.

65. *EA* 1, p.18; also *EA* 2, p.242.

66. *EA* 2, p.242. It is not surprising that Newman scholars disagree. See Henry Tristram, "Cardinal Newman and Baron von Hügel," 240 (1966), pp.295–302; paper originally read by Tristram in 1945 and edited for publication by Stephen Dessain. The paper has some inaccuracies concerning vH's contacts with Newman.

67. *EA* 2, pp.211–13.

68. *EA* 2, p.242.

69. *RG*, p.104.

70. James Luther Adams, "Letter from Friedrich von Hügel to William James," *Downside Review* 98 (1980), p.230.

71. *SL*, pp.35–36.

SPIRITUAL LEGACY

9

T he literary critic Martin Burgess Green suggests that "The Baron's systems are not (we gather) of the sort to much outlast his time and place. The mind we see at work within them is."[1] Green sees von Hügel as "out of touch with the liveliest sensibilities of his own time" and suggests that his imagination was Victorian, illustrating this by drawing parallels between von Hügel's Catherine of Genoa and George Eliot's Dorothea Brooke.[2] But von Hügel's personality, especially as it emerges in his long letters to friends, remains strong and vibrant. Green sums up why we still need von Hügel:

> We need von Hügel's instinctive love of life and reverence for the splendors of the human personality, his readiness to trust that critical impulse which is the most faithful servant of those splendors, his readiness to demand the best in natural things, and to care about and for that best.[3]

While agreeing with Green that the person remains significant while his work is dated, I have argued that there are retrievable aspects of von Hügel's writings that remain helpful, especially in terms of spirituality. It was von Hügel's genius to use the personal in order to understand religion itself. The three elements of religion enable us to appreciate von Hügel as a person but they also serve as a corrective to reductionistic one-dimensional views of religion.

Von Hügel lived in a very different world from that of the late twentieth century and certainly many of his questions and concerns are not ours. For persons living at the end of the twentieth century his world and his ways of viewing it are too neat. Von Hügel deliberately drew on his own experience as a source for his theology. This is both its strength and its limitation. It is a strength in rooting von Hügel's theology in the concrete circumstances of his life. However, there are limitations, and even distortions, to his experience as to anyone's, which should be acknowledged. These limitations in turn suggest the need for some correctives to his thought.

While one hesitates to correct as imposing a figure as Friedrich von Hügel, one of the characteristics of his approach to life was "teachableness." He was always ready to learn, whether it was how to ride a bicycle, read Hebrew, or explore new methodology.[4] He was also convinced that one's personal experience needed to be tested against the corporate "reality."

This chapter will consider the influence which von Hügel's thought has continued to have and indicate some of its limitations. It will then offer some tentative suggestions for correctives and indicate how his thought might be expanded. This expansion builds on von Hügel's insights while overcoming some of the ways that his thought is no longer helpful.

Influence

As we have seen, von Hügel was a spiritual teacher and guide during his lifetime. Probably because of his association with modernism and the clericalism of the Catholic Church of his day, his influence was stronger among persons of other churches and religious traditions than it was among his fellow Catholics. In the years since his death his influence has continued among both Catholics and Protestants. Evidence for this may be seen in the collections of his writings which have been published and reprinted and in the many doctoral theses which have studied his thought.[5] His addresses on the "Life of Prayer" published in the Second Series of his *Essays and Addresses on the Philosophy of Religion* were reissued in a separate form in 1927 and reprinted in 1960 with the note that "These addresses are perhaps the pages in his works that should prove most helpful in guiding souls along the way of the spiritual life on which he himself was one of the most shining lights in our days."[6] In a review of a work on von Hügel, Alban Goodier wrote: "No writer in our time, probably few in any time, have been hailed and approved by more different schools than the late Baron von Hügel."[7] A. Hazard Dakin in his 1934 work, *Von Hügel and the Supernatural,* commented on the vitality and increase of his influence in Britain, the United States, and Germany.[8]

A number of contemporary theologians have drawn on von Hügel, among them William Thompson, Nicholas Lash, and David Tracy. Thompson used the thought of von Hügel as the focus for his chapter on "Adoration's Centrality in Theology and Christology" in *Christology and Spirituality*.[9] Lash devoted two chapters to von Hügel's thought in his study of religious experience.[10] In an important essay on theological method Tracy used von Hügel's three elements of religion as a basis for his study of contemporary Catholic theological method, referring to these fundamental elements as "the most fruitful hypothesis for understanding the Roman Catholic tradition."[11] But Tracy also pointed out the need for Catholic thought "to be open to constant revision as the acknowledgment of the fuller plurality and often radical ambiguity of all three of Hügel's elements comes more clearly into view."[12] In a study of "Recent Catholic Spirituality" Tracy drew on Newman and von Hügel as two influential and representative Catholic figures who in their work and spirit provide the foundations of modern Catholic spirituality.[13] Tracy returned to von Hügel and Newman as two modern Catholic and ecumenical thinkers "for their classic analysis of the fuller complexity of Roman Catholic identity."[14]

Spiritual writers have also found a rich resource in von Hügel's thought. Gerald Hughes in his book, *God of Surprises*, used von Hügel's elements of religion to understand spiritual development from childhood to adulthood. He suggested that much of the present tension within the Catholic Church is between those who assume that the institutional is the only element in the Church and others who are demanding more of the critical and mystical elements.[15] Joseph Whelan in assessing von Hügel's contribution to spirituality saw it as "a cumulative, open-ended moment in the history of prayer and secularity as incarnational, worldly mysticism. As a record of life and love, it is a stage on the way, and as doctrine, it is work in progress."[16]

Religious educators have used von Hügel's work as a framework for their task. His insistence that religious development requires not only an institutional element but a critical reflective self-appropriation of faith and a mystical element that fosters personal religious experience provides a basis for a holistic approach to religious education which seems particularly necessary today when there is danger of focusing only on the institutional.[17]

Because of his ecumenical involvement in an unecumenical age, von Hügel has been seen as a prophetic figure for the ecumenical movement. As a "big Christian" von Hügel challenges all narrow-minded sectarianism.[18] He developed a theological rationale for the recognition of other churches and religions and he lived an ecumenical spirituality.[19] His generous spirit of acceptance of the other and his respect for God's action, not only in each person's life but in their religious institutions, provide inspiration for those who labor ecumenically.

Literary figures have found inspiration in von Hügel's work. Flannery O'Connor wrote to a friend: "The old man I think is the most congenial spirit I have found in English Catholic letters, with more to say, to me anyway, than Newman."[20] Graham Greene was influenced by selections from *The Mystical Element* which he was reading when he wrote *The End of the Affair*.[21] W. B. Yeats was also reading *The Mystical Element* when he wrote his poem "Vacillation," with its references to von Hügel.[22]

Yeat's poem provided Martin Burgess Green with inspiration for his essays, *Yeat's Blessings on von Hügel*. Von Hügel had been an important figure in Green's conversion to Catholicism "just because he showed how much secular freedom could be reconciled with a limited and limiting creed."[23] Green presents von Hügel as "one of the great heroes of liberal humanism, one of the synthesizers of modern Western culture."

> His work was in a dozen ways, an attempt to put together as many as possible separated elements of that culture; to put England together with the rest of Europe, Catholicism with other religions, religion itself with philosophy, the past with the present, science with the arts, morality with sensibility, and so on.[24]

Green rightly points out that this was a work of synthesis, not of systematization.

Broad vision and balance are characteristic of von Hügel's thought. His critical studies of religion, his efforts to bring about renewal within the Catholic Church, his concern for the life of the Spirit, all contribute to this vision of religion as a rich and varied reality. His holistic spirituality as lived in his own life and shared with his contemporaries can continue to inspire us. At the same time it is necessary to critique his work and to extend some of his insights in order that they may be useful for our times.

Limitations

Von Hügel was shaped by the period and class to which he belonged with its understandings of gender, race, class, and culture. His world, which had developed out of Greek culture, was the Western world, shaped by Greek philosophy, the Bible, the Christian classics, especially Augustine, and the Enlightenment. Probably few scholars have as thoroughly incorporated these influences into their thought as did von Hügel. In the first chapter of *The Mystical Element* he described the three chief forces of Western civilization as Hellenism, Christianity, and science. This was the rich tradition which he passed on to his children and to others who turned to him for guidance. The fact that this tradition developed in a patriarchal world in which power was vested in a few privileged white males was not questioned or even recognized by von Hügel and his contemporaries. This world view is being challenged today, but as David Tracy points out:

> The Western temptation to believe in its own intellectual superiority and thereby certainty is dying as slowly, and admittedly as dangerously, as the Western colonial period itself.[25]

The modern world that von Hügel embraced has been largely replaced by the postmodern world with its chorus of different voices. The sane, reasonable voice of the Baron belongs to a different era. The view which he presented as a global perspective is now seen as a privileged Western European world view. When von Hügel referred to "the human race as a whole" he focused on modern Western Europe. Little attention was given to the marginalized and oppressed "others" in the Western tradition itself and in the other great civilizations. When he considered non-European peoples it was from a position of superiority. In *The German Soul* he condemned territorial expansion in Europe as "a moral wrong and a political mistake" but justified territorial expansion outside of Europe "only by the conferment of sterling and large benefits, not necessarily upon the races thus subjecting, but upon the races thus subjected."[26] He presumed that the subjecting race knew what was good for those whom they were subjecting.

In spite of his Eurocentric bias, von Hügel's writings reveal an amazing openness to "the other" based on a deep respect for God's action among all peoples and the beginning of an awareness that the Eurocentric Christian world view needed to be expanded. In the *Reality of God* he challenged his readers "to enlarge Augustine's literary storehouse, and to bear in mind Indian and Persian, Egyptian, Greek, and Roman sighings after God."[27] He appreciated the contribution of different races to Christianity, beginning with the Jews, and expressed the hope that "such great races as the Hindu, the Chinese, and the Japanese will, please God, still come, and whilst gaining so much themselves, may also give of their specific best."[28] Von Hügel recognized Hinduism, Buddhism, and Islam as vehicles of God's love although he considered them inferior religions. His respect for "the other" needs to be further expanded and his Eurocentrism corrected.

The task of correcting bias includes challenging stereotypical attitudes toward race, class, and gender which are reflected in von Hügel's writing. In *The Mystical Element* he described abuses of the three elements of religion found among different races. What von Hügel calls race would now be referred to as ethnicity or culture.

> And whole races have tended and will tend, upon the whole, to one or other of these three excesses: e.g. the Latin races, to Externalism and Superstition; the Teutonic races, to the two Interiorisms, Rationalism and Fanaticism.[29]

Concerning the English he had this to say:

> For the average Englishman does not think much or feel keenly. Do not molest him in his sports and his politics, and he will hardly notice that he is leaving all such thinking and feeling, as regards religion, hence the deepest life, to the Priests, or even, simply, to God Almighty alone.

He imputed to his "German-Scotch blood" the fact that he found "a life without much thought and interiority" to be "*something intolerably childish and philistine.*"[30]

Von Hügel was aware of the dangers of nationalism, a topic which he developed in "The Difficulties and Dangers of Nationality."[31] In spite of certain stereotypical attitudes toward different nationalities he embraced the diversity of the human family.

For myself, I am deeply grateful to God that I most truly owe, and that I am keenly aware that I owe, to all the great typical races and nations far too much ever to condemn any one of them root and branch. What, above all, would my religion be without its Jewish figure? What would my Theology be without the Greeks? What would my Church Order be without the Italians? How much poorer would be my devotional life without the German *Imitation!* without the French Fénelon! without the Spanish St. Teresa! without the English Mother Julian! I want them all, and I rejoice in them all.[32]

Von Hügel was particularly appreciative of the Jewish race, emphasizing the Jewishness of Jesus, his mother and disciples. Not only did he embrace diversity but he seems to have been comfortable with persons from different ethnic and racial backgrounds.

Von Hügel enjoyed privileges of class. This was part of the "givenness" of his life which he simply accepted and used responsibly. He was charitable toward the poor, and encouraged his daughters and those whom he directed to visit the poor, regretting that his deafness prevented him from doing so himself.[33] He also was aware of the Marxist critique of industrial society but when he alluded to the social problems of his day it was with a certain detachment. In *Eternal Life* he discussed socialism and admitted that the socialists "can and do call the forcible attention of the classes, and of the bureaucrats, ever so averse to facing reality, to the grave troubles and requirements of the masses," a situation which had led Cardinal Manning to support the workers in England and Leo XIII to articulate a Catholic social teaching in his encyclical *Rerum Novarum* (1891).[34] In this context von Hügel referred to the influence of culture on religion:

The problem (of poverty) is not simply intensified for us, it is radically changed; and this change has made us realize, more clearly than ever before, the great dependence of the chances and articulation of religion upon the various social conditions of the average human beings addressed by it.[35]

As a philosopher of religion von Hügel considered ignorance of the nature and history of religion to be the cause of the rejection of religion and the acceptance of a materialistic world view by a large part of the population. In response to the changing economic and social situation in Europe he warned that Christianity must avoid "any exclusive Other-Worldliness, all quietistic suffering and listless waiting," and embrace the "Immanentism and the Incarnational Doctrine of Christianity."[36]   But this was only one movement; there was also needed the sense of eternal life, of the transcendent in the immanent, of the eternal in the temporal.[37] As von Hügel grew older he focused more on the second movement.   At times this attitude seemed an escape from the realities of the world around him.   As Flannery O'Connor pointed out, in his desire to accept everything, to be cut off from nothing, he was more inclined to accept injustices than to try to remove them.[38] Is it not also possible that he had a class bias that prevented him from seeing the kind of massive change that would be required if the basic human needs of all classes were to be met?

Von Hügel, who had three daughters and numerous women friends, took women's intellectual development seriously, although he had certain stereotypical views of women as well as of different ethnic groups and classes. In *The Mystical Element* he wrote of the distribution of the three elements:

> Women generally tend either to an excess of the external, to superstition; or of the emotional, to fanaticism. Men, on the contrary, appear generally to incline to an excess of the intellectual, to rationalism and indifference.[39]

He "explained" Catherine's largeness and narrowness in stereotypical male/female terms. She was at times "too much a man, as one absorbed in great but purely general, super-personal ideas which were making her forget both her own and her fellow-creature's minor wants"; in other moods she was "too much a woman, as one engrossed in her own purely individual, small and fanciful troubles and trials."[40] He warned Gwendolen Greene to avoid "lopsidedness," a fault that he saw in women.[41] He even discouraged her from reading some of his own works which were the writings of "a masculine mind," and as such "contain far more sheer thinking than is suited to a woman—even a woman with as rarely much intellect as yourself, Child."[42]   His relationships with a number of highly intelligent women, as well as with his three daughters, do not seem to have seriously challenged his stereotypes.

While accepting the gender stereotypes of his day von Hügel also seems to have understood some of the struggles of women. When

Mildred Mansel, Juliet's mother, was arrested as one of 120 suffragettes trying to enter the House of Commons to interview the Prime Minister, he noted in his diary that he had written to encourage her "to keep spirit during the next ten days for the sake of the cause itself and her own balance."[43] In a letter written in 1912 to Margaret Clutton he acknowledged that he had only recently come to appreciate that women are "fellow-fighters, pure with my purity, tempted with my temptations, however differently within the identity."[44]

Nicholas Lash has warned against the "dangerously seductive" nature of patterns of ideas:

> In religion, as elsewhere, fascination with pattern—with, for example, the interplay and dialectic of forces and elements, woven (by von Hügel) from a vast array of information from ancient philosophy, from the history of the Christian Church, and from modern thought—can distract us from the unpatternable particularity of particular circumstance, suffering, and joy.[45]

Lash suggests that von Hügel offers his own corrective: "the vivid, continuous sense that God . . . is the true originator and the true end of the whole movement" and "the continuous sense of the ever necessary, ever fruitful . . . Cross of Christ—the great law and fact that only through self-renunciation and suffering can the soul win its true self."[46] A contemporary spirituality would want to add a social and political dimension to this personal piety.

Although von Hügel emphasized the autonomy of the secular, he was more interested in and critical of contemporary ecclesiastical structures than of the political and social structures of his day. Whelan refers to the narrowness of his social and political consciousness.[47] Even the "big" Christian's world was too small. One cannot fault von Hügel for being a man of his age, a Victorian European gentleman. The acknowledgment of limitations of time and place emphasize the contextual nature of his theology and spirituality with their focus on historical concreteness.

Correctives and Expansion

The Historical Element

One of von Hügel's major contributions was his insistence on the historical nature of Christianity. An early study of von Hügel refers to him as "a living bond between tradition and the modern spirit."[48] This seems an apt description for one who struggled for responsible self-direction within the Roman Catholic Church during a repressive period in its history. Von Hügel discovered within the tradition liberating aspects which he was able to use.

> We shall never know this our *now*, with full vividness and fruitfulness, unless we know this now's *then*, its past.[49]

The task of discovering liberating aspects also can be undertaken with von Hügel himself. We need to recognize that the *then* has been interpreted too narrowly. We can know our *now* by extending von Hügel's notion of the *then* to include the stories of other groups.

Von Hügel was right in his insistence on the importance of history, a theme which has been developed by twentieth-century theology. One thinks particularly of the work of Chenu, Congar, Lonergan, and Rahner. Building on their work, but moving beyond them, liberation theologies and feminist theologies insist that history must include the concrete struggles of whole groups and societies which have been subsumed, suppressed, and ignored in the Christian story.[50]

Von Hügel, who shared the nineteenth-century approach to history with its emphasis on development and progress, had a naive faith in "historical facts" which did not recognize the interpretative nature of the historical task. Nor did he recognize the discontinuities as well as the continuities of human history. David Tracy suggests a "new hermeneutics of mystical retrieval through prophetic suspicion . . . the retrieval of the sense of history as rupture, break, discontinuity in apocalyptic; the retrieval of the social systemic expression of sin over individual sins; the retrieval of the concrete praxis of discipleship in and for the oppressed."[51]

A retrieval of the negative aspects of human history would serve as a corrective to von Hügel's nineteenth-century view of history as progress. No contemporary spirituality can ignore the realities of the Holocaust and the atrocities of our century, including the ravishing of the earth itself. These too are part of the history of Christianity. Von Hügel looked to the cross of Christ as the answer to the meaning of suffering but he ignored the social imbeddedness of much suffering. Contemporary theology and spirituality challenge the Christian to heed the "dangerous memory" of suffering endured not only by individuals but by whole peoples.

Von Hügel's openness to other traditions was remarkable for his period. He approached the other with a willingness to learn while clearly stating his own position. He certainly should be recognized as a pioneer in interreligious dialogue. However, he also shared with his contemporaries the assumption of the cultural superiority of Western Christianity. Such an assumption can no longer be made in our dialogue both within the Church and with other religions. Tracy suggests that "we are fast approaching the day when it will not be possible to attempt a Christian systematic theology except in serious conversation with the other great ways."[52] As we enter into this dialogue we need to examine our assumptions about "the other." Often this other is no longer in a distant time or place but is a close neighbor. We are challenged by the radical pluralism which we experience. It is a heightened form of the tension or friction which von Hügel saw as both necessary and potentially redemptive. The plurality and ambiguity that characterize the postmodern age are part of our "givenness."[53]

The Intellectual Element

Von Hügel emphasized the purifying dimension of science, including historical criticism, and applied it to his study of the origins and development of the Christian Church. In the critical spirit of von Hügel we can continue to use history, but a more inclusive history than that which he drew upon, as well as employ new tools from the social sciences to critique all expressions of institutional religion, including power structures within the Church.

The value that von Hügel assigned to the intellectual element and to the role of the scholar and of scholarship as a necessary ingredient of a vibrant spirituality continues to be important. His emphasis on the intellectual has been seen by some as elitist.[54] It is true that few people have the leisure and the financial resources to spend a lifetime pursuing their scholarly interests. But the recognition that the pursuit of scholarship is a service to society as well as a ministry within ecclesial communities needs to be affirmed even as it is critiqued and expanded.

Von Hügel's insistence on freedom or "elbow room" for scholarship and on the self-correcting power of the community are important insights. In hindsight David Tracy maintains:

The silencing of the Catholic Modernists was not merely intellectually self-defeating and ethically and religiously unsettling; it was also unnecessary, as the parallel history of liberal Protestant thought in the same period shows. Critical inquiry, left to the self-correcting power of the entire community of inquiry, can and should be trusted to provide whatever corrections it may eventually need.[55]

It was this kind of correction that von Hügel struggled for during his lifetime. He sent his own work to scholars from different backgrounds and welcomed their critique. He in turn carefully studied the work of other scholars and then wrote long commentaries which always began with what he had appreciated in the work and concluded with suggested changes which he hoped the author would consider.

We have seen how von Hügel worked with persons from a variety of disciplines and moved freely from one discipline to another. The need for interdisciplinary work is emphasized today. No one discipline is adequate to understand the complex issues of our day nor can one scholar master many disciplines. Bernard Lonergan suggests different functional specialties as a way to overcome the problem of rigid discipline divisions.[56] The team approach brings its own tensions as well as benefits to participants, a lesson which von Hügel learned long ago. His willingness to share his scholarly work and that of his friends with a wide circle of scholars from different countries and different religious traditions is truly impressive. He did this through personal visits and an amazing correspondence. One cannot help but think of how he would have used the electronic resources available today.

Von Hügel recognized the need for critical appropriation of the tradition, something which he exemplified in all his writings but particularly in his work on Catherine. A hermeneutic of suspicion would push the critique further by examining the very notions of rationality that formed the basis for his critique. Von Hügel, whose approach to science was positivistic, shared the nineteenth-century fascination with science. Those who live in a nuclear age are more aware of its inadequacies and its potential for destruction. A hermeneutic of suspicion is needed to evaluate both the use and abuse of science. Von Hügel was shaped by the classical tradition but was open to the new approaches to learning of his day, particularly psychology and the comparative study of religion. His methods are dated but his openness to new ways of searching for the truth continues to challenge us.

Von Hügel's appreciation for all of creation offers a foundation for an ecological spirituality. He delighted in plant and animal life and took pleasure in the many leveled richness and complexity of life. He saw all of creation as interdependent and as a reflection of God. He also had a profound respect for the autonomy of matter. Here too his science is dated, but his openness to new approaches and his appreciation for the complexities of creation can inspire the contemporary scholar.

Questions about what is scholarship and how it is related to religion remain. Von Hügel's answers will no longer satisfy, but his insistence on the contribution of scholarship to religious life for the individual as well as for church and society remains important. So also is his reminder that the work of scholarship can be both costly and purifying.

The Mystical Element

Not only is von Hügel's world too neat but his understanding of God as the Supreme Reality is also too neat. The God whom von Hügel sees as the object of religion is the God of classical theism, a God no longer credible for many postmodern Christians. Von Hügel met the problems of unbelief in his day by his insistence on what he called the Reality of God, God who is both transcendent and immanent, and who could be discovered through one's experience in the world. His niece remembered him saying: "I don't care about ideas, I want facts. God is not an idea. He is a fact."[57] Reflecting on his experience, and using the tools of the Enlightenment, he developed his philosophy of religion and grew in a profound faith in the Reality of God which guided his life. But new foci of experience are opening up new ways of thinking about God. Elizabeth Johnson has described four such foci which each in turn challenge the God of Western classical theism: the excess of suffering, women's experience, other religions, and contemporary science.[58]

Von Hügel saw that suffering could be transformative but he did not face the reality of misery on a massive scale that characterizes the twentieth century. Although he stressed our interrelatedness, his own experience of suffering was personal, involving himself and his immediate family. He lived through the First World War, but from a safe distance. This distanced approach is no longer possible as television brings the horror of war, starvation, and cruelty into our homes. The reality of massive suffering and evil such as the Holocaust challenge contemporary believers to rethink their understanding of suffering and God. For von Hügel, using the arguments of philosophy, there is overflowing sympathy in God but not suffering.[59] Liberation and feminist theologies would want to add an analysis of the causes of suffering and would argue that sympathy is not enough. Faith in God demands action on behalf of those who suffer and a God who is with the sufferer. Von Hügel's sympathetic God is inadequate in the face of misery on a massive scale.

Von Hügel's reality of God does not reflect the experience of many women who are searching for ways of thinking about God and praying which include their experience as women. Feminist theologians such as Sallie McFague and Elizabeth Johnson have critiqued patriarchal understandings of God which come to us through the tradition and they have explored alternative symbols for the divine.[60] Although von Hügel used the male pronoun to refer to God, he avoided images of father and king, drawing on images such as "the Unconditional, the Abiding, the Prevenient, the Beginning and the End and Crown of light and life and love."[61] There is an openness to critique and a willingness to explore new expressions in von Hügel's thought. In his last book he offered his own critique of the tradition, justifying it by his remark:

> For what is the consciousness of history and of its often perplexing influences but the sense that we are still at school, still in training, and still requiring patient discriminations until the perfect day break for us in the Beyond?[62]

Von Hügel was convinced that we must continue our attempts "at analyzing and theorizing our full human experience and its implications."[63]

> The needs of the human mind and of the human spirit, the qualities of the daisy, the butterfly, lizard, swallow, and sheep, and above all, the intimations of the thus otherwise awakened religious sense are still with us and still quite unexhausted.[64]

This commitment to search for ever deeper understanding of the mystery of God was an abiding characteristic of von Hügel's thought.

Feminist theological discourse is probing some hitherto unexplored dimensions of these unexhausted intimations of the divine mystery.

We have seen von Hügel's openness to other religions as a source for his philosophy of religion. He appreciated "how dear and true and good can be and are the lesser lights, the lesser helps God nowhere forgets to give His children."[65] He urged his readers to remain open and to "smile in welcome towards all the winds that blow in God's great heaven."[66] Today those winds come from new directions and demand a new kind of openness to God's revelation among all religions. This is a blessing for us as well as a challenge as Tracy has pointed out:

> We are also blessed to live in a period where the other great religious traditions—both the other Christian churches, the Jewish traditions, a resurgent Islamic tradition, the profound and polycentric Buddhist, Hindu, neo-Confucian, Taoist traditions, and all the great indigenous traditions throughout the world can finally be heard by us and learned from as genuine others, if we will it.[67]

Von Hügel used the science of his day, especially the work of Darwin, in his reflections on the reality of God. Contemporary science with its chaos theory challenges the orderly evolutionary development that reflected a wise Creator God. Theology needs to enter into dialogue with the new cosmology in order to discover new ways of thinking about the mystery of the universe and its Creator.

In the spirit of openness which characterized von Hügel's own search for the reality of God, contemporary women and men have a wealth of experience on which to draw in our search for the living God. Von Hügel insisted that the mystical element was not a rare gift of privileged persons but an aspect of all mature religion and one which requires personal freedom. The inner freedom which von Hügel struggled to maintain comes from trust in God and is God's gift. But there are certain basic conditions necessary in order for persons to be free to respond. The liberation theologian, Gustavo Gutiérrez, refers to the countless people in the world who are "non-persons." Von Hügel's mystical element is for all persons—but countless people in our world lack what is necessary in order to be able to make a free personal religious response. A contemporary spirituality needs not only to struggle for personal freedom but to facilitate social and political changes which will enable others to achieve this freedom for themselves.

Much of von Hügel's writings, with their practical examples, may no longer speak to us, rooted as they are in a past that seems remote. But the fact that his philosophy of religion and his spirituality were based on his concrete experience as spouse, parent, and friend can remind us that we also need to take seriously the concrete realities of our lives in our spiritual journey. Like von Hügel we can reflect on the Catholic tradition in all its plurality, and allow it to enter into dialogue with other traditions. And we can embrace, even as we are embraced by, the reality of God. There is a profound wisdom in the teachings of von Hügel that the thoughtful reader can take, adapt, and use. This was always von Hügel's hope, as he expressed it to a friend: "Let these poor things go down and take root and produce fruit, if and where and when the God Who is so kind to the birds and to the plants cares to bless them to this degree."[68]

NOTES

1. Martin Green, *Yeat's Blessings on von Hügel: Essays on Literature and Religion* (London: Longmans, 1967), p.7.

2. Ibid., pp.9–10.

3. Ibid., pp.89–90.

4. In his diary for 22 November 1897 while in Rome he notes his first bicycle lesson. We have seen how he studied Hebrew in a highly disciplined way for many years and undertook a rigorous study of biblical criticism, especially German criticism.

5. For anthologies of vH's writings and unpublished theses on vH, see Kelly, *Von Hügel's Philosophy of Religion*, pp.24–26. Kelly lists 28 theses written before 1983. Many more have been written since that date.

6. *The Life of Prayer* (London: J. M. Dent & Sons, 1927; reprinted 1960), p.3.

7. Alban Goodier, "Baron Friedrich von Hügel," *Dublin Review* 196 (1935), pp.73–84; quote from p.73.

8. A. Hazard Dakin, *Von Hügel and the Supernatural* (London: SPCK, 1934), p.vii.

9. Thompson, pp.101–20.

10. Lash, *Easter in Ordinary*, pp.141–77.

11. Tracy, "The Uneasy Alliance Reconceived: Catholic Theological Method, Modernity, and Postmodernity," *Theological Studies* 50 (1989), p.548.

12. Ibid., p.556.

13. Tracy, "Recent Catholic Spirituality: Unity Amid Diversity." In *Christian Spirituality: Post-Reformation and Modern*, ed. by Louis Dupré and Don E. Saliers (New York: Crossroad, 1989), pp.143–73.

14. Tracy, "Roman Catholic Identity and the Ecumenical Dialogues," *On Naming the Present: God, Hermeneutics, and Church* (Maryknoll, N.Y.; Orbis, 1994), p.85.

15. Gerard W. Hughes, *God of Surprises* (New York: Paulist Press, 1985), pp.10–25.

16. Whelan, *Spirituality of von Hügel*, p.211.

17. Wilkie Au, "Holistic Catechesis: Keeping Our Balance in the 1990's," *Religious Education* 86 (1991), pp.347–60, uses vH's categories of the institutional, the critical, and the mystical as a corrective to the emphasis on the institutional in *Catechism of the Catholic Church* (Vatican City: Libreria Editrice Vaticana, 1992; English trans., 1994).

18. David Cairns described vH as a "big Christian." See Chapter 7 above.

19. See Chapter 7 above for vH's ecumenical spirituality. Also Ruddle, "Ecumenical Dimension in the Work of von Hügel"; Hanbury, "Von Hügel and the Ecumenical Movement"; and *Spirituality in Ecumenical Perspective*, ed. by E. Glenn Hinson.

20. Letter to anonymous friend, July 1956 in *The Habit of Being: Letters of Flannery O'Connor*, ed. Sally Fitzgerald (New York: Vintage, 1980), p.85.

21. David Leon Higdon, "Saint Catherine, Von Hügel, and Graham Greene's *The End of the Affair*," *English Studies: A Journal of English Language and Literature* 62 (1981), pp.46–52.

22. Yeats wrote: "Must we part, von Hügel, though much alike, for we/ Accept the miracles of the saints and honor sanctity?" The poet ends with the words: "So get you gone, von Hügel, though with blessings on your head." *Poems of W. B. Yeats*, Selected with an Introduction by A. Norman Jeffares (London: MacMillan Education, 1962), pp.242–43. See also T. R. Henn, *The Lonely Tower: Studies in the Poetry of W. B. Yeats* (London: University Paperbacks, 1950, 1965), pp.169–171.

23. Green, *Yeat's Blessings on von Hügel: Essays on Literature and Religion*, p.5.

24. Ibid., p.6.

25. Tracy, "Catholic Theological Method," *Theological Studies* 50 (1989), p.551.

26. *GS*, p.14.

27. *RG*, p.36.

28. *EA2*, p.270.

29. *ME* 1. p.59.

30. "The Parent as Spiritual Director," p.54; emphasis is vH's.

31. *EA* 2, pp.255-76.

32. *EA* 2, p.271.

33. See Chapter 6 for vH's encouragement to Evelyn Underhill to get herself "gently and gradually interested in the poor." In a letter to Gertrud in Rome, 6 January 1898, at a time when she was going through a crisis of faith, her father encouraged her to be with the poor and added that deafness kept him from doing so himself. vHP, Downside Abbey Archives, MS 1272 (uncatalogued).

34. *EL*, pp.303–23; quote from p.313.

35. *EL*, p.314.

36. *EL*, p.316.

37. *EL*, pp.316–17.

38. William M. Kirkland, "Baron von Hügel and Flannery O'Connor," *The Flannery O'Connor Bulletin* 18 (1989), pp.38.

39. *ME* 1, p.58.

40. *ME* 1, p.221.

41. *LTN*, p.97.

42. *LTN*, p.87.

43. Diary, 1 July 1909.

44. "The Parent as Spiritual Director," p.86.

45. *Easter in Ordinary*, p.175.

46. *ME* 2, p.395; quoted by Lash, p.176.

47. Whelan, p.220.

48. Maurice Nédoncelle, *Baron Friedrich von Hügel: A Study of His Life and Thought* (London: Longmans, Green & Co., 1937), p.192.

49. *EA* 2, p.65.

50. For developments in historical studies, see *New Perspectives on Historical Writing*, ed. Peter Burke (University Park, PA: Pennsylvania State University Press, 1991).

51. *Dialogue with the Other: The Inter-Religious Dialogue* (Leuven: Peeters Press; Grand Rapids, MI: William B. Eerdmans, 1990), pp.119–20.

52. Ibid., p.xi.

53. In *Plurality and Ambiguity* (San Francisco: Harper & Row, 1988) Tracy argues that radical pluralism and a heightened sense of ambiguity are typical of all postmodern movements.

54. Kelly, *Von Hügel's Philosophy of Religion*, p.211.

55. Tracy, "Catholic Theological Method," *Theological Studies* 50 (1989), p.552.

56. Bernard Lonergan, *Method in Theology* (New York: Herder and Herder, 1972).

57. *LTN*, p.xviii.

58. Lecture given at University of Notre Dame, 8 March 1995.

59. *EA2*, pp.167–213, See also Chapter 7 above.

60. Sallie McFague, *Models of God: Theology for an Ecological, Nuclear Age* (Philadelphia: Fortress Press, 1987); Elizabeth A. Johnson, *She Who Is: The Mystery of God in Feminist Theological Discourse* (New York: Crossroad, 1992).

61. *RG*, p.18.

62. *RG*, p.20.

63. *RG*, p.22.

64. *RG*, p.23.

65. *RG*, p.21.

66. *RG*, p.30.

67. *On Naming the Present*, p.5.

68. vH to Mrs. Lillie, 29 November 1922, *SL*, p.363.

APPENDIX

FRIEDRICH VON HÜGEL, *THE MYSTICAL ELEMENT OF RELIGION AS STUDIED IN ST. CATHERINE OF GENOA AND HER FRIENDS* (London: Dent, 1908)

CHAPTER II
THE THREE ELEMENTS OF RELIGION
INTRODUCTORY

We have found then that all life and all truth are, for all their unity, deeply complex, for us men at all events; indeed that they are both in exact proportion to their reality. In this, our second chapter, I should like to show the complexity special to the deepest kind of life, to Religion; and to attempt some description of the working harmonization of this complexity. If Religion turned out to be simple, in the sense of monotone, a mere oneness, a whole without parts, it could not be true; and yet if Religion be left too much a mere multiplicity, a mere congeries of parts without a whole, it cannot be persuasive and fully operative. And the several constituents are there, whether we harbor, recognize, and discipline them or not; but these constituents will but hinder or supplant each other, in proportion as they are not something each recognized in their proper place and rank, and are not each allowed and required to supplement and to stimulate the other. And though no amount of talk or theory can, otherwise than harmfully, take the place of life, yet observation and reflection can help us to see where and how life acts: what are the causes, or at least the concomitants, of its inhibition and of its stimulation and propagation, and can thus supply us with aids to action, which action will then, in its turn, help to give experimental fulness and precision to what otherwise remains a more or less vague and empty scheme.

I. THE THREE ELEMENTS, AS THEY SUCCESSIVELY APPEAR IN THE CHILD, THE YOUTH, AND THE ADULT MAN.

Now if we will but look back upon our own religious life, we shall find that, in degrees and in part in an order of succession varying indefinitely with each individual, three modalities, three modes of apprehension and forms of appeal and of outlook, have been and are at work within us and around.[1]

1. Sense and Memory, the Child's means of apprehending Religion.

In the doubtless overwhelming majority of cases, there came first, as far as we can reconstruct the history of our consciousness, the appeal to our infant senses of some external religious symbol or place, some picture or statue, some cross or book, some movement of some attendant's hands and eyes. And this appeal would generally have been externally interpreted to us by some particular men or women, a Mother, Nurse, Father, Teacher, Cleric, who themselves would generally have belonged to some more or less well-defined traditional, institutional religion. And their appeal would be through my senses to my imaginative faculty first, and then to my memory of that first appeal, and would represent the principle of authority in its simplest form.

All here as yet works quasi-automatically. The little child gets these impressions long before itself can choose between, or even is distinctly conscious of them; it believes whatever it sees and is told, equally, as so much fact, as something to build on. If you will, it believes these things to be true, but not in the sense of contrasting them with error; the very possibility of the latter has not yet come into sight. And at this stage the External, Authoritative, Historical, Traditional, Institutional side and function of Religion are everywhere evident. Cases like that of John Stuart Mill, of being left outside of all religious tradition, we may safely say, will ever remain exceptions to help prove the rule. The five senses then, perhaps that of touch first, and certainly that of sight most; the picturing and associative powers of the imagination; and the retentiveness of the memory, are the side of human nature specially called forth. And the external, sensible, readily picturable facts and the picturing functions of religion correspond to and feed this side, as readily as does the mother's milk correspond to and feed that same mother's infant. Religion is here, above all, a Fact and Thing.

2. Question and Argument, the Youth's mode of approaching Religion.

But soon there wakes up another activity and requirement of human nature, and another side of religion comes forth to meet it. Direct experience, for one thing, brings home to the child that these sense-informations are not always trustworthy, or identical in its own case and in that of others. And, again, the very impressiveness of this external religion stimulates indeed the sense of awe and of wonder, but it awakens curiosity as well. The time of trustful questioning, but still of questioning, first others, then oneself, has come. The old impressions get now more and more consciously sought out, and selected from among other conflicting ones; the facts seem to clamor for reasons to back them, against the other hostile facts and appearances, or at least against those men in books, if not in life, who dare to question or reject them. Affirmation is beginning to be consciously exclusive of its contrary: I begin to feel that I hold *this,* and that *you* hold *that;* and that I cannot do both; and that I do the former, and exclude and refuse the latter.

Here it is the reasoning, argumentative, abstractive side of human nature that begins to come into play. Facts have now in my mind to be related, to be bound to other facts, and men to men; the facts themselves begin to stand for ideas or to have the latter in them or behind them. The measuring-rod seems to be over all things. And religion answers this demand by clear and systematic arguments and concatenations: this and this is now connected with that and that; this is true or this need not be false, because of that and that. Religion here becomes Thought, System, a Philosophy.

3. Intuition, Feeling, and Volitional requirements and evidences, the Mature Man's special approaches to Faith.

But yet a final activity of human nature has to come to its fullest, and to meet its response in a third side of Religion. For if in Physiology and Psychology all action whatsoever is found to begin with a sense-impression, to move through the central process of reflection, and to end in the final discharge of will and of action, the same final stage can be found in the religious life. Certain interior experiences, certain deep-seated spiritual pleasures and pains, weaknesses and powers, helps and hindrances, are increasingly known and felt in and through interior and exterior action, and interior suffering, effort, and growth. For man is necessarily a creature of action, even more than of sensation and of reflection; and in this action of part of himself against other parts, of himself with or against other men, with or against this or that external fact or condition, he grows and gradually comes to his real self, and gains certain experiences as to the existence and nature and growth of this his own deeper personality.

Man's emotional and volitional, his ethical and spiritual powers, are now in ever fuller motion, and they are met and fed by the third side of religion, the Experimental and Mystical. Here religion is rather felt than seen or reasoned about, is loved and lived rather than analyzed, is action and power, rather than either external fact or intellectual verification.

II. EACH ELEMENT EVER ACCOMPANIED BY SOME AMOUNT OF THE OTHER TWO. DIFFICULTY OF THE TRANSITIONS FROM ONE STAGE TO THE OTHER.

Now these three sides of the human character, and corresponding three elements of Religion, are never, any one of them, without a trace or rudiment of the other two; and this joint presence of three such disparate elements ever involves tension, of a fruitful or dangerous kind.[2]

1. *Utility of this joint presence.*

In the living human being indeed there never exists a mere apprehension of something external and sensible, without any interior elaboration, any interpretation by the head and heart. We can hardly allow, we can certainly in nowise picture to ourselves, even an infant of a few hours old as working, and being worked upon, by nothing beyond these sense-perceptions alone. Already some mental, abstractive, emotional-volitional reaction and interpretation is presumably at work; and not many weeks or months pass before this is quite obviously the case. And although, on the other hand, the impressions of the senses, of the imagination and the memory are, normally, more numerous, fresh, and lasting in early than in later years, yet up to the end they continue to take in some new impressions, and keep up their most necessary functions of supplying materials, stimulants, and tests to the other powers of the soul.

Thus, too, Religion is at all times more or less both traditional and individual; both external and internal; both institutional, rational, and volitional. It always answers more or less to the needs of authority and society; of reason and proof; of interior sustenance and purification. I believe because I am told, because it is true, because it answers to my deepest interior experiences and needs. And, everything else being equal, my faith will be at its richest and deepest and strongest, in so far as all these three motives are most fully and characteristically operative within me, at one and the same time, and towards one and the same ultimate result and end.

2. The two crises of the soul, when it adds Speculation to Institutionalism, and Mysticism to both.

Now all this is no fancy scheme, no petty or pretty artificial arrangement: the danger and yet necessity of the presence of these three forces, the conflicts and crises within and between them all, in each human soul, and between various men and races that typify or espouse one or the other force to the more or less complete exclusion of the other, help to form the deepest history, the truest tragedy or triumph of the secret life of every one of us.

The transition from the child's religion, so simply naive and unselfconscious, so tied to time and place and particular persons and things, so predominantly traditional and historical, institutional and external, to the right and normal type of a young man's religion, is as necessary as it is perilous. The transition is necessary. For all the rest of him is growing—body and soul are growing in clamorous complexity in every direction: how then can the deepest part of his nature, his religion, not require to grow and develop also? And how can it permeate and purify all the rest, how can it remain and increasingly become "the secret source of all his seeing," of his productiveness and courage and unification, unless it continually equals and exceeds all other interests within the living man, by its own persistent vitality, its rich and infinite variety, its subtle, ever-fresh attraction and inexhaustible resourcefulness and power? But the crisis is perilous. For he will be greatly tempted either to cling exclusively to his existing, all but simply institutional, external position, and to fight or elude all approaches to its reasoned, intellectual apprehension and systematization; and in this case his religion will tend to contract and shrivel up, and to become a something simply alongside of other things in his life. Or he will feel strongly pressed to let the individually intellectual simply supplant the institutional, in which case his religion will grow hard and shallow, and will tend to disappear altogether. In the former case he will, at best, assimilate his religion to external law and order, to Economics and Politics; in the latter case he will, at best, assimilate it to Science and Philosophy. In the first case, he will tend to superstition; in the second, to rationalism and indifference.

But even if he passes well through this first crisis, and has thus achieved the collaboration of these two religious forces, the external and the intellectual, his religion will still be incomplete and semi-operative, because still not reaching to what is deepest and nearest to his will. A final transition, the addition of the third force, that of the emotional-experimental life, must yet be safely achieved. And this again is perilous: for the two other forces will, even if single, still more if combined, tend to resist this third force's full share of influence to the uttermost. To the external force this emotional power will tend to appear as akin to revolution; to the intellectual side it will readily seem mere subjectivity and sentimentality ever verging on delusion. And the emotional-experimental force will, in its turn, be tempted to sweep aside both the external, as so much oppressive ballast; and the intellectual, as so much hair-splitting or rationalism. And if it succeeds, a shifting subjectivity, and all but incurable tyranny of mood and fancy, will result,—fanaticism is in full sight.

III. PARALLELS TO THIS TRIAD OF RELIGIOUS ELEMENTS.

If we would find, applied to other matters, the actual operation and co-operation, at the earliest stage of man's life, of the identical powers under discussion, we can find them, by a careful analysis of our means and processes of knowledge, or of the stages of all reflex action.

I. *The three constituents of Knowledge.*

Even the most elementary acquisition, indeed the very possibility, of any and all certitude and knowledge, is dependent for us upon the due collaboration of the three elements or forces of our nature, the sensational, the rational, the ethico-mystical.[3]

There is, first, in the order of our consciousness and in the degree of its undeniableness, the element of our actual impressions, the flux of our consciousness as it apprehends particular sights and sounds, smells and tastes and touches; particular sensations of rest and movement, pleasure and pain, memory, judgment, and volition, a flux, "changeless in its ceaseless change." We have so far found neither a true object for thought, nor a subject which can think. And yet this element, and this alone, is the simply, passively received, the absolutely undeniable part of our experience—we cannot deny it if we would. And again, it is the absolutely necessary prerequisite for our exercise or acquisition, indeed for our very consciousness, of the other two means or elements, without which there can be no real knowledge.

For there is, next in the logical order of the analysis of our consciousness and in the degree of its undeniableness, the element of the various forms of necessary thought, in as much as these are experienced by us as necessary. We can, with Aristotle, simply call them the ten categories; or we can, with greater precision and extension, group them, so far with Kant, under the two main heads of the two pure "aesthetic" Perceptions of time and space, on the one hand; and of the various "analytic" Forms of judgment and of the Categories of Unity, Reality, Substance, Possibility, etc., on the other hand. Now it can be shown that it is only by means of this whole second element, only through the co-operation of these "perceptions" and forms of thought, that any kind even of dim feeling of ordered succession or of system, of unity or meaning, is found by our mind in that first element. Only these two elements, found and taken together, present us, in their interaction, with even the impression and possibility of something to reason *about*, and something *wherewith* to reason.

The second element then differs from the first in this, that whereas the first presents its contents simply as actual and undeniable, yet without so far any necessity or significance: the second presents its contents as both actual and necessary. By means of the first element I see a red rose, but without any feeling of more than the fact that a rose, or at least this one, *is* red; it might quite as well be yellow or blue. By means of the second element, I think of a body of any kind, not only as actually occupying some particular space and time, but as *necessarily* doing so: I feel that I *must* so think of it.

And yet there is a third and last element necessary to give real value to the two previous ones. For only on the condition that I am willing to trust these intimations of necessity, to believe that these necessities of my subjective thought are objective as well, and correspond to the necessities of Being, can I reach the trans-subjective, can I have any real knowledge and experience of anything whatsoever, either within me or without. The most elementary experience, the humblest something to be granted as really existing and as to be reasoned from, is thus invariably and inevitably composed for me of three elements, of which only the first two are directly experienced by me at all. And the third element, the ethico-mystical, has to be there, I have to trust and endorse the intimations of necessity furnished by the second element, if anything is to come of the whole movement.

Thus, here also, at the very source of all our certainty, of the worth attributable to the least or greatest of our thoughts and feelings and acts, we already find the three elements: indubitable sensation, clear thought, warm faith in and through action. And thus life here already consists of multiplicity in unity; and what in it is absolutely indubitable, is of value only because it constitutes the indispensable starting-point and stimulation for the apprehension and affirmation of realities not directly experienced, not absolutely undeniable, but which alone bear with them all the meaning, all the richness, all the reality and worth of life.

2. *The three links in the chain of Reflex Action.*

We can also find this same triad, perhaps more simply, if we look to Psychology, and that most assured and most far-reaching of all its results, the fact and analysis of Reflex Action. For we find here that all the activities of specifically human life begin with a sense-impression, as the first, the one simply *given* element; that they move into and through a central process of mental abstraction and reflection, as the second element, contributed by the mind itself; and that they end, as the third element, in the discharge of will and of action, in an act of free affirmation, expansion, and love.

In this endless chain composed of these groups of three links each, the first link and the last link are obscure and mysterious; the first, as coming from without us, and as still below our own thought; the third, as going out from us, and seen by us only in its external results, never in its actual operation, nor in its effect upon our own central selves. Only the middle link is clear to us. And yet the most mysterious part of the whole process, the effect of it all upon the central self, is also the most certain and the most important result of the whole movement, a movement which ever culminates in a modification of the personality and which prepares this personality for the next round of sense-perception, intellectual abstraction, ethical affirmation and volitional self-determination—acts which light and love, fixed and free, hard and cold and warm, are so mysteriously, so universally, and yet so variously linked.

IV. DISTRIBUTION OF THE THREE ELEMENTS AMONGST MANKIND AND THROUGHOUT HUMAN HISTORY.

Let us now watch and see where and how the three elements of Religion appear among the periods of man's life, the human professions, and the races of mankind; then how they succeed each other in history generally; and finally how they exist among the chief types and phases of the Oriental, Classical Graeco-Roman, and Judaeo-Christian religions.

1. *The Elements: their distribution among man's various ages, sexes, professions and races.*

We have already noticed how children incline to the memory side, to the external, social type; and it is well they should do so, and they should be wisely helped therein. Those passing through the storm-and-stress period insist more upon reason, the internal, intellectual type; and mature souls lay stress upon the feelings and the will, the internal, ethical type. So again, women generally tend either to an excess of the external, to superstition; or to the emotional, to fanaticism. Men, on the contrary, appear generally to incline to an excess of the intellectual, to rationalism and indifference.

Professions, too, both by the temperaments which they presuppose, and the habits of mind which they foster, have various affinities. The fighting, administrative, legal and political sciences and services, readily incline to the external and institutional; the medical, mathematical, natural science studies, to the internal-intellectual; the poetical, artistic, humanitarian activities, to the internal-emotional.

And whole races have tended and will tend, upon the whole, to one or other of these three excesses: e.g. the Latin races, to Externalism and Superstition; the Teutonic races, to the two Interiorisms, Rationalism and Fanaticism.

2. *Co-existence and succession of the Three Elements in history generally.*

The human race at large has evidently been passing, upon the whole, from the exterior to the interior, but with a constant tendency to drop one function for another, instead of supplementing, stimulating, purifying each by means of the other two.

If we go back as far as any analyzable records will carry us, we find that, in proportion as religion emerges from pure fetishism, it has ever combined with the apprehension of a Power conceived, at last and at best, as of a Father in heaven, that of a Bond with its brethren upon earth. Never has the sacrifice, the so-to-speak vertical relation between the individual man and God, between the worshipper and the object of his worship, been without the sacrificial meal, the communion, the so-to-speak lateral, horizontal relations between man and his fellow-man, between the worshippers one and all. Never has religion been purely and entirely individual; always has it been, as truly and necessarily, social and institutional, traditional and historical. And this traditional element, not all the religious genius in the world can ever escape or replace: it was there, surrounding and molding the very pre-natal existence of each one of us; it will be there, long after we have left the scene. We live and die its wise servants and stewards, or its blind slaves, or in futile, impoverishing revolt against it: we never, for good or for evil, really get beyond its reach.

And yet all this stream and environment of the traditional and social could make no impression upon me whatsoever, unless it were met by certain secret sympathies, by certain imperious wants and energies within myself. If the contribution of tradition is *quantitatively* by far the most important, and might be compared to the contribution furnished by the Vocabulary to the constitution of definite, particular language—the contribution of the individual is, *qualitatively* and for that individual, more important still, and might be compared to the contribution of the Grammar to the constitution of that same language: for it is the Grammar which, though incomparably less in amount than the Vocabulary, yet definitely constitutes any, and every language.

And there is here no necessary conflict with the claim of Tradition. It is true that all real, actual Religion is ever an act of submission to some fact or truth conceived as not only true but as obligatory, as coming from God, and hence as beyond and above our purely subjective fancies, opinings, and wishes. But it is also true that, if I could not mentally hear or see, I should be incapable of hearing or seeing anything of this kind or of any other; and that without some already existing interior affinity with and mysterious capacity for discriminating between such intimations—as either corresponding to or as traversing my existing imperious needs and instincts—I could not apprehend the former as coming from God. Without, then, such non-fanciful, non-wilful, subjective capacities and dispositions, there is for us not even the apprehension of the existence of such objective realities: such capacities and dispositions are as necessary pre-requisites to every act of faith, as sight is the absolute pre-requisite for my discrimination between black and white. Hence as far back as we can go, the traditional and social, the institutional side of religion was accompanied, in varying, and at first small or less perceptible degrees and forms, by intellectual and experimental interpretation and response.

3. *The Three Elements in the great Religions.*

Even the Greek religion, so largely naturalistic up to the very end, appears, in the centuries of its relative interiorization, as a triad composed of a most ancient traditional cultus, a philosophy of religion, and an experimental-ethical life; the latter element being readily exemplified by the Demon of Socrates, and by the Eleusinian and Orphic Mysteries.

In India and Tibet, again, Brahminism and Buddhism may be said to have divided these three elements between them, the former representing as great an excess of the external as Buddhism does of abstruse reasoning and pessimistic emotion. Mahometanism, while combining, in very imperfect proportions, all three elements within itself, lays special stress upon the first, the external element; and though harbouring, for centuries now and more or less everywhere, the third, the mystical element, looks, in its strictly orthodox representatives, with suspicion upon this mysticism.

Judaism was slow in developing the second, the intellectual element; and the third, the mystical, is all but wholly absent till the Exilic period, and does not become a marked feature till later on, and in writers under Hellenistic influence. It is in the Book of Wisdom, still more in Philo, that we find all three sides almost equally developed. And from the Hasmonean period onwards till the destruction of Jerusalem by Titus, we find a severe and ardent external, traditional, authoritative school in the Pharisees; an accommodating and rationalizing school in the Sadducees; and, apart from both, more a sect than a school, the experimental, ascetical, and mystical body of the Essenes.

But it is in Christianity, and throughout its various vicissitudes and schools, that we can most fully observe the presence, characteristics, and interaction of these three modalities. We have already seen how the New Testament writings can be grouped with little or no violence, according to the predominance of one of these three moods, under the heads of the traditional, historic, external, the "Petrine" school; the reasoning, speculative-internal, the Pauline; and the experimental mystical-internal, the Johannine school. And in the East, up to Clement of Alexandria, in the West up to St. Augustine, we find the prevalence of the first type. And next, in the East, in Clement and Origen, in St. Gregory of Nyssa, in the Alexandrian and the Antiochene school generally, and in the West, in St. Augustine, we find predominantly a combination of the second and third types. The Areopagitic writings of the end of the fifth century still further emphasize and systematize this Neo-Platonic form of mystical speculation, and become indeed the great treasure-house from which above all the Mystics, but also largely the Scholastics, throughout the Middle Ages, drew much of their literary material.

And those six or seven centuries of the Middle Ages are full of the contrasts and conflicts between varying forms of Institutionalism, Intellectualism, and Mysticism. Especially clearly marked is the parallelism, interaction, and apparent indestructibleness of the Scholastic and Mystical currents. Abelard and St. Bernard, St. Thomas of Aquin and the great Franciscan Doctors, above all the often largely latent, yet really ceaseless conflict between Realism and Nominalism, all can be rightly taken as caused by various combinations and degrees, insufficiencies or abnormalities in the action of the three great powers of the human soul, and of the three corresponding root-forms and functions of religion. And whereas during the prevalence of Realism, affective, mystical religion is the concomitant and double of intellectual religion; during the later prevalence of Nominalism, Mysticism becomes the ever-increasing supplement; and at last, ever more largely, the substitute, for the methods of reasoning. "Do penance and believe in the Gospel" becomes now the favorite text, even in the mouth of Gerson (who died in 1429), the great Nominalist Doctor, the Chancellor of the then greatest intellectual centre upon earth, the University of Paris. A constant depreciation of all dialectics, indeed largely of human knowledge generally, appears even more markedly in the pages of the gentle and otherwise moderate Thomas of Kempen (who died in 1471).

Although the Humanist Renaissance was not long in carrying away many minds and hearts from all deeper consciousness and effort of a moral and religious sort, yet in so far as men retained and but further deepened and enriched their religious outlook and life, the three old forms and modalities reappear, during the earlier stages of the movement, in fresh forms and combinations. Perhaps the most truly comprehensive and Christian representative of the new at its best, is Cardinal Nicolas of Coes, the precursor of modern philosophy. For he combines the fullest adhesion to, and life-long labor for, External Institutional authority, with the keenest Intellectual, Speculative life, and with the constant temper and practice of experimental and Mystical piety. And a similar combination we find in Blessed Sir Thomas More in England, who lays down his life in defense of Institutional Religion and of the authority of the visible Church and its earthly head; who is a devoted lover of the New Learning, both Critical and Philosophical; and who continuously cultivates the Interior Life. A little later on, we find the same combination in Cardinal Ximenes in Spain.

But it is under the stress and strain of the Reformation and Counter-Reformation movements that the depth and vitality of the three currents get specially revealed. For in Germany, and in Continental Protestantism generally, we see (immediately after the very short first "fluid" stage of Luther's and Zwingli's attitude consequent upon their breach with Rome) the three currents in a largely separate condition, and hence with startling distinctness. Luther, Calvin, Zwingli, different as are their temperaments and both their earlier and later Protestant attitudes and doctrines, all three soon fall back upon some form and fragmentary continuation, or in its way intensification, of Institutional Religion—driven to such conservatism by the iron necessity of real life and the irrepressible requirements of human nature. They thus formed that heavy untransparent thing, orthodox Continental Protestantism. Laelius and Faustus Socinus attempt the construction of a purely Rationalistic Religion, and capture and intensify the current of a clear, cold Deism, in which the critical mind is to be supreme. And the Anabaptist and other scattered sects and individuals (the latter represented at their best by Sebastian Frank) attempt, in their turn, to hold and develop a purely interior, experimental, emotional-intuitive, ecstatic Religion, which is warm, indeed feverish and impulsive, and distrusts both the visible and institutional, and the rational and critical.

In England the same phenomenon recurs in a modified form. For in Anglicanism, the most characteristic of its parties, the High Church school, represents predominantly the Historical, Institutional principle. The Latitudinarian school fights for the Rational, Critical, and Speculative element. The Evangelical school stands in close spiritual affinity to all but the Unitarian Nonconformists in England, and represents the Experimental, Mystical element. We readily think of Laud and Andrewes, Pusey and Keble as representatives of the first class; of Arnold, Stanley and Jowett as figures of the second class; of Thomas Scott, John Newton and Charles Simeon as types of the third class. *The Tracts for the Times, Essays and Reviews,* and (further back) Bunyan's Works, would roughly correspond to them in literature.

And this trinity of tendency can also be traced in Catholicism. Whole Religious Orders and Congregations can be seen or felt to tend, upon the whole, to one or the other type. The Jesuits can be taken as predominantly making for the first type, for fact, authority, submission, obedience; the Dominicans for the second type, for thought, a philosophico-speculative, intellectual religion; the Benedictines, in their noble Congregation of St. Maur, for a historico-critical intellectual type; the French Oratory, for a combination of both the speculative (Malebranche) and the critical (Simon, Thomassin); and the Franciscans, for the third, for action and experimental, affective spirituality.

And yet none of these Orders but has had its individuals, and even whole secondary periods, schools, and traditions, markedly typical of some current other than that specially characteristic of the Order as a whole. There are the great Critics and Historians of the Jesuit Order: the Spanish Maldonatus, the New Testament Scholar, admirable for his time, and helpful and unexhausted still; the French Denys Petau, the great historian of Christian Doctrine and of its development; the Flemish Bollandists, with their unbroken tradition of thorough critical method and incorruptible accuracy and impartiality. There are the great Jesuit Mystics: the Spanish Venerable Balthazar Alvarez, declared by St. Teresa to be the holiest mystical soul she had ever known; and the Frenchmen, Louis Lallemant and Jean Joseph Surin. There are those most attractive figures, combining the Scholar and the Mystic: Blessed Edmund Campion, the Oxford Scholar and Elizabethan Martyr; and Jean Nicolas Grou, the French translator of Plato, who died in exile in England in 1800. The Dominicans have, from the first, been really representative of external authority as well as of the speculative rational bent; and the mystical side has never been wanting to them, so amongst the early German Dominicans, Tauler and Suso, and many a Dominican female Saint. The Benedictines from the first produced great rulers; such striking types of external authority as the Pope-Saints, Gregory the Great and Gregory VII (Hildebrand), and the great

Benedictine Abbots and Bishops throughout the Middle Ages are rightly felt to represent one whole side of this great Order. And again such great mystical figures as St. Hildegard of Bingen and the two Saints Gertrude are fully at home in that hospitable Family. And the Franciscans have, in the Conventuals, developed representatives of the external authority type; and in such great philosopher-theologians as Duns Scotus and Occam, a combination which has more of the intellectual, both speculative and critical, than of the simply ascetical or even mystical type.

And if we look for individual contrasts, we can often find them in close temporal and local juxtaposition, as in France, in the time of Louis XIV, in the persons of Bossuet, Richard Simon, and Fénelon, so strikingly typical of the special strengths and limitations of the institutional, rational, experimental types respectively. And yet the most largely varied influence will necessarily proceed from characters which combine not only two of the types, as in our times Frederick Faber combined the external and experimental; but which hold them all three, as with John Henry Newman in England or Antonio Rosmini in Italy.

V. CAUSES OPERATIVE IN ALL RELIGION TOWARDS MINIMIZING OR SUPPRESSING ONE OR OTHER ELEMENT, OR TOWARDS DENYING THE NEED OF ANY MULTIPLICITY.

Let us end this chapter with some consideration of the causes and reasons that are ever tending to produce and to excuse the quiet elimination or forcible suppression of one or other of the elements that constitute the full organism of religion, and even to minimize or to deny altogether the necessity of any such multiplicity.

1. *The religious temper longs for simplification.*

To take the last point first. How obvious and irresistible seems always, to the specifically religious temper, the appeal to boundless simplification. "Can there be anything more sublimely, utterly simple than religion?" we all say and feel. In these regions, if anywhere, we long and thirst to see and feel all things in one, to become ourselves one, to find the One Thing necessary, the One God, and to be one with Him for ever. Where is there room here, we feel even angrily, for all these distinctions, all this balancing of divers faculties and parts? Is not all this but so much Aestheticism, some kind of subtle Naturalism, a presumptuous attempting to build up bit by bit in practice, and to analyze part from part in theory, what can only come straight from God Himself, and, coming from Him the One, cannot but bear the impress of His own indistinguishable Unity? And can there be anything more unforcedly, unanalyzably simple than all actual religion—and this in exact proportion to its greatness? Look at St. Francis of Assisi, or St. John Baptist; look above all at the Christ, supremely, uniquely great, just because of His sublime simplicity! Look at, feel, the presence and character of those countless souls that bear, unknown even to themselves, some portion of this His impress within themselves, forming thus a kind of indefinitely rich extension of His reign, of the kingdom of His childlikeness. Away then with everything that at all threatens to break up a corresponding simplicity in ourselves! Poverty of spirit, emptiness of heart, a constant turning away from all distraction, from all multiplicity both of thought and of feeling, of action and of being; this, surely, is the one and only necessity for the soul, at least in proportion to the height of her spiritual call.

2. *Yet every truly living Unity is constituted in Multiplicity.*

Now in all this there is a most subtle mixture of truth and of error. It is profoundly true that all that *is* at all, still more all personality, and hence above all God, the Spirit of spirits is, just in that proportion, profoundly mysteriously One, with a Unity which all our best thinking can only distantly and analogously represent. And all religion will ever, in proportion as it is vigorous and pure, thirst after an ever-increasing Unification, will long to be one and to give itself to the One,—to follow naked the naked Jesus. Yet all the history of human thought and all the actual experience of each one of us prove that this Unity can be apprehended and developed, by and within our poor human selves, only in proportion as we carefully persist in stopping at the point where it can most thoroughly organize and harmonize the largest possible multiplicity of various facts and forces.

No doubt the living soul is not a whole made up of separate parts; still less is God made up of parts. Yet we cannot apprehend this Unity of God except in multiplicity of some sort; nor can we ourselves become rightly one, except through being in a true sense many, and very many, as well. Indeed the Christian Faith insists that there is something most real actually corresponding to this our conception of multiplicity even and especially in God Himself. For it as emphatically bids us think of Him as in one sense a Trinity as in another a Unity.

And it is one of the oldest and most universal of Christian approaches to this mystery, to conceive it under the analogy of the three powers of the soul. God the Father and Creator is conceived as corresponding to the sense-perception and Imagination, to Memory-power; God the Son and Redeemer, as the Logos, to our reason; and God the Holy Spirit as corresponding to the effective-volitional force within us; and then we are bidden to remember that, as in ourselves these three powers are all united in One personality, so in God the Three Persons are united in One substance and nature. Even the supremely and ineffably simple Godhead is not, then, a mere, undifferentiated One.

And if we take the case of our Lord, even when He is apprehended in the most abstract of orthodox ways: we get either the duality of natures, God and Man; or a trinity of offices, the Kingly, the Prophetic, and the Priestly—these latter again corresponding roughly to the External, the Intellectual, and the Mystical element of the human soul. And even if we restrict ourselves to His Humanity, and as pictured in any one Gospel, nay in the earliest, simplest, and shortest, St. Mark, we shall still come continually upon a rich multiplicity, variety, and play of different exterior and interior apprehensions and activities, emotions and sufferings, all profoundly permeated by one great end and aim, yet each differing from the other, and contributing a different share to the one great result. The astonishment at the disciples' slowness of com- prehension, the flash of anger at Peter, the sad reproachfulness towards Judas, the love of the children, the sympathy with women, the pity towards the fallen, the indignation against the Pharisees, the rejoicing in the Father's revelation, the agony in the Garden, the desolation on the Cross, are all *different* emotions. The perception of the beauty of the flowers of the field, the habits of plants and of birds, of the varieties of the day's early and late cloud and sunshine, of the effects of storm and rain; and again of the psychology of various classes of character, age, temperament, and avocation; and indeed of so much more are all *different* observations. The lonely recollection in the desert, the nights spent in prayer upon the mountains, the preaching from boats and on the lake-side, the long foot journeyings, the many flights, the reading and expounding in the Synagogues, the curing the sick and restoring them to their right mind, the driving the sellers from the Temple-court, and so much else, are all *different* activities.

And if we take what is or should be simplest in the spiritual life of the Christian, his intention and motive; and conceive this according to the evidence of the practice of such Saints as have themselves revealed to us the actual working of their souls, and of the long and most valuable series of controversies and ecclesiastical decisions in this delicate matter, we shall again find the greatest possible Multiplicity in the deepest possible Unity. For even in such a Saint as St. John of the Cross, whose own analysis and theory of the interior life would often seem all but directly and completely to exclude the element of multiplicity, it is necessary ever to interpret and supplement one part of his teaching by another, and to understand the whole in the light of his actual, deliberate, habitual practice. This latter will necessarily ever exceed his explicit teaching, both in its completeness and in its authority. Now if in his formal teaching he never wearies of insisting upon detachment from all things, and upon the utmost simplification of the intentions of the soul, yet he occasionally fully states what is ever completing this doctrine in his own mind—that this applies only to means and not to the end, and to false and not to true multiplicity. "The spiritual man," he writes in one place, "has greater joy and comfort in creatures, if he detaches himself from them; and he can have no joy in them, if he considers them as his own." "He," as distinct from the unspiritual man, "rejoices in their truth," "in their best conditions," "in their substantial worth." He "has joy in all things."[4] A real multiplicity then exists in things, and in our most purified apprehension of them; varied, rich joys related to this multiplicity are facts in the life of the Saints; and these varied joys may legitimately be dwelt on as incentives to holiness for oneself and others. "All that is wanting now," he writes to Donna Juana de Pedraca, his penitent, "is that I should forget you. But consider how that is to be forgotten which is ever present to the soul."[5] An affection then, as pure as it was particular, was ever in his heart, and fully accepted and willed and acknowledged to its immediate object, as entirely conformable to his own teaching. St Teresa, on the other hand, is a character of much greater natural variety, and yet it is she who has left us that most instructive record of her temporary erroneous ideal of a false simplicity, in turning away, for a number of years, from the consideration of the Humanity of Christ. And a constant, keen interest in the actual larger happenings of her time, in the vicissitudes of the Church in her day, was stamped upon all her teaching, and remained with her up to the very end.

Perhaps the most classic expression of the true Unity is that implied by St. Ignatius of Loyola, when he tells us that "Peace is the simplicity of order." For order as necessarily implies a multiplicity of things ordered as the unity of the supreme ordering principle. Fénelon, doubtless, at times, especially in parts of his condemned *Explication des Maximes des Saints*, too much excludes, or seems to exclude, the element of multiplicity in the soul's intention. Yet, both before and after this book, some of the clearest and completest statements in existence, as to the true unity and diversity to be found in the most perfect life, are to be found among his writings. In his Latin Epistle to Pope Clement XI he insists upon the irreducible element of multiplicity in the motives of the very highest sanctity.

For he maintains first that, though "in the specific act of Love, the chief of the theological virtues, it is possible to love the absolute perfection of God considered in Himself, without the addition of any motive of the promised beatitude," yet that "this specific act of love, of its own nature, never excludes, and indeed most frequently includes, this same motive of beatitude." He asserts next that though, "in the highest grade of perfection amongst souls here below, deliberate acts of simply natural love of ourselves, and even supernatural acts of hope which are not commanded by love mostly cease," yet that in this "habitual state of any and every most perfect soul upon earth, the promised beatitude is desired, and there is no diminution of the exercise of the virtue of hope, indeed day by day there is an increase in this desire, from the specific motive of hope of this great good, which God Himself bids us all, without exception, to hope for." And he declares finally that "there is no state of perfection in which souls enjoy an uninterrupted contemplation, or in which the powers of the soul are bound by an absolute incapacity for eliciting the discursive acts of Christian piety; nor is there a state in which they are exempted from following the laws of the Church, and executing all the orders of superiors."[6]

All the variety, then, of the interested and of the disinterested; of hope and fear and sorrow; of gratitude and adoration and love; of the Intuitive and Discursive; of Recollection and external Action, is to be found, in a deeper, richer, more multiple and varied and at the same time a more unified unity, in the most perfect life; and all this in proportion to its approach to its own ideal and normality.

Indeed the same multiplicity in unity is finely traced by St. Bernard, the great contemplative, in every human act that partakes of grace at all. "That which was begun by Grace, gets accomplished alike by both Grace and Free Will, so that they operate mixedly not separately, simultaneously not successively, in each and all of their processes. The acts are not in part Grace, in part Free Will; but the whole of each act is effected by both in an undivided operation."[7]

VI. THE SPECIAL MOTIVES OPERATING IN EACH ELEMENT TOWARDS THE SUPPRESSION OF THE OTHER ELEMENTS.

Now the elements of Multiplicity and Friction and of Unity and Harmonization, absolutely essential to all life, everywhere and always cost us much to keep and gain. But there are also very special reasons why the three great constituents of religion should, each in its own way, tend continually to tempt the soul to retain only *it*, and hence to an impoverishing simplification. Let us try and see this tendency at work in the two chief constituents, as against each other, and in combination against the third.

1. *In the Historical and Institutional Element, as against all else.*
We have seen how *all* religiousness is ever called into life by some already existing religion. And this religion will consist in the continuous commemoration of some great religious facts of the past. It will teach and represent some divine revelation as having been made, in and through such and such a particular person, in such and such a particular place, at such and such a particular time; and such a revelation will claim acceptance and submission as divine and redemptive in and through the very form and manner in which it was originally made. The very particularity, which will render the teaching distinctively religious will hence be a certain real, or at least at first apparent, externality to the mind and life of the recipient, and a sense of even painful obligation answered by a willing endorsement. All higher religion ever is thus personal and revelational; and all such personal and revelational religion was necessarily first manifested in unique conditions of space and time; and yet claims, in as much as divine, to embrace all the endless conditions of other spaces and other times.

And this combination of a clearly contingent constituent and of an imperiously absolute claim is not less, but more visible as we rise in the scale of religions. The figure of our Lord is far more clear and definite and richly individual than are the figures of the Buddha or of Mahomet. And at the same time Christianity has ever claimed for Him far more than Buddhism or Mohammedanism have claimed for their respective, somewhat shadowy founders. For the Buddha was conceived as but one amongst a whole series of similar revealers that were to come; and Mahomet was but the final prophet of the one God. But Christ is offered to us as the unique Savior, as the unique revelation of God Himself. You are thus to take Him or leave Him. To distinguish and interpret, analyze or theorize Him, to accept Him provisionally or on conditions—nothing of all this is distinctively religious. For, here as everywhere else, the distinctive religious act is, as such, an unconditional surrender. Nowhere in life can we both give and keep at the same time; and least of all here, at life's deepest sources.

With this acceptance then, in exact proportion as it is religious, a double exclusiveness will apparently be set up. I have here found my true life—I will turn away then from all else, and will either directly fight, or will at least starve and stunt, all other competing interests and activities—I will have here a (so to speak) *spatial,* a *simultaneous* exclusiveness. Religion will thus be conceived as a thing amongst other things, or as a force struggling amongst other forces; we have given our undivided heart to it—hence the other things must go, as so many actual supernumeraries and possible supplanters. Science and Literature, Art and Politics must all be starved or cramped. Religion can safely reign, apparently, in a desert alone.

But again, Religion will be conceived, at the same time, as a thing fixed in itself, as given once for all, and to be defended against all change and interpretation, against all novelty and discrimination. We get thus a second, a (so to speak) *temporal, successive* exclusiveness. Religion will here be conceived as a thing to be kept literally and materially identical with itself, and hence as requiring to be defended against any kind of modification. Conceive it as a paste, and all yeast must be kept out; or as wine, and fermentation must be carefully excluded. And indeed Religion here would thus become a stone, even though a stone fallen from heaven, like one of those meteorites worshipped in Pagan antiquity. And the two exclusivenesses, joined together, would give us a religion reduced to such a stone worshipped in a desert.

Now the point to notice here is, that all this seems not to be an abuse, but to spring from the very essence of religion—from two of its specific inalienable characteristics—those of externality and authority. And although the extreme just described has never been completely realized in history, yet we can see various approximations to it in Mohammedan Egypt, in Puritan Scotland, in Piagnone Florence, in

Spain of the Inquisition. Religion would thus appear fated, by its very nature, to starve out all else, and its own self into the bargain.

What will be the answer to, the escape from, all this, provided by religion itself? The answer and escape will be provided by the intrinsic nature of the human soul, and of the religious appeal made to it. For if this appeal must be conceived by the soul, in exact proportion to the religiousness of both, as incomprehensible by it, as exceeding its present, and even its potential, powers of comprehension; if again this appeal must demand a sacrifice of various inclinations felt at the time to be wrong or inferior; if it must come home to the soul with a sense of constraining obligation, as an act of submission and of sacrifice which it ought to and must make: yet it will as necessarily be conceived, at the same time, and again in exact proportion to the religiousness both of the soul and of the appeal, as the expression of Mind, of Spirit, and the impression of another mind and spirit; as the manifestation of an infinite Personality, responded and assented to by a personality, finite indeed yet capable of indefinite growth. And hence the fixity of the revelation and of the soul's assent to it, will be as the fixity of a fountain-head, or as the fixity of river-banks; or again as the fixity of a plant's growth, or of the gradual leavening of bread, or as that of the successive evolution and identity of the human body. The fixity, in a word, will be conceived and found to be a fixity of orientation, a definiteness of affinities and of assimilative capacity.

Only full trust, only unconditional surrender suffice for religion. But then religion excites and commands this in a person towards a Person; a surrender to be achieved not in some thing, but in some one—a some one who *is* at all, only in as much as he is living, loving, growing; and to be performed, not towards some thing, but towards Some One, Whose right, indeed Whose very power to claim me, consists precisely in that He is Himself absolutely, infinitely and actually, what I am but derivatively, finitely and potentially.

Thus the very same act and reasons which completely bind me, do so only to true growth and to indefinite expansion. I shall, it is true, ever go back and cling to the definite spatial and temporal manifestations of this infinite Spirit's personality, but I shall, by this same act, proclaim His eternal presentness and inexhaustible self-interpreting illumination. By the same act by which I believe in the revelation of the workshop of Nazareth, of the Lake of Galilee, of Gethsemane and Calvary, I believe that this revelation is inexhaustible, and that its gradual analysis and theory, and above all its successive practical application, experimentation, acceptance or rejection, and unfolding, confer and call forth poignant dramatic freshness and inexhaustible uniqueness upon and within every human life, unto the end of time.

All this takes place through the present, the *hic et nunc*, co-operation of the living God and the living soul. And this ever-to-be reconquered, ever-costing and checkered, ever "deepenable" interpretation, is as truly fresh as if it were a fresh revelation. For all that comes from the living God, and is worked out by living souls, is ever living and enlivening: there is no such thing as mere repetition, or differentiation by mere number, place, and time, in this Kingdom of Life, either as to God's action or the soul's. Infinite Spirit Himself, He creates an indefinite number of, at first largely but potential, persons, no one of which is identical with any other, and provokes and supports an indefinite number of ever different successive acts on the part of each and all of them, that so, through the sum-total of such sources and streams of difference, the nearest creaturely approach may be achieved to the ocean of His own infinite richness.

2. *In the Emotional and Volitional Element, as against the Historical and Institutional Element.*

Now the tendency of a soul, when once awake to this necessary freshness and interiority of feeling with regard to God's and her own action, will again be towards an impoverishing oneness. It will now tend to shrink away from the External, Institutional altogether. For though it cannot but have experienced the fact that it was by contact with this External that, like unto Antaeus at his contact with Mother Earth, it gained its experience of the Internal, yet each such experience tends to obliterate the traces of its own occasion. Indeed the interior feeling thus achieved tends, in the long run, to make the return to the contact with the fact that occasioned, and to the act that produced it, a matter of effort and repugnance. It seems a case of "a man's returning to his mother's womb"; and is indeed a new birth to a fuller life, and hence humiliating, obscure, concentrated, effortful, a matter of trust and labor and pain and faith and love—a true death of and adieu to the self of this moment, however advanced this self may seem—a fully willed purifying pang. Only through such dark and narrow Thermopylae passes can we issue on to the wide, sunlit plains. And both plain and sunshine can never last long at a time; and they will cease altogether, if they are not interrupted by this apparent shadow of the valley of death, this concrete action, which invariably modifies not only the soul's environment, but above all the soul itself.

Thus does a simply mental prayer readily feel, to the soul that possesses the habit of it, a complete substitute for all vocal prayer; and a generally prayerful habit of mind readily appears an improvement upon all conscious acts of prayer. Thus does a general, indeterminate consciousness of Christ's spirit and presence easily feel larger and wider, to him who has it, than the apparent contraction of mind and heart involved in devotion to Him pictured in the definite Gospel scenes or localized in His Eucharistic presence. Thus again does a general disposition of regret for sin and of determination to do better readily feel nobler, to him who has it, than the apparent materiality and peddling casuistry, the attempting the impossible, of fixing for oneself the kind and degree of one's actual sins, and of determining upon definite, detailed reforms.

Yet, in all these cases, this feeling will rapidly lead the soul on to become unconsciously weak or feverish, unless the soul manfully escapes from this feeling's tyranny, and nobly bends under the yoke and cramps itself within the narrow limits of the life-giving concrete act. The Church's insistence upon *some* vocal prayer, upon *some* definite, differentiated, specific acts of the various moral and theological virtues, upon Sacramental practice throughout all the states and stages of the Christian life, is but a living commentary upon the difficulty and importance of the point under discussion. And History, as we have seen, confirms all this.

3. *In the Emotional and Volitional, singly or in combination with the Historical and Institutional, as against the Analytic and Speculative Element.*

But just as the Institutional easily tends to a weakening both of the Intellectual and of the Emotional, so does the Emotional readily turn against not only the Institutional but against the Intellectual as well. This latter hostility will take two forms. Inasmuch as the feeling clings to historical facts and persons, it will instinctively elude or attempt to suppress all critical examination and analysis of these its supports. Inasmuch as it feeds upon its own emotion, which (as so much pure emotion) is, at any one of its stages, ever intensely one and intensely exclusive, it will instinctively fret under and oppose all that slow discrimination and mere approximation, that collection of a few certainties, many probabilities, and innumerable possibilities, all that pother over a very little, which seem to make up the sum of all human knowledge. Such Emotion will thus tend to be hostile to Historical Criticism, and to all the Critical, Analytic stages and forms of Philosophy. It turns away instinctively from the cold manifold of thinking; and it shrinks spontaneously from the hard opaque of action and of the external. All this will again be found to be borne out by history.

A combination of Institutionalism and Experimentalism against Intellectualism is another not infrequent abuse, and one which is not hard to explain. For if external, definite facts and acts are found to lead to certain internal, deep, all-embracing emotions and experiences, the soul can to a certain extent live and thrive in and by a constant moving backwards and forwards between the Institution and the Emotion alone, and can thus constitute an ever-tightening bond and dialogue, increasingly exclusive of all else. For although the Institution will, taken in itself, retain for the Emotion a certain dryness and hardness, yet the Emotion can and often will associate with this Institution whatever that contact with it has been found to bring and to produce. And if the Institution feels hard and obscure, it is not, like the Thinking, cold and transparent. Just because the Institution appears to the emotional nature as though further from its feeling, and yet is experienced as a mysterious cause or occasion of this feeling, the emotional nature is fairly, often passionately, ready to welcome what it can thus rest on and lean on, as something having a comfortable fixity both of relation and of resistance. But with regard to Thinking, all this is different. For thought is sufficiently near to Feeling, necessarily to produce friction and competition of some sort, and seems, with its keen edge and endless mobility, to be the born implacable foe of the dull, dead givenness of the Institutional, and of the equal givenness of any one Emotional mood. One of the spontaneous activities of the human soul, the Analytic and Speculative faculty, seems habitually, instinctively to labor at depersonalizing all it touches, and thus continually both to undermine and discrown the deeply personal work and world of the experimental forces of the soul. Indeed the thinking seems to be doing this necessarily, since by its very essence it begins and ends with laws, qualities, functions, and parts—with abstractions, which, at best, can be but skeletons and empty forms of the real and actual, and which, of themselves, ever tend to represent all Reality as something static, not dynamic, as a thing, not as a person or Spirit.

Here again the true solution will be found in an ever fuller conception of Personality, and of its primary place in the religious life.

For even the bare possibility of the truth of all religion, especially of any one of the characteristic doctrines of Christianity, involves a group of personalist convictions. Here the human person begins more as a possibility than a reality. Here the moral and spiritual character has to be built up slowly, painfully, laboriously, throughout all the various stages and circumstances of life, with their endless combinations of pleasure and pain, trouble and temptation, inner and outer help and hindrance, success and failure. Here the simply Individual is transformed into the truly Personal only by the successive sacrifice of the lower, of the merely animal and impoverishingly selfish self, with the help of God's constant prevenient, concomitant, and subsequent grace. And here this constantly renewed dropping and opposing of the various lower selves, in proportion as they appear and become lower, to the soul's deepest insight, in the growing light of its conscience and the increasing elevation of the moral personality, involves that constant death to self, that perpetual conversion, that unification and peace in and through a continuous inner self-estrangement and conflict, which is the very breath and joy of the religious life.

Only if all this be so, to a quite unpicturable extent, can even the most elementary Christianity be more than an amiable intruder, or a morbid surplusage in the world. And at the same time, if this be so, then all within us is in need of successive, never-ending purification and elaboration; and the God who has made man with a view to his gradually achieving, and conquering his real self, must have stored means and instruments, for the attainment of this man's true end, in constant readiness, within himself. Now our whole intellectual nature is a great storehouse of one special class of such instruments. For it is clear that the moral and spiritual side of our nature will, more than any other, constantly require three things: Rest, Expression, and Purification. And the intellectual activities will, if only they be kept sufficiently vigorous and independent, alone be in a position sufficiently to supply some forms of these three needs. For they can rest the moral-spiritual activities, since they, the intellectual ones, primarily neglect emotion, action, and persons, and are directly occupied with abstractions and with things. They can and should express the results of those moral, spiritual activities, because the religious facts and experiences require, like all other facts, to be constantly stated and re-stated by the intellect in terms fairly understandable by the civilization and culture of the successive ages of the world. Above all, they can help to purify those moral-spiritual activities, owing to their interposing, by their very nature, a zone of abstraction, of cool, clear thinking, of seemingly adequate and exhaustive, but actually impoverishing and artificial concepts, and of apparently ultimate, though really only phenomenal determinism, between the direct informations of the senses, to which the Individual clings, and the inspirations of the moral and spiritual nature, which constitute the Person.   Thus this intellectual abstractive element is, if neither minimized in the life of the soul, nor allowed to be its sole element or its last, a sobering, purifying, mortifying, vivifying bath and fire.

VII. THREE FINAL OBJECTIONS TO SUCH A CONCEPTION OF RELIGION, AND THEIR ANSWERS.

Now there are three obvious objections to such a conception: with their consideration, this Introduction shall conclude.

1. *This conception not excessively intellectual.*
Does not, in the first place, such a view of life appear preposterously intellectual? What of the uneducated, of the toiling millions? What of most women and of all children? Are then all these, the overwhelming majority of mankind, the objects of Christ's predilection, the very types chosen by Himself of His spirit and of God's ideal for man, precluded from an essential element of religion? Or are we, at the least, to hold that an ethical and spiritual advantage is necessarily attached, and this too for but a small minority of mankind, to a simple intellectual function and activity? If there was a thing specially antagonistic to Christ and condemned by Him, it was the arrogance of the Schools of His day; if there is a thing apparently absent from Christ's own life it is all philosophizing: even to suggest its presence seems at once to disfigure and to lower Him. Is then Reasoning, the School, to be declared not only necessary for some and for mankind at large, but necessary, in a sense, for all men and for the religious life itself?

The answer to all this appears not far to seek. The element which we have named the intellectual is but one of the faculties of every living soul; and hence, in some degree and form, it is present and operative in every one of us. And there is probably no greater difference between these degrees and forms, with regard to this element, than there is between the degrees and forms found in the other two elements of religion. For this intellectual, determinist element would be truly represented by every however simple mental attention to *things* and their mechanism, their necessary laws and requirements. Hence, the Venerable Anna Maria Taigi, the Roman working-man's wife, attending to the requirements and rules of good washing and of darning of clothes; St. Jean Batiste de la Salle, the Breton gentleman, studying the psychology of school-children's minds, and adapting his school system to it; St. Jerome laboring at his minute textual criticism of manuscripts of all kinds; St. Anselm and St. Thomas toiling at the construction of their dialectic systems—all these, amongst endless other cases, are but illustrations of the omnipresence and endless variety of this element, which is busy with the rules and processes that govern things.

And it is impossible to see why, simply because of their superior intellectual gifts and development, men like Clement of Alexandria and Origen, Cassian and Duns Scotus, Nicolas of Coes and Pascal, Rosmini and Newman, should count as necessarily less near to God and Christ than others with fewer of such gifts and opportunities. For it is not as though such gifts were considered as ever *of themselves* constituting any moral or spiritual worth. Nothing can be more certain than that great mental powers can be accompanied by emptiness or depravity of heart. The identical standard is to be applied to these as to all other gifts: they are not to be considered as substitutes, but only as additional material and means for the moral and spiritual life; and it is only inasmuch as they are actually so used that they can effectively help on sanctity itself. It is only contended here that such gifts do furnish additional means and materials for the devoted will and grace-moved soul, towards the richest and deepest spiritual life. For the intellectual virtues are no mere empty name: candor, moral courage, intellectual honesty, scrupulous accuracy, chivalrous fairness, endless docility to facts, disinterested collaboration, unconquerable hopefulness and perseverance, manly renunciation of popularity and easy honours, love of bracing labour and strengthening solitude: these and many other cognate qualities bear upon them the impress of God and of His Christ. And yet they all as surely find but a scanty field of development outside of the intellectual life, as they are not the only virtues or class of virtues, and as the other two elements each produce a quite unique group of virtues of their own and require other means and materials for their exercise.

2. *Such a conception not Pelagian.*

But, in the second place, is not such a view of life Pelagian at bottom? Have we not argued throughout, as if the religious life were to be begun, and carried on, and achieved simply by a constant succession of efforts of our own; and as though it could be built up by us, like to some work of art, by a careful, conscious balancing of part against part? Is not all this pure Naturalism? Is not religion a life, and hence an indivisible whole? And is not this life simply the gift of God, capable of being dimly apprehended at present, but not of being clearly analyzed in its process of formation?

Here again there is a true answer, I think. Simply all and every one of our acts, our very physical existence and persistence, is dependent, at every moment and in every direction, upon the prevenient, accompanying and subsequent power and help of God; and still more is every religious, every truly spiritual and supernatural act of the soul impossible without the constant action of God's grace. Yet not only does all this not prevent the soul from consciously acting on her own part, and according to the laws of her own being; but God's grace acts in and through the medium of her acts, inasmuch as these are good: so that the very same action which, seen as it were from without, is the effect of our own volition, is, seen as it were from within, the effect of God's grace. The more costly is our act of love or of sacrifice, the more ethical and spiritual, and the more truly it is our own deepest self-expression, so much the more, at the same time, is this action a thing received as well as given, and that we have it to give, and that we can and do give it, is itself a pure gift of God.

What then is wanted, if we would really cover the facts of the case, is evidently not a conception which would minimize the human action, and would represent the latter as shrinking, in proportion as God's action increases; but one which, on the contrary, fully faces, and keeps a firm hold of, the mysterious paradox which pervades all true life, and which shows us the human soul as self-active in proportion to God's action within it, according to St. Bernard's doctrine already quoted. Grace and the Will thus rise and fall, in their degree of action, together; and man will never be so fully active, so truly and intensely himself, as when he is most possessed by God.

And since man's action is thus in actual fact mysteriously double, it should ever be so considered by him; and he should, as St. Ignatius of Loyola says, "pray as if all depended on his prayer, and act as if all depended on his action." Hence all man's action, though really incapable of existing for an instant without the aid of God, and though never exclusively his own, can be studied throughout, preliminarily as though it were his exclusive production on its analyzable, human side. And man not only can, he ought to be as reasonably analytic and systematic about this study of his action as he was careful and consistent in its production—in both cases, whilst praying and believing as though it were all from God, he can and should behave also as though this action were exclusively his own. As St. Thomas admirably says: "We attribute one and the same effect both to a natural cause and to a divine force, not in the sense of that effect proceeding in part from God, and in part from the human agent. But the effect proceeds entire from both, according to a different mode: just as, in music, the whole effect is attributed to the instrument, and the same entire effect is referred to man as the principal agent."[8]

3. *Such a conception not Epicurean.*

But, in the last place, is not such a view of life Epicurean? Where is the Cross and Self-Renunciation? Is it not Christ Himself Who has bidden us cut off our right hand and pluck out our right eye, if they offend; Who has declared that he who hateth not his own father and mother for His sake is not worthy of Him; Who has asked, "What doth it profit a man, if he gain the whole world, and suffer the loss of his own soul?" and Who has pronounced a special woe upon the rich, and a special blessing upon the poor in spirit? Does not our view, on the contrary, bid a man attend to his hands and eyes, rather than to their possible or even actual offending, euphemistically described here as "friction"; bid him love his father and mother, even though this introduce a conflict into his affections; bid him take care to gain, as far as may be, the whole of his own possible interior and exterior world, as though this would of itself be equivalent to his saving his soul; and thus bid him become rich and full and complex, an aesthete rather than a man of God? In a word, is not our position a masked Paganism, a new Renaissance rather than the nobly stern old Christianity?

Now here again a true answer is found in a clear intelligence of the actual implications of the position. For if the Intellectual action were here taken as capable of alone, or in any degree directly, forming the foundation of all our other life, so that on a mathematically clear and complete system, appealing to and requiring the abstractive powers alone would, later on, be built, according to our own further determination, the Institutional and Experimental, or both or neither; then such a position, if possible and actualized, would indeed save us the simultaneous energizing of our whole complex nature, and would, so far, well deserve the accusation of unduly facilitating life; it might be taken as, at least, not beginning with the Cross. But here this is not so. For from the first the External and the Mystical elements are held to be at least as necessary and operative as the Intellectual element; and it is impossible to see how the elimination of this latter, and of the ever-expensive keeping it and its rivals each at their own work, could deepen the truly moral sufferings and sacrifices of the soul's life.

If again the Intellectual action were taken, as by Gnosticism of all sorts, as the eventual goal of the whole, so that the External and Mystical would end by being absorbed into the Intellectual, our Knowledge becoming coextensive with Reality itself, then we might again, and with still deeper truth, be accused of eliminating the element of effort and of sacrifice—the Cross. But here, on the contrary, not only the Intellectual alone does not begin the soul's life or build up its conditions, but the Intellectual alone does not conclude and crown it. Eternally will different soul-functions conjoin in a common work, eternally will God and the souls of our fellows be for us realities in diverse degrees outside of and beyond our own apprehension of them, and eternally shall we apprehend them differently and to a different degree by our intelligence, by our affection, and our volition. Hence, even in eternity itself we can, without exceeding the limits of sober thinking and of psychological probability, find a field for the exercise by our souls of something corresponding to the joy and greatness of noble self-sacrifice here below. The loving soul will there, in the very home of love, give itself wholly to and be fulfilled by God, and yet the soul will possess an indefinitely heightened apprehension of the immense excess of this its love and act above its knowledge, and of God Himself above both. And here again it is impossible to see how the elimination of the intellectual element, which becomes thus the very measure of the soul's own limitations, and of the exceeding greatness of its love and of its Lover, would make the conception more efficaciously humbling and Christian.

Both at the beginning, then, and throughout, and even at the end of the soul's life, the intellectual element is necessary, and this above all for the planting fully and finally, in the very depths of the personality, the Cross, the sole means to the soul's true Incoronation.

NOTES

1.   I have found much help towards formulating the following experiences and convictions in Professor William James's striking paper, "Reflex Action and Theism," in *The Will to Believe*, pp.111–114, 1897.

2.   I have been much helped towards the general contents of the next four sections by that profoundly thoughtful little book, Fechner's *Die drei Motive und Grunde des Glaubens*, 1863, and by the large and rich conception elaborated by Cardinal Newman in his Preface to *The Via Media*, 1877, Vol. I, pp. xv–xciv.

3.   See, for this point. the admirably clear analysis in J. Volkelt's *Kant's Erkenntnisstheorie*, 1879, pp. 160–234. This book is probably the most conclusive demonstration extant of the profound self-contradictions running through Kant's Epistemology.

4.   *Works of St. John of the Cross*, translated by David Lewis, Vol.1, ed.1889, p.298.

5.   *Ibid.* Vol. II, ed. 1890, pp.541, 542.

6.   Oeuvres de Fénelon, Paris, Lebel, Vol. IX, 1828, pp.632, 652, 668.

7.   *Tractatus de Gratia et Libero Arbitrio*, cap. xiv, 47.

8.   *Summa c. Gentiles*, iii, c.70, in fine.

SELECTED
BIBLIOGRAPHY

T he following bibliography includes only those writings of von Hügel which were used for this study. For a more complete bibliography, see James J. Kelly, *Baron Friedrich von Hügel's Philosophy of Religion* (Lueven: University Press, 1983), pp. 14–26.

1. Archives and Manuscript Collections

Archives of the Archdiocese of Westminster.
    Papers of Cardinal Herbert Vaughan (1892–1903).
    Papers of Cardinal Francis Bourne (1903–1935).
Archives of the Diocese of Southwark.
    Vigilance Committee File.
British Library, London.
    Von Hügel-Tyrrell Correspondence. Add. MSS 44927–44931.
    Von Hügel-Petre Correspondence. Add. MSS 45361–45362.
    Letters to Maude Petre from various correspondents. Add. MSS45744–45745.
    Petre Papers, Letters of George Tyrrell to Maude Petre (1898–1908). Add. MS 52367.
    George Tyrrell's correspondence (1900–1908); material concerning Tyrrell's death (1909–1933). Add. MS 52368. Maude Petre's Diaries (1900–1942). Add MSS 52372–52379.
    Letters of Bremond to Maude Petre. Add. MS 52380.
    Correspondence of Maude Petre; correspondence of James A. Walker, Petre's literary executor. Add. MS 52381.

St. Andrews University Library.
   Von Hügel Papers. Diaries 43 vols, 1877–79, 1884–1900, 1902–25.
   Von Hügel's will. MS B3280.H8.
   Letters to numerous correspondents, including:
   Blondel, Maurice MS B3280.H8 (1895–1924).
   Bremond, Henri MS 30284 (1899–1923).
   Chapman, Adeline MS 37194 (1901–1921).
   Clutton, Ralph and Margaret MS 30994–5 (1912–13).
   Lilley, Alfred L. MSS 30513–30580 (1903–1925).
   Mansel, Juliet MS 37194 (1910–1921).
   Mansel, Mildred MS 37194 (1910–1915).
   Osborne, Charles MS 37018/1–5 (1906–1910).
   Smith, Norman Kemp MS 30420 (1919–1924).
   Underhill, Evelyn MS 5552 (1921–1924).
   Ward, James MS 30498 (1902–1923).
   Lilley Papers. Letters of Tyrrell to Lilley (1903–1909).
   Letters of Maude Petre to Lilley (1904–1942).
   Wilfrid Ward Family Papers. Letters of Maude Petre to Ward
        (1897–1910) MS 38347,vii,235
   Letters of von Hügel to Ward MS 38347,vii,143.
   Letters to von Hügel from various correspondents including:
   Bishop, Edmund MSS 2210–2234 (1904–1913).
   Blondel, Maurice MSS 2235–2289 (1895–1924).
   Huvelin, Henri MSS 2690–2704 (1886–1904).
   Inge, William Ralph MSS 2705–2710 (1911–1923).
   James, John George MS 2711 (1909).
   Newman, John Henry MSS 2884–2900 (1874–1884).
   Petre, Maude MS 2910 (1883).
Downside Abbey Archives, Stratton on the Fosse, Bath
   Von Hügel Papers. MS 1272 (uncatalogued).
   Notes on Pauline von Hügel.
   Letters of Tyrrell to Gertrud (1897–98).
   Letters of von Hügel to Gertrud.
   Letters of von Hügel to Hildegard.
   Letters from E. Gardner to Hildegard.
   Letter from Sr. Thekla to Hildegard.
   Edward C. Butler Papers. Butler–von Hügel correspondence.
Balliol College Library, Oxford
   Caird, Edward Modern MSS collection, Box 2.

Bodleian Library, Oxford
    Dawson, Albert   MS Eng. Lett. c. 196 f. 62.
    Gardner, Percy   MS Eng. Lett. c. 55 fs. 195–229.
    Hopkins, Gerard MS Eng. Misc. a.8 f. 68.
    Marvin, Francis MS Eng. Lett. c. 263–267.
    Sanday, William MS Eng.Misc.d.123(2)fs. 610–13.
    Zimmern, Alfred   MS Zimmern 15 fs. 37–42.

2. Published Writings of Friedrich von Hügel

"Carl von Hügel, The Story of the Escape of Prince Metternich,"
    National Review 1 June 1883, pp. 588–605.
"Chronique," *Bulletin critique* 6:2 (May 1885), pp. 175–78; 7:6 (March
    1886), pp. 117–18; 7:7 (April 1886), p. 135; 7:24 (December 1886),
    pp. 477–78; 12:6 (March 1891), pp. 119–20; 12:24 (December
    1891), pp. 278–79.
"The Spiritual Writings of Père Grou, S.J." *Tablet* 74 (December 1889),
    pp. 900-901; 1029–31.
"The Papal Encyclical and Mr. Gore," *Spectator* 3438 (19 May 1894), pp.
    684–85.
"Fénelon's 'Spiritual Letters'," *Tablet* 83 (June 1894), pp. 857–58.
"The Roman Catholic View of Inspiration," *Spectator* 3440 (2 June
    1894), p. 750.
"The Church and the Bible: The Two Stages of Their Inter-Relation,"
    Dublin Review 115 (October 1894), pp. 313–41; 116 (April 1895),
    pp. 306–37; 117 (October 1895), pp. 275–304.
"L'Abbé Duchesne and Anglican Orders," *Tablet* 84 (November 1894),
    p. 776.
"Professor Eucken on the Struggle for Spiritual Life," *Spectator* 3568 (14
    November 1896), pp. 679–81.
"The Comma Johanneum," *Tablet* 89 (5 June 1896), pp. 896–97.
"Caterina Fiesca Adorna, the Saint of Genoa, 1447–1510," *Hampstead
    Annual* (1898), pp. 70–85.
"A Proposito dell'Abate Loisy," *Studi Religiosi* 1 (July–August, 1901),
    pp. 348–50.
"The Case of Abbé Loisy," *The Pilot* 9 (9 January 1904), pp. 30–31.
"The Case of M. Loisy," *The Pilot* 9 (23 January 1904), p. 94.
"The Abbé Loisy and the Holy Office," *The Times* (2 March 1904), p.
    15 (signed Romanus).

"Introduction to letters by Bailey Saunders and Loisy," *The Times* (30 April 1904), p. 6.

"Du Christ éternel et de nos christologies successives." *La Quinzaine* 58(1904), pp. 285–312.

"Discussions: M. Loisy's Type of Catholicism," *Hibbert Journal* 3 (April 1905), pp. 599–600.

"Experience and Transcendence," *Dublin Review* 138 (April 1906), pp. 357–79.

The Papal Commission and the Pentateuch. With Charles A. Briggs. London: Longmans, Green & Co., 1906.

"The Relations Between God and Man in *The New Theology* of Rev. R. J. Campbell," *Albany Review* 1 (September 1907), pp. 650–68.

"The Abbé Loisy," *Tablet* 3 (7 March 1908), pp. 378–79.

Review, *Les Evangiles Synoptiques*, *Hibbert Journal* 6 (July 1908), pp. 926–30.

"L'Abate Loisy e il problema dei Vangeli Sinottici," *Il Rinnovamento* 3 (January-June 1908), pp. 209–34; 4 (July-December 1908), pp. 1–44; 5 (January-June 1909), pp. 396–423 (signed H).

The Mystical Element of Religion As Studied in Saint Catherine of Genoa and Her Friends. 2 vols. London: Dent, 1908; 2nd edn, 1923; reprint edn, 1927.

"The Death-Bed of Father Tyrrell," *Tablet* 114 (31 July 1909), p. 182.

"The Late Father Tyrrell and the Faith," *Tablet* 114 (6 November 1909), p. 738.

"Father Tyrrell: Some Memorials of the Last Twelve Years of His Life." *Hibbert Journal* 8 (1910), pp. 233–52.

"John, The Apostle," *The Encyclopedia Britannica*, 11th ed., v. 15 (1911), pp. 432–33; "John, Gospel of St.," v. 15 (1911), pp. 452–58; "Loisy, Alfred Firmin," v. 16 (1911), pp. 926–28.

Eternal Life: A Study of Its Implications and Applications. Edinburgh: T. T. Clark, 1912.

"The Religious Philosophy of Rudolf Eucken," *Hibbert Journal* 10 (April 1912), pp. 660–77.

"Father Tyrrell," *Tablet 120* (30 November 1912), pp. 866–67.

"Julius Wellhausen," *Times Literary Supplement* 842 (7 March 1918), p. 117.

The German Soul in its Attitude towards Ethics and Christianity. The State and War. London, Paris, Toronto: J. M. Dent & Sons, 1916.

"Eudoxe Irénée Mignot," *Contemporary Review* 113 (1918), pp. 520–21.

Essays and Addresses on the Philosophy of Religion. London: Dent, 1921.

"Apologist of Religion,'" *Times Literary Supplement* 1040 (22 December 1921), p. 860.

"Louis Duchesne," *Times Literary Supplement* 1062 (25 May 1922), p. 342.

"Ernst Troeltsch," *Times Literary Supplement* 1106 (29 March 1923), p. 216.

Ernst Troeltsch. *Christian Thought: Its History and Application.* Ed. with an Introduction by F. von Hügel. London: University of London Press, 1923.

"Der Mystiker und die Kirche aus anlass des Sâdhu," *Das Hochland* 22 (December 1924), pp. 320–30.

Some Letters of Baron von Hügel. Ed. F. R. Lillie. Chicago: Privately printed, 1925.

Essays and Addresses on the Philosophy of Religion. Second Series. Ed. Edmund Gardner. London: Dent, 1926.

Selected Letters 1896–1924. Ed. with a Memoir by Bernard Holland. London: Dent, 1927.

The Life of Prayer. London: Dent, 1927.

Letters from Baron Friedrich von Hügel to a Niece. Edited with an Introduction by Gwendolen Greene. London: Dent, 1928.

The Reality of God and Religion and Agnosticism. Ed. Edmund Gardner. London: Dent, 1931.

Mansel, Juliet. "A Letter from Baron von Hügel," *Dublin Review* 222 (July 1951), pp. 1–11.

Abercombie, Nigel. "Friedrich von Hügel's Letters to Edmund Bishop," *Dublin Review* 227 (January-October 1953), pp. 68–78, 179–89, 285–98, 419–38.

Whelan, Joseph P. "Friedrich von Hügel's Letters to Martin D'Arcy," *Month* n.s.42 (July-August 1969), pp. 23–36.

Whelan, Joseph P. "The Parent as Spiritual Director: A Newly Published Letter of Friedrich von Hügel," *Month* n.s.2 (August-September 1970), pp. 52–57, 84–87.

James J. Kelly, "On the Fringe of the Modernist Crisis: Correspondence of von Hügel and Abbot Cuthbert Butler," *Downside Review* 97 (October 1979), pp. 275–303.

James J. Kelly, "The Modernist Controversy in England: The Correspondence between Friedrich von Hügel and Percy Gardner, I and II," *Downside Review* 99 (January, April 1981), pp. 40–58, 119–36.

Adams, James Luther. "Letter from Friedrich von Hügel to William James," *Downside Review* 98 (1980), pp. 214–236.

Letters of Baron Friedrich von Hügel and Professor Norman Kemp Smith. Ed. Lawrence F. Barmann. New York: Fordham University Press, 1981.

Anthologies of von Hügel's Writings:

Readings from Friedrich von Hügel. Compiled and introduced by Algar Thorold. London: Dent, 1928.

Baron von Hügel: Man of God. Compiled and introduced by P. Franklin Chambers. London: Collins, 1964; first published in 1945.

Spiritual Counsels and Letters of Baron Friedrich von Hügel. Ed. with an Introduction by Douglas V. Steere. New York: Harper & Row, 1964.

3. Selected Secondary Sources

Almond, Philip C. *Mystical Experience and Religious Doctrine: An Investigation of the Study of Mysticism in World Religions*. Berlin: Mouton, 1982.

Anstein, Walter L. *Protestant Versus Catholic in Mid-Victorian England: Mr. Newdegate and the Nuns*. Columbia & London: University of Missouri Press, 1982.

Appleby, R. Scott. *"Church and Age Unite!" The Modernist Impulse in American Catholicism*. Notre Dame: University of Notre Dame Press, 1992.

Au, Wilkie. "Holistic Catechesis: Keeping our Balance in the 1990s," *Religious Education* 86 (1991), pp. 347–60.

Barmann, Lawrence. *Baron Friedrich von Hügel and the Modernist Crisis in England*. Cambridge: University Press, 1972.

Barmann, Lawrence. "Friedrich von Hügel as Modernist and as More Than Modernist," *The Catholic Historical Review* 75 (1989), pp. 211–32.

Barmann, Lawrence. "Confronting Secularization: Origins of the London Society for the Study of Religion," *Church History* 62 (1993), pp. 22–40.

Barmann, Lawrence, ed. *The Letters of Baron Friedrich von Hügel and Professor Norman Kemp Smith*. New York: Fordham University Press, 1981.

Baum, Gregory, ed. *Journeys: The Impact of Personal Experience on Religious Thought*. New York: Paulist, 1975.

Bedoyère, Michael de la. *The Life of Baron von Hügel*. London: J. M. Dent & Sons, 1951.

Blanchet, Andre. *Henri Bremond 1865-1904*. Paris: Aubier Montaigne, Paris, 1975.

Blunt, Wilfrid Scawen. *My Diaries: Being a Personal Narrative of Events, 1888–1914*, Part II, 1900–1914. London: Martin Secker, 1919.

Bossy, John. *The English Catholic Community 1570–1859*. New York: Oxford University Press, 1976.

Boudens, R. "George Tyrrell: Last Illness, Death and Burial." *Ephemerides Theologicae Lovanienses* 6 (December 1985), pp. 340–54.

Brown, R. K. "Newman and von Hügel: A Record of an Early Morning Meeting," *Month* n.s. 26 (1961), pp. 24–33.

Burke, Peter, ed. *New Perspectives on Historical Writing*. University Park, PN: Pennsylvania State University Press, 1991.

Chadwich, Owen. *The Victorian Church* Part II. London: Adam & Charles Black, 1970.

Clifton, Michael. *Amigo—Friend of the Poor: Bishop of Southwark, 1904–1949*. Leominster, Herefordshire: Fowler Wright Books Ltd., 1987.

Congar, Yves M. J. *Dialogue between Christians: Catholic Contributions to Ecumenism*. Westminster, Maryland: Newman Press, 1966.

Connelly, Gerard. "The Transubstantiation of Myth: Towards a New Popular Nineteenth Century Catholicism," *Journal of Ecclesiastical History* 35 (1984), pp. 78–104.

Crews, Clyde F. *English Catholic Modernism: Maude Petre's Way of Faith*. Notre Dame University Press, 1984.

Dakin, A. Hazard. *Von Hügel and the Supernatural*. London: SPCK, 1934.

Daly, Gabriel. *Transcendence and Immanence: A Study in Catholic Modernism and Integralism*. Oxford: Clarendon, 1980.

Dangerfield, George. *The Strange Death of Liberal England*. London: Constable & Co., 1936.

Daniel-Rops, Henri. *A Fight for God*. London: Dent & Sons, 1966.

Doyle, Peter. "The Education and Training of Roman Catholic Priests in Nineteenth Century England," *Journal of Ecclesiastical History* 35 (1984), pp. 208–19.

Duffy, Eamon. "Will the Real von Hügel Please Stand Up?" *Heythrop Journal* 22 (1981), pp. 49–55.

Dupré, Louis K. *Passage to Modernity: An Essay on the Hermeneutics of Nature and Culture*. New Haven: Yale University Press, 1993.

Egan, Harvey D. *Christian Mysticism: The Future of a Tradition*. New York: Pueblo, 1984.

Egan, Harvey D. *What Are They Saying About Mystics?* New York: Paulist Press, 1982.

Eigelsbach, Jo Ann. *Wilfrid Ward and the Challenge to Faith at the Turn of the Twentieth Century.* Unpublished Doctoral Dissertation, Catholic University of America, 1985.

Eigelsbach, Jo Ann. "The Intellectual Dialogue of Friedrich von Hügel and Wilfrid Ward," *Downside Review* 104 (1986), pp. 144–57.

Falconi, Carlo. *The Popes in the Twentieth Century: From Pius X to John XXIII.* Tr. Muriel Grindrod. London: Weidenfeld & Nicolson, 1967.

Fogazzaro, Antonio. *The Saint.* Tr. from Italian by M. Prichard-Agnetti. London: Hodder & Stoughton, 1906.

Gerson, Theresa Krystyniak. *Maude D. Petre and Catholic Modernism in England.* Unpublished M.A. Thesis, University of St. Michael's College, Toronto, 1975.

Goodier, Alan. "Baron Friedrich von Hügel's Spiritual Outlook," *Month* (1939), pp. 11–21.

Green, Martin, *Yeat's Blessings on von Hügel: Essays on Literature and Religion.* London: Longmans, 1967.

Guinan, Alastair. "Portrait of a Devout Humanist M. l'Abbé Henri Bremond: An Essay Introducing His Life and Thought," *Harvard Theological Review* 47 (January 1954), pp. 15–53.

Hamilton, Robert. "Faith and Knowledge: The Autobiography of Maude Petre." *Downside Review* 85 (1967), pp. 148–59.

Hanbury, Michael. "Baron von Hügel and the Ecumenical Movement," *Month* n.s. 29 (1963), p. 140.

Healy, Charles. "M. Petre: Her Life and Significance." *Recusant History* 15 (1979), pp. 23–42.

Heaney, John J. "The Enigma of the Later von Hügel," *Heythrop Journal* 6 (1965), pp. 145–59.

Heaney, John J. *The Modernist Crisis: von Hügel.* Washington: Corpus Books, 1968.

Henn, T. R. *The Lonely Tower: Studies in the Poetry of W. B. Yeats.* London: University Paperbacks, 1950, 1965.

Higdon, David Leon. "Saint Catherine, Von Hügel, and Graham Greene's *The End of the Affair,*" *English Studies: A Journal of English Language and Literature* 62 (1981), pp. 46–52.

Hinson, E. Glenn, ed. *Spirituality in Ecumenical Perspective.* Louisville, Kentucky: Westminster/John Knox Press, 1993.

Holmes, J. Derek. *More Roman than Rome: English Catholicism in the Nineteenth Century.* London: Burns & Oates, 1978.

Holmes, J. Derek. *The Triumph of the Holy See: A Short History of the Papacy in the Nineteenth Century.* London: Burns & Oates, 1978.

Hughes, Gerard W. *God of Surprises.* New York: Paulist Press, 1985.

Hynes, William J. "A Hidden Nexus between Catholic and Protestant Modernism: C.A. Briggs in Correspondence with Loisy, von Hügel and Genocchi," *Downside Review* 105 (July 1987), pp. 193–223.

Izquierdo, Cesar. "History and Truth: The Exegetical Position of Baron von Hügel," *Downside Review* 108 (1990), pp. 295–312.

James, William. *The Varieties of Religious Experience: A Study in Human Nature.* London: Longmans, 1935.

Johnson, Elizabeth A. *She who Is: The Mystery of God in Feminist Theological Discourse.* New York: Crossroad, 1992.

Kelly, James J. "The Abbé Huvelin's Counsel to Baron Friedrich von Hügel." *Bijdragen, Tijdschriftvoor Filosofie en Theologie* 39 (1978), pp. 59–69.

Kelly, James J. *Baron Friedrich von Hügel's Philosophy of Religion.* Leuven University Press, 1983.

Kelly, James J. "Counseling von Hügel: A Selection of Some Advice Given to von Hügel by the Abbé Huvelin in 1886 and 1893," *Tablet* 223 (1974), pp. 693–95.

Kerlin, Michael J. *Historical Religion in the Thought of Friedrich von Hügel and George Tyrrell.* Rome: Pontificia Universitas Gregoriana, 1966.

Kirkland, William M. "Baron von Hügel and Flannery O'Connor," *The Flannery O'Connor Bulletin* 18 (1989), pp. 28–42.

Kurtz, Lester. *The Politics of Heresy: The Modernist Crisis in Roman Catholicism.* Berkeley: University of California Press, 1986.

Lash, Nicholas. *Easter in Ordinary: Reflections on Human Experience and the Knowledge of God.* Charlottesville: University Press of Virginia, 1988.

Lease, Gary. "Merry del Val and Tyrrell: A Modernist Struggle." *Downside Review* 102 (1984), pp. 133–56.

Leech, Kenneth. *Experiencing God: Theology as Spirituality.* San Francisco: Harper & Row, 1985.

Lemius, J. B. *Catéchisme sur le modernisme d'après l'encyclique Pascendi Domininici Gregis de S.S.Pie X.* Paris: Libairie Saint-Paul, 1907.

Leonard, Ellen. *George Tyrrell and the Catholic Tradition.* London: Darton, Longman and Todd; New York: Paulist Press, 1982.

Leonard, Ellen. *Unresting Transformation: The Theology and Spirituality of Maude Petre.* Lanham: University Press of America, 1991.

Lester-Garland, L.V. *The Religious Philosophy of Baron F. von Hügel.* London: J. M. Dent & Sons, 1933.

Lilley, A. Leslie. *Modernism: A Record and Review.* New York: Scribners, 1908.

Lilley, A. Leslie. *Nature and Supernature: From Epiphany to Easter at St. Mary's, Paddington Green.* London: Francis Griffiths, 1911.

Loisy, Alfred. *Autour d'un petit livre.* Paris: Alphonse Picard, 1903.

Loisy, Alfred. *George Tyrrell et Henri Bremond.* Paris: Nourry, 1936.

Loisy, Alfred. *L'Evangile et L'Eglise.* Paris: Alphonse Picard et fils, 1902. *The Gospel and the Church.* Tr. Christopher Home. London: Pitman, 1904.

Loisy, Alfred. *Mémoires pour servir à l'histoire religieuse de notre temps.* 3 vols. Paris: Nourry, 1931.

Lonergan, Bernard. *Method in Theology.* New York: Herder and Herder, 1972.

Longford, Elizabeth. *A Pilgrim of Passion: The Life of Wilfrid Scawen Blunt.* London: Weidenfeld and Nicolson, 1979.

Loome, Thomas M. "The Enigma of Baron Friedrich von Hügel as Modernist." *Downside Review* 91 (1973), pp. 1334, 123–40, 204–30.

Loome, Thomas M. *Liberal Catholicism, Reform Catholicism, Modernism: A Contribution to a New Orientation in Modernist Research.* Mainz: Matthias-Grünewald Verlag, 1979.

Louis-David, Anne, ed., tr. *Lettres de George Tyrrell à Henri Bremond.* Paris: Aubier Montaigne, 1971.

MacPherson, Duncan. "Baron von Hügel on Celibacy," *Tablet* 223 (1969), pp. 757–58.

Manning, H. E. "The Work and the Wants of the Catholic Church in England," *Dublin Review* n.s.1 (1863), p. 162.

Massa, Mark S. "Mediating Modernism: Charles Briggs, Catholic Modernism, and an Ecumenical 'Plot'," *Harvard Theological Review* 81 (1988), pp. 413–30.

Mathew, David. *Catholicism in England 1535–1935. Portrait of a Minority: Its Culture and Tradition.* London: Catholic Book Club, 1938.

May, J. Lewis. *Father Tyrrell and the Modernist Movement.* London: Eyre & Spottiswoode, 1932.

McClendon, James. *Biography as Theology: How Life Stories Can Remake Today's Theology.* New York: Abingdon Press, 1974.

McFague, Sallie. *Models of God: Theology for an Ecological, Nuclear Age.* Philadelphia: Fortress Press, 1987.

McGrath, John. *Baron Friedrich Von Hügel and the Debate on Historical Christianity (1902-1905)*. San Francisco: Mellen Research University Press, 1993.

McGrath, John. "Fact and Reality: Von Hügel's Response," *Heythrop Journal* 30 (1989), pp. 13–31.

McGrath, John. "The Rights and Limits of History," *Downside Review* 108 (1990), pp. 20–36.

Mitchell, Keith. "Avuncular Counsels: Von Hügel and his *Letters to a Niece*," *Month* 29 (1996), pp. 68–71.

Moore, Andrew. "Edmund Bishop as a Commentator on Modernism," *Downside Review* 101 (1983), pp. 90–107.

Murphy, Nancey. *Theology in the Age of Scientific Reasoning*. Ithaca: Cornell University Press, 1990.

Nédoncelle, Maurice. *Baron Friedrich Von Hügel: A Study of His Life and Thought*. London: Longmans, Green & Co., 1937.

Neuner, Peter. "Lay Spirituality Among the Modernists: Friedrich von Hügel," *Philosophy and Theology* 4 (1989), pp. 53–66.

Newman, John Henry. *The Letters and Diaries of John Henry Newman*. Eds. Charles Stephen Dessain & Thomas Gornall, v. 26, 27. Oxford: Clarendon Press, 1974, 1975.

Newman, John Henry. *Sermons Preached on Various Occasions*. London: Longmans, Green, & Co., 1892.

Newman, John Henry. *A Letter Addressed to His Grace the Duke of Norfolk on the Occasion of Mr. Gladstone's Recent Exposition*. London: B.M. Pickering, 1875.

Norman, Edward. *The English Catholic Church in the Nineteenth Century*. Oxford: Clarendon Press, 1984.

Norman, Edward. *Roman Catholicism in England from the Elizabethan Settlement to the Second Vatican Council*. Oxford: Oxford University Press, 1985.

O'Connell, Marvin R. *Critics on Trial: An Introduction to the Catholic Modernist Crisis*. Washington: Catholic University of America Press, 1994.

O'Connor, Flannery. *The Habit of Being: Letters of Flannery O'Connor*. Ed. Sally Fitzgerald. New York: Vintage, 1980.

Petre, Maude. *Autobiography and Life of George Tyrrell*. 2 vols. London: Edward Arnold, 1912.

Petre, Maude. *Modernism: Its Failure and Its Fruits*. London: T. C.& E.C. Jack, 1918.

Petre, Maude. *The Ninth Lord Petre: Pioneers of Roman Catholic Emancipation.* London: SPCK, 1928.

Petre, Maude. *My Way of Faith.* London: Dent & Sons, 1937

Petre, Maude. *Von Hügel and Tyrrell: The Story of a Friendship.* London: Dent & Sons, 1937.

Petre, Maude. "Friedrich von Hügel: Personal Thoughts and Reminiscences." *Hibbert Journal* 24 (October 1925), pp. 77–87.

Petre, Maude. "George Tyrrell and Friedrich von Hügel in Their Relation to Catholic Modernism." *Modern Churchman* 17 (June 1927), pp. 143–54.

Petre, Maude. "A Religious Movement of the First Years of Our Century." *Horizon* 6 (November 1942), pp. 328–42.

Poulat, Emile. *Histoire, dogme et critique dans la Crise Moderniste.* Paris: Casterman, 1962.

Ramsey, Michael. "Evelyn Underhill," *Religious Studies* 12 (1974), pp. 273–79.

Reynolds, E. E. *The Roman Catholic Church in England and Wales.* Wheathampstead; Anthony Clarke Books, 1973.

Rivière, Jean. *Le Modernisme dans l'Eglise: Etude d'histoire religieuse contemporaine.* Paris: Letouzey et Ané, 1929.

Rollmann, Hans. "Ernst Troeltsch, Friedrich von Hügel and the Student Christian Movement," *Downside Review* 101 (1983), pp. 216–26.

Rollmann, Hans. "Evangelical Catholicity: Friedrich von Hügel, Nathan Söderblom and Friedrich Heiler in Conversation," *Downside Review* 100 (1982), pp. 274–79.

Rollmann, Hans. "Liberal Catholicism, Modernism, and the Closing of the Roman Mind: Franz Xaver Kraus and Friedrich von Hügel," *Downside Review* 109 (1991), pp. 202–16.

Rollmann, Hans. "Von Hügel and Scheler," *Downside Review* 101 (1983), pp. 30–42.

Ruddle, Patrick J. "The Ecumenical Dimension in the Work of Baron Friedrich von Hügel," *Ephemerides Theologicae Lovanienses* 50 (1974), pp. 231–54.

Sabatier, Paul. *Modernism: The Jowett Lectures 1908.* Tr. C. A. Miles. London: T. Fisher Unwin, 1908.

Sagovsky, Nicholas. *"On God's Side": A Life of George Tyrrell.* Oxford: Clarendon Press, 1990.

Sagovsky, Nicholas. "Von Hügel and the Will to Believe," in *The Critical Spirit and the Will to Believe: Essays in Nineteenth-Century*

Literature and Religion, Ed. David Jasper and T. R. Wright. London: Macmillan, 1989, pp. 206–17.

Schiefen, Richard J. *Nicholas Wiseman*. Shepherdstown: Patmos Press, 1984.

Schneiders, Sandra M. "Spirituality in the Academy," *Theological Studies* 50 (December 1989), pp. 676–97.

Schoenl, William. *The Intellectual Crisis in English Catholicism: Liberal Catholics, Modernists, and the Vatican in the Late Nineteenth and Early Twentieth Centuries*. New York, London: Garland Publications, 1982.

Schoenl, William. "Von Hügel After the Modernist Crisis," *Clergy Review* 63 (1978), pp. 211–19.

Schoof, Mark. *A Survey of Catholic Theology 1800–1970*. Tr. N. D. Smith. New York: Paulist, 1970.

Schultenover, David. *A View from Rome: On the Eve of the Modernist Crisis*. New York: Fordham University Press, 1991.

Schultenover, David. "George Tyrrell: Caught in the Archives of the Society of Jesus." in *Three Discussions: Biblical Exegesis, George Tyrrell, Jesuit Archives*. Eds. Ronald Burke, George Gilmore. Mobile, AL: Spring College, 1981, pp. 85–114.

Schultenover, David. *George Tyrrell: In Search of Catholicism*. Shepherdstown: Patmos, 1981.

Schweitzer, Albert. *The Kingdom of God and Primitive Christianity*. Tr. L.A. Garrard. London: A. & C. Black, 1968.

Schweitzer, Albert. *The Mystery of the Kingdom of God: The Secret of Jesus' Messiahship and Passion*. Tr. and Introduction by Walter Lowrie. London: A. & C. Black, 1914.

Sherry, Patrick. "Von Hügel: Philosophy and Spirituality," *Religious Studies* 17 (1981), pp. 1–18.

Sherry, Patrick. "Von Hügel's Retrospective View of Modernism," *Heythrop Journal* 28 (1987), pp. 179–91.

Steere, Douglas V. "Spirituality of von Hügel," *Worship* 47 (1973), pp. 540–46.

Thompson, William M. *Christology and Spirituality*. New York: Crossroad, 1991.

Tracy, David. *Dialogue with the Other: The Inter-Religious Dialogue*. Leuven: Peeters Press; Grand Rapids, MI: William B. Eerdmans, 1990.

Tracy, David. *On Naming the Present: God, Hermeneutics, and Church*. Maryknoll, N.Y.: Orbis, 1994.

Tracy, David. *Plurality and Ambiguity*. San Francisco: Harper & Row, 1988.

Tracy, David. "Recent Catholic Spirituality: Unity amid Diversity." In *Christian Spirituality: Post-Reformation and Modern*, ed. by Louis Dupré and Don E. Saliers. New York: Crossroad, 1989, pp. 143–73.

Tracy, David. "The Uneasy Alliance Reconceived: Catholic Theological Method, Modernity, and Postmodernity," *Theological Studies* 50 (1989), pp. 548–70.

Trevor, Meriol. *Prophets and Guardians: Renewal and Tradition in the Church*. London: Hollis & Carter, 1969.

Tristram, Henry. "Newman and von Hügel," *Dublin Review* 240 (1966), pp. 295–302.

Troeltsch, Ernst. *The Absoluteness of Christianity and the History of Religions*. Tr. David Reid. Richmond, VA: John Knox Press, 1971.

Tyrrell, George. *A Jesuit Friendship: Letters of George Tyrrell to Herbert Thurston*. Ed. Robert Butterworth. London: Roehampton Institute, 1988.

Tyrrell, George. *A Much-Abused Letter*. Printed and circulated privately in 1904 as "A Letter to a Friend, a Professor of Anthropology in a Continental University." Reprinted under Tyrrell's name with an Introduction and an Epilogue. London: Longmans, 1906.

Tyrrell, George. *Christianity at the Cross-Roads*. London: Longmans, 1909.

Tyrrell, George. *External Religion: Its Use and Abuse*. London: Sands, 1899.

Tyrrell, George. *The Faith of the Millions*. Two series. London: Longmans, 1901.

Tyrrell, George. *Hard Sayings: A Selection of Meditations and Studies*. London: Longmans, 1898.

Tyrrell, George. *Lex Credendi: A Sequel to Lex Orandi*. London: Longmans, 1906.

Tyrrell, George. *Lex Orandi: Or Prayer and Creed*. London: Longmans, 1903.

Tyrrell, George. *Medievalism: A Reply to Cardinal Mercier*. London: Longmans, 1908.

Tyrrell, George. *Nova et Vetera: Informal Meditations for Times of Spiritual Dryness*. London: Longmans, 1897.

Tyrrell, George. *Oil and Wine*. Printed and privately circulated in 1902. London: Longmans, 1907.

Tyrrell, George. *The Church and the Future*. Privately printed in 1903 and signed Hilaire Bourdon. Reprinted under Tyrrell's name with an Introduction by M.D. Petre. London: Priory Press, 1910.

Tyrrell, George. *Through Scylla and Charybdis: or The Old Theology and the New*. London: Longmans, 1907.

Underhill, Evelyn. *The Essentials of Mysticism and Other Essays*. New York: E. P. Dutton & Co., 1960; first published in 1920.

Underhill, Evelyn. *Mixed Pastures: Twelve Essays and Addresses*. Freeport, NY: Books for Libraries, 1933.

Underhill, Evelyn. *Mysticism: A Study of the Nature and Development of Man's Spiritual Consciousness*. London: Methuen and Co., 1911; reprinted 1930.

Vaughan, Herbert. *Letters of Herbert Cardinal Vaughan to Lady Herbert Lea, 1867–1903*. Ed. Shane Leslie. London: Burns & Oates, 1942.

Vidler, Alec R. "An Abortive Renaissance: Catholic Modernists in Sussex," in *Renaissance and Renewal in Christian History*. Ed. Derek Baker. Oxford: Basil Blackwell, 1977, pp. 377–92.

Vidler, Alec R. *The Modernist Movement in the Roman Catholic Church: Its Origin and Outcome*. Cambridge University Press, 1934.

Vidler, Alec R. *Twentieth Century Defenders of the Faith*. London: SCM Press, 1965.

Vidler, Alec R. *A Variety of Catholic Modernists*. Cambridge University Press, 1970.

Walker, James A. "Maude Petre: A Memorial Tribute." *Hibbert Journal* 41 (April 1943), pp. 340–346.

Watkin, E. I. *Roman Catholicism in England from the Reformation to 1950* London: Oxford University Press, 1957.

Ward, Maisie. *Insurrection Versus Resurrection*. Vol. II of *The Wilfrid Wards and the Transition*. London: Sheed and Ward, 1938.

Ward, Wilfrid. "The Character Study in Autobiography and in Fiction." *Last Lectures*. London: Longmans, 1918.

Ward, Wilfrid. *William George Ward and the Catholic Revival*. London: MacMillan & Co., 1893.

Weaver, Mary Jo. *Letters from a "Modernist": The Letters of George Tyrrell to Wilfrid Ward*. Shepherdtown: Patmos Press, 1981.

Whelan, Joseph P. *The Spirituality of Friedrich von Hügel*. London: Collins, 1971.

Yeats, W. B. *Poems of W. B. Yeats*. Introduction and notes by A. Norman Jeffares. London: MacMillan Education, 1962.

Yzermans, Vincent A., ed. *All Things in Christ: Encyclicals and Selected Documents of Saint Pius X*. Westminster: Newman, 1954.

Index

DATE DUE